9 73.91
H33h

70017

A HOTBED OF TRANQUILITY

A HOTBED OF TRANQUILITY

My Life in Five Worlds

BY BROOKS HAYS

With an Appreciation by Donald G. Herzberg

THE MACMILLAN COMPANY, NEW YORK

COLLIER-MACMILLAN LTD., LONDON

First Printing

The Macmillan Company, New York
Collier-Macmillan Canada Ltd., Toronto, Ontario
PRINTED IN THE UNITED STATES OF AMERICA

TO MARION

known generally as Mrs. Hays, but advertised rather widely
by me as "Little Manager" or "L. M.," in reality co-author,
for it was she who inspired my exertions and she who
polished the rough lumber that I supplied.

SPECIAL NOTE

*This book is Mr. Hays' creation. It is not ghost-written,
but both the author and publisher are grateful to
Mr. Donald G. Herzberg for his participation in the planning
and development of the manuscript as well as for some of the stories.*

Contents

Brooks Hays: An Appreciation

BY DONALD G. HERZBERG

OLIVER WENDELL HOLMES once said that "A man ought to share in the action and emotion of his time at peril of being judged not to have lived." Justice Holmes would have been pleased with Brooks Hays. All men in public life meet situations that can be decided expediently—few men in public life choose to do what is morally right, regardless of personal cost. At a time when most other southern leaders chose the expedient of following the passions of the mob, Brooks Hays attempted to lead and persuade men, because he believed in the moral right rather than the popular issue.

A distinguished southern senator, in attempting to justify his silence on civil rights matters, pointed out the fact that Brooks Hays had spoken up—and where, he asked, was Hays today?

Brooks Hays no longer holds public office as a result of his moral stand on civil rights, but by his precept and quiet courage he has demonstrated the ultimate answer to the most pressing domestic problem we face. He is a living symbol of what can be done to bring together Americans of all faiths and different colors.

Brooks Hays has been concerned with the problems of people from his earliest days—working on youth and educational problems as an assistant attorney general of Arkansas, through his days with the NRA and the Resettlement Agency of the Department of Agriculture, and in Congress, where he served eight terms.

His civic and church activities underscore his concern for people. Brooks was president of the Arkansas Conference of Social Work, one of five members of the Little Rock Public

Welfare Agency during the depths of the depression, and president of the Southern Baptist Convention, where he worked diligently toward racial as well as religious tolerance.

Brooks is a consummate politician in the finest sense of the word. He empathizes with people and their problems. His characteristics include a willingness to speak up and try to educate his followers.

Immediately after the 1958 election, when a highly questionable and openly distorted write-in campaign had cost Brooks his seat in Congress, a committee of Rutgers professors went to Washington to invite the former Congressman to be the Arthur T. Vanderbilt Professor of Public Affairs. He had been the committee's unanimous choice to fill this chair, which was designed to give distinguished public officials an opportunity to participate in academic undertakings. Politics and Education share common characteristics and processes, often making the transition from politics to teaching easy for the consummate politician. Thus the Rutgers group believed Brooks Hays could make the transition from the Capitol to the campus.

Among the many qualities in Brooks Hays that had attracted the Rutgers group were a few that were pointed out at a testimonial dinner given by his friends shortly after his defeat. Senator Monroney said: "We are here because we know Brooks Hays for what he is—a man who will not leave the path which conscience sets. His loyalty to those ultimate virtues of love and courage has set a high mark in our political life. A prefabricated sticker may mutilate a ballot but not his record. . . . Brooks Hays has lost nothing. It is his nation and colleagues in the Congress who are the losers—for he has brought into our lives the example of a courageous Christian leader."

At the same dinner Billy Graham eulogized Brooks, calling him "one of those rare jewels that has helped lift the word 'politics' out of the mud, slime, and mire, to help it have a new meaning in modern America."

In culmination his friends presented Brooks with a scroll:

The National Committee to Honor Brooks Hays presents to you, Brooks Hays, this scroll to honor you:
We salute you first as a human being, a very human being, whose

gift of laughter has spread its clean, homely wit far and wide among all who know you.

We salute you as an educator, an expositor of truth, a clarifier of the complex, an inspiration to youth.

We salute you as a lawyer, who sees clearly what the rule of law can mean to a people, an apostle of constitutionalism sensitive to its new meanings in a changing age.

We salute you as a statesman. Your many terms in Congress have combined the wisdom of conciliation, and a gallant greatness in devotion to principle. A party man on appropriate occasions, at heart you have been greater than party.

We salute you as a man of courage, never more than in this day, a day which some may count a day of defeat, but which to us is a day of victory.

We salute you as a man of faith. We count this the greatest of all, because we know that it is to you of all things most precious. The love of others for you, as your love for them, knows no boundaries of creed in the consciousness of the common fatherhood of God.

Brooks responded in a speech which revealed the basic philosophy of government that has guided him throughout his life:

While I honor the office of representative, I am convinced that under the circumstances the loss of my seat in Congress is not too big a price to pay.

Is there a standard to which the just and prudent may repair? There is. First, it seems to me, is an appreciation of what the rule of law means in sustaining our liberties and our property. The point does not need laboring, but the times do call for reminders that the Constitution provides a method for change and that until changed, unpopular as well as popular laws must be respected. Odium does not attach to lawful protests against statutes or decisions. Defiance is another matter.

Secondly, we must have a firm commitment to the democratic tradition as expressed in our procedures and institutions. Our public school system must be preserved. Without it the freedom that flowers from an educated citizenry would perish. James Madison put it succinctly: "Without popular education, popular government will be a farce or a tragedy, perhaps both." We know that there can be no government *of* and *for* the people without government *by* the people.

Citizens of a racial minority, who meet the qualifications prescribed for electors, should not be denied a vote because of race. This, too, is basic.

The third imperative is disciplined freedom. This embraces the right to maintain private schools at private expense, not as a substitute for public education but as a privilege in American life that not only adds to our cultural enrichment but helps to preserve the independence of viewpoint that makes freedom possible. This principle grants to both the proponents and opponents of proposed changes the right to organize, and their rights are not forfeited by methods and manners that are not admirable, so long as they are not illegal.

Finally, there must be a due concern for the preservation of our common faith—the faith which sustains our position of world leadership. If there were not other and higher motivations we would still be inspired to bind up the nation's wounds by the knowledge that a ruthless force is loose in the world and that our failure at this point would be exploited. The door that religion alone can open leads to a pure passageway of peace and justice.

Brooks told the Rutgers committee, in his warm, friendly, and always humorous manner, that while he would like to join his old friend Dr. Lewis Webster Jones (then president of Rutgers and formerly president of the University of Arkansas) in a "government in exile," he believed he still had some things left to do in government service.

In 1959 President Eisenhower named him a member of the Board of Directors of the Tennessee Valley Authority. In the months before the election of 1960 Senator Kennedy found Brooks' advice on religious issues helpful. As a leading Protestant, Brooks could interpret certain viewpoints.

In 1961 President Kennedy named him Assistant Secretary of State for Congressional Affairs, in which capacity Brooks worked closely with Adlai Stevenson and Secretary of State Dean Rusk.

In 1962 President Kennedy transferred Brooks to the White House as a Special Assistant, whose concern was civil rights. After President Kennedy's assassination he continued to serve President Johnson in that capacity.

In all the intervening years the Rutgers committee continued to pursue Brooks, and in 1964 he finally joined us at Rutgers.

At the same time he continued as a consultant to the White House.

The Washington *Post* commented editorially on Hays' appointment to Rutgers:

The first of President Kennedy's men to leave the White House is one of the gentlest spirits in this hard-boiled town. Rutgers University will not be easily forgiven for abducting Brooks Hays from us. . . . His office has been next to that of Arthur M. Schlesinger, Jr., in the East Wing . . . he has tried as he once put it to offer an answer from an Arkansas cornfield to the cerebral questions that preoccupied the President's staff.

The *Arkansas Gazette* also had some editorial comment:

Rutgers seems to have some sort of vogue for the unstuffy scholar-doer, who is a pearl beyond price and, when found, one of the adornments of our civilization. Dr. (Lewis Webster) Jones, now the president of the National Conference of Christian and Jews, was and is such a man. His successor as president of Rutgers, Dr. Mason Gross, while tweeded, mustached and properly Keyed, once moon-lighted for a time as the good-humored arbiter of a popular network quiz show. Brooks Hays' last formal teaching assignment was at Sunny Point, in Pope County, but the intervening years have been spent as a student as well as a practitioner of the arcane art of politics, and he should fit in just fine in the congenial academic atmosphere at New Brunswick. We rather envy the students who will be exposed there for the first time to the former Little Rock district congressman's special anecdotal gifts. Mr. Hays can make of the ambulant tombstone vote in old-time Yell County, a story that at once is both as mysterious and as explicable as the story of Burke and Hare, the celebrated Scottish medical school suppliers, and a whole lot funnier. At the same time, his listeners are aware that *he* is aware that graveyard voting is no funnier in its essentials than grave-robbing, and that this is merely one of his ways of saying so.

At Rutgers, Brooks joined the Eagleton Institute of Politics. The institute, privately endowed, has as its central concern the education of young people in politics and government.

The graduate program, designed to train students at the master's level for non-civil-service careers in politics and government, is a unique one in this country. For two years Brooks joined in teaching my Eagleton seminar on Practical Politics.

One learns the full measure of a man, watching him in the classroom working with young people. He has the rare touch that bridges the age difference. Brooks' message was that a life of politics is a high calling, which demands the best in us. He taught with his wonderful brand of humor.

The Eagleton Fellows responded to Brooks, and he responded to them. While Brooks has left us now for other university work, he still returns to Rutgers to work with the Eagleton students— and the Hays' magic never fails to work.

While Brooks Hays was at Eagleton, he taught us a great deal. I suspect from time to time we taught him. We tend to be an irreverent group, an informal group, and Brooks good-humoredly participated in the give-and-take.

No appreciation of Brooks would be complete without a tribute to his wife, Marion. After more than forty years of married life she can still laugh at Brooks' stories, as if she were hearing them all for the first time. There is no doubt that Brooks' iron courage and resolution stem from the support that his "little manager" has given him. Her unswerving loyalty and love have been his greatest strength and comfort through the years. Her way with young people went far toward making Brooks' stay at Rutgers so successful.

Once, at a meeting of college students, one of them asked Brooks just what he thought was the American Dream. Spontaneously, he responded:

It is the anticipation that some time we will be able to say here is equality and freedom, here is brotherhood and justice.

The dream is of compassion expressing itself in society's concern for those who fall by the way in a competitive system.

It is imagination perfecting the mechanisms of government.

It is sensitivity to the claim of righteousness in human affairs.

It is the hope that triumphs here will strengthen values shared with people around the world.

It is human kindness so penetrating the nation that every man, no matter how incapacitated, will feel that he is wanted.

It is the vision of opened doors of opportunity.

It is insistence upon government *by* as well as *for* and *of* the people.
It is the hope of human dignity made secure.
It is the longing for acknowledgment of the human family's oneness.
It is the vision of a citizenry drawn together in mutual confidence,
facing common evils and exalting a common faith in God.
This is my conception of the American Dream.

In the pages that follow, he has attempted to set that dream
to laughter. Brooks has almost perfect pitch, when it comes to
capturing American folk humor, and his ability to capture and
record the humor of American politics is legendary. In these
days almost every comedian has a stable full of writers who
write every joke, and when burlesque houses and vaudeville—
the training ground for American humorists—are a thing of the
past, political humor is the last stronghold of spontaneous
American humor.

A HOTBED OF TRANQUILITY

1

A Funny Thing Happened on My Way: Campaigning

ONE SUMMER MORNING—nearly two score years ago, when I was young and foolish—I came into the kitchen, where my wife was getting breakfast.

"I have an announcement to make," I said.

"Oh. Does it concern me, the children, the house, or the office?"

"None of those. It . . ."

"In that case, will you have orange juice or grapefruit?"

"Either one. Now, listen—this is important."

She went on pouring juice for the children and getting them to the table, while I plowed single-mindedly ahead, referring to the week I had just had with Senator Joe T. Robinson, listening to his speeches and observing his oratorical style. He was campaigning for the Roosevelt-Garner ticket, and I had just been elected Democratic National Committeeman for Arkansas, and so was expected to attend to a lot of chores, especially raising money in that depression-ridden year. I toured Arkansas with him in a Lincoln car, driven by Mrs. Robinson, and had a brief platform appearance at each engagement. I was impressed with his serious hard-hitting, hew-to-the-line delivery, and I had asked him about it. I told him that I had noticed he very seldom used an anecdote or joke in his speeches and asked if this was intentional.

He said it was. He had deliberately renounced humor because he feared audiences would remember only the jokes and forget the serious content of his talks. He made this resolution, he said, one night as he was leaving the school ground where he had spoken. In the dark, as he was unhitching his horse, he heard some of the farmers who had been at the "speaking" chuckling over his yarns.

"There wasn't a word said," Senator Robinson complained to me, "about the serious side of my speech! I decided then and there that I would drop humor, in all its forms, from my speeches."

This reasoning impressed me, and I felt that a technique that was good enough for the Democratic leader of the United States Senate, was good enough for me—I, too, would be a serious speaker.

It was not until I was nearly through my "important announcement" that my wife got the drift. "And so I've decided to cut all humor out of my speeches in the future, and . . ."

She whirled around and stared at me. "*What did you say?*"

"I said I was going to be a serious speaker. Like Senator Robinson, you know. Don't you think that would be a good idea?"

"No, I don't. I think it's a terrible idea! Why, you'd be leaving out the choicest ingredient. Just because they didn't start discussing the senator's weighty points doesn't mean they didn't learn anything. I'll bet the thing that kept them listening through the dull parts was the humor. It's . . . why, it's the *saving grace!*"

Thus my new-made resolution practically died aborning and went into the rubbish heap, and I continued to develop my own individual style, in which humor has been an ally and a friend.

As a result, this book is the harvest of many years in public life, innumerable appearances on the "stump" and the platform, and some rich associations with interesting people of all creeds, races, and political persuasions.

It is not just a joke book. That may be a disappointing announcement to certain of my friends, who have laughed at my yarns, urged me to put them in a book, and even promised to buy it! This country does not need another anthology of funny stories; it is liberally supplied with them already. I prefer to dedicate my efforts in support of a thesis I have long held: that

humor, to be truly effective, must be related to a philosophy of
life, and should contribute to the expression of ideas. So this
book puts a special emphasis on the place that humor has in
government, politics, and related areas.

In this imperfect world of ours, the strains and stresses of
life could destroy man's happiness if he lacked the quality of
humor. Politics is one of the great sources of tensions. Humor
can become a cohesive force, and laughter a healing exercise;
and in this decade of civil strife and serious problems beyond the
seas, when frustration engenders bitterness and passions arise,
this precious quality of humor may be our saving grace. It may
strengthen our faith and enable us to enjoy companionship, even
with those who are on opposing sides. If this volume should be
an influence, however feeble, to the realization of this hope, I
shall be very happy.

Many of the stories that I have included came out of the life
of the South's rural people, with whom I have been identified
from boyhood. I have plagiarized, of course, as all lovers of
humor must do, but I trust that the special flavor of the frontier,
and of the Arkansas hill country in particular, as I discovered it,
may be found in these pages. The hill country people are my
people. I have laughed with them since I was able to laugh.
And they taught me to laugh at myself, and even abided my
laughing at them on occasion. Their folklore is part of the warp
and woof of my philosophy. The elements of affection and
loyalty are in this relationship—even during those periods when
so many of them either did not understand me, or if they understood, did not quite approve of me.

I was once asked by a newsman, after I had become a member
of Congress, if I could pinpoint the origin of my interest in
politics.

I said, "Yes, I can. You'll have to give the credit—or blame, if
you like that better—to the Easter bunny, in 1904."

He said, "How's that?" looking as if he thought he had not
heard correctly, so I filled him in.

This dynamic century was less than half a dozen years old—
and so was I—when my latent interest in a subject which had
always engaged my family was awakened by the Easter rabbit.

In my nest on that particular Easter morning I found a most intriguing egg. It was a beautiful smooth purple, and on one side was the face of a gentleman who was much in the public eye, for he was the Democratic nominee for President, Alton B. Parker. My family, and indeed all of our neighbors, were rock-ribbed Democrats, so I knew both the face and the name of the nominee. I also knew the Republican nominee was Teddy Roosevelt. But the Easter bunny had unerringly laid in my nest the right egg! I was seized by a sudden urge of patriotism, tempered by a burst of personal ambition.

"You see," I explained to the newsman, "I decided that morning that some day I'd like to have *my* picture on an Easter egg, and the route to that happy event seemed to be a political career."

The newsman smilingly asked, "Did you make it? That is, did the rabbit cooperate?"

"Well, no, the rabbit didn't. But an understanding woman friend, hearing me make a reference in a speech to my youthful ambition, took care of it the following Easter. She sent me a big chocolate egg, with a picture of me pasted on one side."

As far back as I can remember, I was interested in the techniques of speakers, with special attention to their use of humor. As a debater in high school, I began to prepare myself for one of the prime essentials of a public career—the ability to confront an audience. That was much more important then than now, when a speaker may read from a manuscript, sitting at ease in an air-conditioned studio. In those days, before even the radio had been invented, political rallies were held where candidates for public office gathered to bring their causes to the people, and these speakers offered a rich field for study of picturesque speech, though most often they presented examples of what not to do.

Our state's two United States senators, who were both masters of old-time southern oratory, as well as other political figures were friends of my father. So it was natural that political speaking engaged my attention, and was the laboratory as well as the inspiration for this great adventure called politics.

As I have already indicated, the senior senator, Joe T. Robinson, the wheel horse of the New Deal, deliberately eschewed humor in his addresses, though he gave an enthusiastic response to the wit of others. Senator Thaddeus Caraway, on the other hand, was extremely effective in his use of earthy humor, as he regaled Arkansas audiences, who delighted in his incisive wit and homespun stories.

I remember one of his typical yarns, and the cotton-country drawl in which he told it.

"We had a fellow in our town named Charlie Johnson. He weighed about 130 pounds. Cut off his feet and his Adam's apple, and he'd weigh about 30. He went to see his sweetheart one evening. She weighed 250 pounds, give or take a pound here and there. She sat down on Charlie's lap, and then musta' forgot about him for a spell. Finally, she recalled where she was, and said, 'Honey, are you tired?'

'Well, I *wuz* tired about two hours ago,' he answered. 'I'm paralyzed now.'"

The one area in which I have used humor sparingly is campaigning. One reason for this is that humor in campaign talks runs the risk of injuring the feelings of others, and even when done skillfully, can backfire.

I had my exposure early to the public's unreliable sense of humor, when Secretary of Labor Frances Perkins offered me a job, and I said I had turned it down because it was bad enough to have to take orders from a woman at home—to have the same situation at the office would be too much. I did not expect to be taken seriously by anyone, but I learned that there is a type of mind which can never enjoy a joke at its own expense.

A joke told by the speaker on himself, however, is quite a different matter, and never fails to receive an appreciative response. I learned to expect grins from farmers when I explained how I had been drawn into public life.

"I decided to be a 'statesman,'" I confided, "when I was picking peaches on my Uncle Will's farm, and the thermometer stood at 110° in the shade. There is something about the feel of peach fuzz on the back of your neck, Ladies and Gentlemen, that makes that an easy decision."

I think that Thaddeus Caraway probably owed his victory in the 1920 senatorial election—when he defeated the incumbent

Senator W. F. Kirby—to his qualities as an entertainer, although he also had the advantage of a good issue. That issue was Kirby's vote opposing the arming of merchant vessels prior to the declaration of war against Germany, which invoked Woodrow Wilson's angry denunciation of him as one of the "willful men."

The campaign literature of both candidates was weighted with references to this issue, but it is my opinion that most voters were less interested in the charge and Senator Kirby's answer (that he supported the war effort vigorously, even winning praise from President Wilson) than in the easy-to-listen-to speeches of Mr. Caraway. The average Arkansas voter was not familiar enough with the controversy between Woodrow Wilson and the Senate dissidents to care much about it, but he warmed to Caraway, who called himself "the plain man from Jonesboro," who had lived close to the soil, and who was skillful in conveying that fact to his audiences.

I attended a Confederate reunion near the close of the 1920 campaign, a time when Civil War veterans were still numerous enough to be considered factors in elections. A rather pompous friend of Senator Kirby's made a deadly serious speech in behalf of the senator's candidacy and wound up with what he may have regarded as an unanswerable prediction, "And so, on August the ninth, Thaddeus H. Caraway will be buried so deep beneath an avalanche of votes for Kirby that his political sun will be forever set!"

Before the orator had time even to add "Thank you" and sit down, a high-pitched voice, emanating from a highly respected Confederate veteran on a back seat, added a rider so devastating that the fine vocal effort of Senator Kirby's friend fell flatter than a punctured balloon, "Mebbe he will—and mebbe he won't." To the accompaniment of uncontrollable laughter, the speaker uncomfortably took his seat.

To some seekers of public office the campaign itself is stimulating and exciting. "Follower of the campaign trail" is a sentimental cognomen bestowed by veterans of brush arbors and country picnics on those to whom the appeal of the hustings is as authentic as the call of the wild to the wolf or the smell of smoke to the firehorse. Once a man has experienced the give and take of the battle, the roar of the crowd, and the aura of glamour that surrounds the candidate, he is usually as stage-struck as any theatrical neophyte. There is a little ham in the shyest politician.

There are, actually, some points of similarity between good actors and successful campaigners, for a sense of showmanship is a part of the stock in trade of each. It was one of Huey Long's greatest assets, as it has been of many a spellbinder, enabling him to hypnotize an audience and mold it to his will. A man whose purposes are good has need of some of the same talents of showmanship. He should be able to stir the emotions as well as the mind, to lift the spirit, to make his hearers laugh, and sometimes to bring them close to tears.

SHOWMANSHIP

A political rally should be good clean fun. To be entertained rather than instructed is what the majority of the audience want, and the man who can do this best is the lucky possessor of an ace in the hole. This I concede with reluctance, since political education is one of the needs of the hour, but I do so with the rider that even humor should be a means, not an end.

The late Alben Barkley was adept at making audiences laugh, and he will long be remembered for his delightful stories. One that could be used in a variety of ways to make a point, but which was worth telling for no reason at all, has the extra advantage of being about a well-known person. To cite names, places, and circumstances is always effective, as these lend authenticity to even the most absurd situation.

Fes Whitaker, a local politician, Barkley said, was running for county jailer of Letcher County, Kentucky, right after the Spanish-American War. Fes had a set speech. He said, referring to the Battle of San Juan Hill: "Teddy Roosevelt came to me that morning and he said, 'Fes, that Hill must be taken today.' I said, 'Teddy, it is just as good as took.' Teddy went on to tell me, 'You see, Fes, there must be a million Cubians up there.' Well, I agreed and then we fought 'em. We fought 'em all day. We must have killed 500,000 Cubians. When it was over, Teddy says to me, 'Fes, this day is destined to live in history.' And I said 'That's right, Teddy.' Then he said, 'And

Fes, one of us is des-tyned to be President of the United States.'
I said, 'Teddy, *you* be President of the United States and let
me be the county jailer of Letcher County, Kentucky.'"

Claud A. Swanson, who had a brilliant career in politics,
being governor of Virginia, United States senator, and Secretary
of the Navy, was also successful at making politics fun. He had
a keen sense of humor, and he created some of his own anecdotes. His summation of what is needed to be a successful
campaigner is still quoted:

1. Don't buy your ticket till you hear the train whistle.
2. Be strong *for* something nobody can be against.
3. When in doubt, do right.
4. Never use one word when five will do.
5. Always stand by the Party. If a storm comes, shift the ballast
   and try to save the ship. But if you see she's sinking, follow
   the rats!

Tom Heflin, the flamboyant senator from Alabama, was a
natural entertainer and was adept in the use of another "gim-
mick," at which most southern campaigners excel—he poured
gratitude and affection over his hearers with a lavish hand. He
was particularly good before Alabama rural audiences at typical,
old fashioned, before-radio-or-television political rallies. These
rallies with "dinner on the grounds" at noon and "speaking" in
the afternoon, with its inevitable accompaniment of buzzing
flies, barking dogs, and crying babies, have all but disappeared
from our American political scene.

At one of these rallies Heflin, as the candidate for re-election
to the United States Senate, was the last speaker. When Tom's
turn came, he began (using one of his organ tones), "Mah
friends, I've come out here to ask your help in my race for a
second term in the U. S. Senate. But first I want to thank you
folks in Gifford Township for your support. You've always been
mighty good to me. Mighty good, and now I ask it again. I don't
think ah'm a selfish man. Ah'm not asking for *all* your votes. I'm
just asking for a portion. Mah friends, that reminds me of one
time when the preacher came to dinner, when I was a boy.
When there was company for dinner, my brother and I never
got to eat at the first table. We always had to wait till the grown

folks were through. On this occasion, we were having chicken pie—a mouth-watering chicken pie—mah friends. I had seen it go to the table, its golden brown flaky crust both hiding and promising the delicious chicken gravy treat beneath. I was even hungrier than usual, as I stood in the pantry with my brother and peered through a crack in the door. I was younger and smaller than he and couldn't see much. I heard my mother say, 'Brother Yarbrough, will you have some chicken pie?'

"The preacher answered with enthusiasm, 'Yes, ma'am! I certainly will.' My mother moved the pie over so he could help himself. 'Thank you ma'am, I'll just take a portion.'

"I said to my brother, 'How much is a portion?'

"With his eye still glued to the crack, he answered emphatically, 'Darn near all of it!' "

Former Mayor William O'Dwyer of New York City, also a great showman, had one technique that never failed to get him a warm response. He used to campaign with what appeared to be a set of notes for a speech. As he got up to talk, O'Dwyer would look out over his audience. Inevitably he would spot some great friends. After a series of hellos to a number of them, he'd smile and say, "With so many friends in this audience, I don't need these," and he would ostentatiously tear up the *notes*. Then he'd say, placing his hand over his heart, "To you, I can speak from down here."

Old reporters swear that once they put together the crumpled and torn notes and found them to be a shopping list.

Sometimes a joke or gibe aimed at the speaker can be fielded by him and returned with devastating effect. A laugh gained in this way, at the expense of the opposition, is sweet indeed. One time, when William Howard Taft was campaigning, someone threw a head of cabbage at him. It fell on the platform at Taft's feet. He was quick-witted enough to turn the incident to advantage.

"I see," he remarked, "that one of my adversaries has lost his head." The audience roared its approval.

William J. Bryan, who was normally a rather solemn and pontifical speaker, once found himself with an audience, but no platform from which to address it. The only thing nearby that would offer any elevation was a manure-spreader, and he quickly mounted it, and at the same time availed himself of the opportunity to attack his opposition in no very dainty way: "Ladies and gentlemen, this is the first time I have ever addressed an audience from a Republican platform."

This was in fact a rather rough era, and Speaker Thomas Reed was only reflecting the tone of the decade when he made a similar riposte. One of the most distinguished as well as hardboiled politicians the United States has produced, he was campaigning in Maine for the Republican ticket. As he spoke, one heckler was particularly irksome and disagreeable in what was plainly an effort to get the speaker to lose his temper. Finally the heckler himself lost his temper and yelled, "Aw, go to hell!" Reed responded with studied politeness, "I have traveled in many parts of this great and lovely state. I have had the honor to address many groups, but this is the first time I have ever received an invitation to the Democratic headquarters."

When the speaker makes himself the butt of a joke, it is a sure-fire way to get a laugh. One simple little story I told many times, because it never failed me. I usually told it like this:

Many years ago there was a Congressman from North Carolina named Strange. When he was in his last illness and knew he was not going to recover, he said to his son, "I've decided what I want on my tombstone: 'Here lies an Honest Congressman.'"

"And then your name?" prompted the young man.

"No," said his father solemnly, but with a little twinkle in his eye, "that won't be necessary. People who read it will say, 'That's Strange.'"

Paradoxical it may be, but audiences also seem to like to cry. To bring them to it, however, is not so easy as it is to cause laughter, and the speaker who can stir them to tears not unreasonably thinks himself a very clever fellow.

I still enjoy telling, though it happened many years ago, how I turned the tables on a friend who was tramping the campaign trail with me one long ago summer. He was helping me try to become governor of Arkansas by driving me about the state in a Model T Ford, and by giving me advice on my speeches. He felt that he was more practical than I, and he feared that I was talking over the heads of most of my rural audiences.

"Brooks," he said one day, "you've got to get down on a lower intellectual level. You're appealing to their minds—you've got to appeal to their hearts. You've got to make 'em cry."

This had never been a part of my weaponry, and I remonstrated.

"Tell 'em your enemies are persecuting you," Bill urged.

I decided to try to do something with that theme in the next speech. It was not done well. I was too new in the role, but it was a stimulant, and I stepped up the tempo with each repetition of the pathetic efforts of the Hays family to survive against the machinations of the enemy.

As first presented, it went something like the following, but I shudder to recall today the picture of starvation and suffering that must have been conjured up in succeeding speeches, as I conformed to my friend's promptings to "make 'em cry":

"My friends, I have been fighting your battles ever since I was old enough to take part in these struggles for the people's rights. And you know that I have had to pay the price for standing by you. After that second race for governor against the vicious and powerful highway machine, I knew I would have no rest from their persecutions. I had challenged them once too often. They determined to destroy me. They were not content to defeat me. They decided to take my law practice from me. They told the clients of my firm that to employ me would be regarded as an unfriendly act by every member of their statewide organization, and that they would find a way to punish anyone who helped me. And their scheme worked. They were powerful as well as ruthless. They were responsible for the collapse of my law business.

"Yes, they made good their threats that followed my promise if elected governor to clean the state house out, from the tip of the shining dome to the dark recesses of the bottom basement. I fought them once too often, and I tell you now that, because I have stood by you, there have been times in this terrible depression when I haven't been able to put enough food on the table to nourish the bodies of my little children."

After three or four performances of that ilk, I "begged" the adviser's permission to change tactics.

"Why, Bill," I implored, "I can't afford to exploit my family

like that. Listen," I said, as we drove toward the next appointment, "just now, at Knoxville, I saw my old friend Brother
Garwein wiping his eyes. He was *crying.*"

"Brother Garwein, the devil!" said Bill. "I have been crying
myself ever since we left Hartman, fifty miles up the road."

HAZARDS ON THE CAMPAIGN TRAIL

A hazard of the campaign trail is the unexpected development,
the unlooked-for question, the attempt to embarrass, or simply
the wry twist of fate.

Experience, of course, makes a politician more adept at parry-
ing thrusts, and even, with a little luck, turning them to good
account.

In 1928, in my campaign for the governorship, I had a personal
example of the need to think quickly as I was closing the campaign with a big rally in the City Park in Little Rock, in an
outdoor gathering place called The Band Shell.

A tremendous crowd greeted me, partly attributable to the
fact that I had challenged the *establishment* when I was only
twenty-nine, and the people were curious about "this pre-
sumptuous young fellow." At one point in my talk, the children
down in front were interfering a bit with proceedings, and one
of my staff was trying to quiet them.

I had an idea: "Please don't interfere with the children, Mr.
Holland," I interjected. "They don't have to listen to this dull
speech about state affairs. They have already made up their
minds about this race. If the children of Arkansas could vote tomorrow, I would win by the biggest majority ever received,
because they know who bears the interests of childhood close
to his heart. They know who would promote the welfare of
young people in the office of governor."

A man told me later that his wife said after the meeting, "That
man gets my vote! That's the man I want for governor."

I offer this incident not as an example of excellent ad-libbing
(I have done better in my forty years of campaigning), but to
suggest that the speech instructors are right in saying that actors,
ministers, and candidates must never let an unscheduled interruption divert an audience's attention from the stage. "Hold the
audience—do something—say something to preserve your posi-

tion as center of the stage." This guideline was given emphasis in my speech classes at Little Rock's YMCA evening school during the depression (which provided grocery money for my family in the lean years). I had several aspirants to political office among my students, one a candidate for governor—a shy and inexperienced speaker. In the occasional pauses in his class speeches, when he was in what I termed an air pocket, I would insist that he "not just stand there—say something as you struggle to pursue a train of thought, even if it's merely 'now I repeat, etc.' " I must have done pretty well in this lesson, because when I attended one of his meetings and listened to his vigorous attack on certain practices in government and the individuals guilty of them, I was fascinated by the phrase he used to come out of an air pocket. He had stated his indictment well. But when he started to put on the clincher, his flow of words suddenly stopped. He had just said, "A man who will do that . . ." then there was silence—agonizing to me, his old instructor— but he must have remembered my advice, "say something," for he added, finally, "a man who'll do that—well, he ain't made out of the real he-American stuff." It was an individualized application of the parlance of the day, and it did the job.

Many instances of campaign humor came from the extemporaneous utterances, sometimes inspired by an incident, sometimes by the lapses of mind—the subjective qualities in the conflicts of political life.

Senator Charles Sumner of Massachusetts proved himself a master of the lightning-speed counterthrust when he was making a speech to a group of preachers just prior to the Civil War. One of them asked why he didn't go into the South with his antislavery speeches, since it was there that slavery existed.

Sumner shot back his answer. "You are trying to save souls from hell, aren't you? Then why don't you go there?"

In more recent times, two of my own colleagues succeeded in by-passing direct hits by a little fast footwork. One of these, Senator Tom Connally of Texas, was running for re-election. He was speaking in a little east Texas town, where interest in one of the proposed cotton subsidy plans was keen. At the end of the speech a listener called out, "How do you stand on the cotton issue?"

Tom promptly said, "I'm okay on that one. Are there any other questions?"

The other colleague, Congressman Charles A. Eaton of New Jersey, an ordained Baptist minister, had a little experience, due to the prohibition amendment, which he enjoyed recounting.

In the middle of a speech he was interrupted by a listener, who demanded, "Now wait a minute, Congressman! I've got a question. What about prohibition?"

"The fact that he had not said whether he was for retention of prohibition or for repeal gave me an opening," said Congressman Eaton later, "and I quickly seized it.

"Looking him straight in the eye, I put sternness and courage into my voice as I said, 'I shall not evade. I shall not dodge. I shall not equivocate. My answer is yes!'"

A favorite story in the Capitol cloak rooms involved the economy issue. Ross Collins, a representative from Mississippi, was hard pressed on the issue of his vote, as member of the House Appropriations Committee, in favor of a three-million-dollar purchase of some valuable books and documents from Russia in 1933. Domestic conditions were terrible—unemployment, drought, etc.—money so scarce that it was "dynamite" for his opponent to be talking about Collins' vote for three million dollars to Russia. When Ross got back to Mississippi, to campaign, his friends told him he was licked unless he answered it.

"Just say it's a lie," they urged.

Instead, he handled it this way. "That's right. I voted for buying those documents. If I had to vote on it again, I'd be willing to pay even a little more for them. We got a real bargain! Did you know that among them is the only manuscript of the New Testament in the world in Jesus' handwriting!" (I have suspected Ross of making this up.)

A Mississippi congressman of some years ago was affectionately called "Private" John Mills Allen. He was called "Private" because of one of his very earliest speeches. Called upon suddenly to explain how the South happened to lose the war, he found himself on a platform completely surrounded by former Confederate officers of high rank. "Ladies and Gentlemen," he began slowly, "as I look about me, I see on my right Major——, Captain——, and Colonel——, and on my left General——,

Major——, and Colonel——, all high-ranking officers of the Confederate Army, in which I was only a private in the rear ranks. Now, ladies and gentlemen, I was asked to account for the Confederacy's failure in the late conflict, but I will be brief. I will ask you to look at these officers, and at me, and to draw your own conclusions." Allen kept on being elected by the other private soldiers in Mississippi.

A midwestern governor, in the thirties, was once asked, from the floor, such an embarrassing question about his personal life that, although he was an experienced and fluent speaker, it nearly got the best of him. He had a well-deserved reputation as a *bon vivant,* gourmet, and all-around playboy, and one night a few of his chickens returned to roost.

He was addressing a church group, and in spite of being a bit overstimulated he made a brilliant speech. Questions followed, which he handled with ease and skill, until a woman stood up, and fixing the governor with a quelling eye, said sternly, "Governor, I have heard that you drink too much and are too fond of women, and I just want to know—Is this true?"

There was a gasp from the audience at the frankness of the question. Then all eyes sought the governor's face. There was complete silence in the hall for several seconds.

When he finally broke it, it was to say, looking limpidly at the questioner, "Sister, pray for me!"

Al Smith had just addressed the chairman and was about to begin a speech when someone from the gallery called out, "Take a full minute, Al, and tell 'em all you know."

"I'll just tell 'em all we *both* know," Governor Smith instantly responded, "It won't take any longer."

Two instances come to my mind in which the man on the stump could think of no adequate rejoinder, and it was the audience, or an individual, who had the last word. One of these, when Senator Thad Caraway's friend took care of his opponent, I have already described.

The other concerned Congressman Hamp Fulmer of South Carolina, chairman of the House Agriculture Committee, who followed the usual custom in South Carolina, of going with his opponent and speaking from the same platform with him. A camp meeting in South Carolina, in other words, is a public festival. Mr. Fulmer's opponent, in the grand climax of his speech, shouted, "And so I ask you, 'what's he ever done?' " referring to Mr. Fulmer, of course.

A voice came loud and clear from the back of the room, "I'll tell you one thing he's done. He's licked the pants off of ever'body who ever put his head up against him!"

One time in Norfolk, Virginia, I was scheduled to speak for Adlai Stevenson in a debate with Hugh Scott, then a congressman and now a senator from Pennsylvania, who was to speak for Eisenhower. On the way to the auditorium, Congressman Porter Hardy of Virginia warned me that I wouldn't find the people very friendly toward the Stevenson cause. This I found to be the understatement of the year.

Hugh and I both gave our prepared speeches, and I got light applause at the end, just enough for politeness. My friend Hugh's applause was thundering. Then the chairman invited questions. The first one was addressed to me. An elderly gentleman got up and, with his voice quivering with indignation and his hand upraised in a gesture of condemnation, he said, "I want to ask Congressman Hays to name one way—just one—in which Adlai E. Stevenson differs from Harry S Truman!" A ripple of pleased laughter swept through the hall.

I named not just one, but several. The audience would have none of them. They shook their heads. Some gave audible *no*'s. They almost booed. So I gave up and said:

"I see I'm not convincing any of you. So I'll just wrap this one up by saying that if the gentleman will forgive my frankness, he reminds me of a woman in Little Rock who was also very partisan. But she confessed her sin. She said to her Presbyterian pastor, 'Dr. Boggs, I know I'd be a better woman and a better Christian if I could just hate sin and the devil like I hate Harry S Truman!' "

This time I got the laughter.

Sometimes a candidate overdoes some reference to his freedom from the secondary personal vices (even the primary ones) such as use of liquor, tobacco, and card playing. It happened once to an otherwise admirable candidate for state office in Arkansas, who sensed that his opponent was vulnerable on these points. The candidate was eager to capitalize on the situation.

Hoping the contrast would be evident, he said, in a joint debate, "And I have never known the taste of whiskey, my lips have never touched tobacco, and I have never played a game of cards or gone to a horse race in my whole life."

His opponent was quick to gain the advantage this puritanism gave him. He saw that the faces of his auditors, composed of more common clay, registered no warmth of approval. His reply: "My opponent says he's never gambled on a horse race, never played a game of poker, never taken a little nip, and never inhaled the fragrant smoke of a good cigar. Well, that young man doesn't know what he's missed, does he?"

Laughter from an audience should not mislead a candidate into believing that he has revealed brilliant wit. Human nature, having a certain kindness toward harassed politicians, produces a sympathetic response to his exertions, even to feeble ones. Moreover, audiences are often glad for a break in what is generally a dry dissertation in public problems.

At Mt. Vernon, Arkansas, in one of my gubernatorial races, something happened which is still remembered, though it was nearly forty years ago. In one of my rare mentions of an opponent's name, and just as I mentioned it, a noble representative of the male animal that symbolizes the Democratic party, grazing a few feet from the open window near my table, decided to participate. He emitted the loudest "Yawnkee" sound I ever heard from the throat of a jackass, gradually fading into the familiar "hee-haw" that clearly identified the genus and the gender. The crowd was convulsed rather satisfactorily in response to my comment: "Well, now, I'm glad my opponent has a friend in the community to speak up for him."

INTRODUCTIONS: HELP OR HANDICAP?

Introductions at their best may be wonderful springboards for a speaker, occasionally giving his confidence a needed boost, or giving him a clue as to how to quickly establish rapport with the audience. In the hands of an inept or insensitive chairman they often become liabilities.

In my first campaign for the governorship, my youth kept cropping up in the political conversations. How often I felt the truth of that observation that youth is wasted on young people!

They can neither enjoy it nor appreciate it, until they are old enough to miss it. I would have unhesitatingly bartered five years at the end of my life, if it had been possible, to be able to add them to my current age.

The chairmen at my meetings would frequently make some reference to my age, sometimes apologetically, in the manner of one glossing over an obvious physical liability, like a cleft palate or a cast in the eye. Sometimes they tried to make me out a white knight riding to the rescue of an infirm and corrupt party.

One old gentleman at a small town really did not mess around with tact or subterfuges. He gave the table a smart rap with his gavel, and announced, "Ladies and gentlemen, we got a candidate for governor here this mornin'. I ain't for him. I think he's too young. But I ask you to give him a good hearin' just the same."

I had to drag myself up out of that sand trap even to start at taw, to use the marble players' term. But I turned it to advantage. In my speech, as I concluded each count of my indictment of the record of my opponent, the governor, I would pause to smile broadly and with a friendly gesture toward the chairman say, "And our good friend, the chairman, hasn't told you *that* about his candidate, has he?"

"No, he ain't," someone yelled, and the crowd was at least momentarily on my side.

The poor judgment and bad taste of a supporter may be very costly to the candidate. One such case has become a political horror story, for it actually cost the Republican Presidential candidate the election in 1880.

In October of that year Republican Presidential candidate James G. Blaine allowed Samuel O. Burchard, a Presbyterian minister, to state unchallenged that "we are Republicans and do not propose to leave our party and identify with the party whose antecedents have been rum, rebellion, and Romanism!"

That remark cost Blaine New York State in a close vote and elected Grover Cleveland President.

Four years later the remark was still widely remembered and gave Governor Zebulon Vance of North Carolina a witty retort, when friends counseled against his proposed marriage to an attractive lady who happened to be a Catholic.

When he told some political advisers of his plans, they tried to dissuade him. North Carolina, being strongly Protestant, "will not look with favor on this," they warned. Some insisted such an alliance would be political suicide.

Governor Vance was not impressed.

"I know what I'm doing," he told them. "And don't try to talk me out of it. If you're thinking of rum, rebellion, and Romanism, let me just tell you I've survived the first two, and now I intend to try the third!"

William Jennings Bryan was once the victim of an overly long, however well-intentioned, introduction. In fact the introduction used so much time in cataloging the Great Commoner's virtues and accomplishments, all Bryan could do was get up and speak for a few minutes before running off to catch his train.

As he left, he heard a member of the audience talking to a friend, "Wonderful speech," he said.

"Yep," said the other fellow, "and the baldheaded fellow who followed him weren't so bad either."

Sometimes introductions are boorish and rude in ill-fated attempts to be funny. Will Rogers was to speak at a Democratic rally. The governor, who was to have presided and introduce Rogers, was suddenly taken ill. The lieutenant governor had taken his place. In an ill-timed effort to be funny the lieutenant governor said in introducing Will, "I'll not try to make any jokes because I am about to call on the biggest joke in California. Like all conceited actors he is, I see, whispering to his companion now instead of listening to me and trying to learn something."

Rogers responded: "First of all, ladies and gentleman, I want to apologize. It is quite true I was whispering to the lady next to me, and I feel very bad about it. I am sorry about it. The reason it made such a disturbance was that I asked her a question. I asked her, 'Who is that man talking?' And she said, 'I don't know.' And then she turned to the gentleman and asked him, and then he turned and asked the gentleman next to her, and then he turned and asked the lady next to him, and then—well, it had to go all the way down the aisle and over there by the door, and then when they found out, it had to come all the way back: 'Why, it's the lieutenant governor.' That sounds pretty big when you say it, and that's why it made such a disturbance. And then I says to the lady, I says, 'Oh, it's the lieutenant governor, is it? Well, what does he do?' 'Oh, he don't do anything,' she said. 'What do you mean,' I said, 'don't do anything? Don't he even get up in the morning?' 'Oh, yes,' she said, 'he gets up every morning and inquires whether the governor is any worse.'"

Occasionally an introduction can be the device to attempt to smooth over a difficult situation. In September of 1964 Presidential candidate Barry Goldwater was invited by some Republican political scientists to address the annual convention of the American Political Science Association in Chicago. While the speech was in no way a part of the formal proceedings, there were some political scientists who objected, on general principles, to the senator's appearance. Others, however, felt that it was perfectly appropriate. The sponsors of Senator Goldwater's appearance wanted to have a person known not to be a supporter of the senator to introduce him. Don Herzberg agreed to be that person and introduce Senator Goldwater.

"I am delighted to welcome our speaker this afternoon. Aside from Woodrow Wilson and John F. Kennedy, the best our members have been able to achieve are some University presidencies and a few scattered deanships. Thus to have a card-carrying APSA member reach the exalted position you have achieved, Senator, makes this a singular occasion.

"The American Political Science Association, is home to many people. We are scholars, researchers, teachers, administrators (none of these, incidentally are mutually exclusive) and indeed, many of us like to believe that we are doers in the world of politics. The more we become so involved, the more we know that conflict in the United States takes place within the framework of our great, two-party system. Our association, which has as one of its own basic commitments to seek an understanding of the political life of this country, will always, I hope, strive to have the principals of these two parties present their views to us.

"Because of what you have done for the association, in view of your present position in American public life, you need no introduction to this assembly of individuals who apparently pursue politics here in Chicago as avidly as they pursue it back home in Alabama, New York, Michigan, or Arizona.

"Ladies and gentlemen, members of the Political Science Association, I am honored to present the Republican nominee for President, a senator of the United States, the Honorable Barry M. Goldwater of Arizona."

THE ART OF WITTY RESPONSE

Appropriate responses to introductions call for a certain *savoir-faire*, and an experienced speaker is usually fortified by having in his repertoire some stock quips, with which he may meet a variety of situations. I have some old standbys, which I have called upon after receiving a very warm and flattering introduction, and like Old Faithful geyser they have never disappointed me. Referring to the chairman's compliments, I have said, "I shall only thank him for this friendly presentation. If I try to say more, I fear I will bungle as the preacher did when we surprised him with the gift of a new automobile. He said, 'I don't appreciate this, but I sure do deserve it.'"

A brief bon mot that produces at least a smile, is: "That is the second best introduction I have ever had. The best one was when, because the fellow who was supposed to introduce me failed to show up, I had to introduce myself."

If the chairman has used the word "distinguished," I may tell of my first participation in Congressional debate. It was several months before I got up enough courage to address the speaker. The revered Carl Vinson of Georgia had the floor. I said, "Mr. Speaker, will the gentleman from Georgia yield?"

He bowed from the waist. "I am happy to yield to the *distinguished* gentleman from Arkansas." I was so overwhelmed that I forgot my question!

Some years ago I quit telling, because I had worn it threadbare, an incident my audiences seemed to enjoy, probably because it was drawn from the lore of baseball, which is the great American pastime.

A sure-fire way to answer a flattering introduction a generation ago was to invoke the name of the great Hall of Fame baseball pitcher Walter Johnson, although today, I suppose, we'd substitute Sandy Koufax. A young rookie was facing the feared fast ball of Johnson for the first time. The rookie was scared to death and justifiably so, for the first ball was a typical Big Train special. The rookie didn't even see it.

"Strike one," the umpire called.

The rookie turned to him, "Mister Umpire, did you *see* that ball?"

"Sure I saw it—it was a strike."

"Well," said the rookie, "it *sounded* a little *high* to me."

A speaker should always be alert to the possibilities for humor or other advantages that lie in the presence of platform guests. Once at a meeting in Nashville, Tennessee, where I was the speaker, the new mayor of the "metro" city and county government was sitting on my left. Nashville's municipal and Davidson County's governments had just been combined, and the county judge, Beverly Briley, had become mayor of the new unit, which was generally referred to as the "Metro" government. I had asked someone just before the meeting how the new mayor was doing.

"Oh, he's eighteen karat," was the reply.

I quoted this to the audience, and added, "I'm glad we have the Metro Golden Mayor with us."

Wilbur Cross, four times governor of Connecticut, was a magnificent campaigner. He was fond of an opening sentence which never failed to amuse his audience. "Mr. Chairman," he would intone solemnly, "fellow Democrats, and lost Republicans, who have come in here to inquire the way home. . . ."

One time he was scheduled to speak in Middletown on behalf of the local ticket. He was met at the Portland-Middletown line by Professor Wilbert Snow of Wesleyan. Bill Snow gave him a briefing on the other candidates who would be on the platform with him. Included in the platform dignitaries was Elmer Eric Schattschneider, a distinguished political science professor, who was running for city council. Cross was magnificent as he went down the list of platform dignitaries, speaking warmly of "my good friend, Carl Shaffer—everybody knows what a great job Carl has done as mayor," and so on until he got to Schattschneider. "And here is my good old friend Elmer Eric Shatt . . . Schatt . . . ," and try as he would, he could not get out the full name.

In desperation Bill Snow leaped up and whispered in his ear, "Schattschneider."

"My good friend Schattschneider," he finally sputtered out, and then in a loud aside the governor muttered, "That fellow ought to do something about his name if he expects to have a career in politics."

APPEALS TO PREJUDICE AND SYMPATHY

Speeches, or allusions, which are slanted toward a group, or a segment of society, for the purpose of arousing mass prejudice, while a very tempting gambit to speakers of a certain type, do not always achieve the desired results. They are sometimes costly. Senator Goldwater, in his pursuit of the Republican nomination for President, frequently attacked something he called the Eastern Establishment, and once in a fit of pique, he proposed sawing off the entire Eastern Seaboard and letting it sink into the Atlantic Ocean. This intemperate remark may have done him more harm than good.

One of the candidates for governor of Arkansas in the 1966 campaign changed his appeals for support as the moods and situations changed. For example, he had high praise in the fall for an opponent he had earlier castigated as a betrayer of confidences. One of my friends commented, "He reminds me of the Louisianan who, after making his pitch for votes, said, 'Now, mah friends, them's mah sentiments; and if you don't like 'em—I'll change 'em!' "

It was in a quite different context that Jefferson Davis—not the Confederate president, but a governor of Arkansas and a United States senator in the early part of this century—made a whipping boy of the easterner. He campaigned against him as if every resident of the Eastern Seaboard had an Arkansas residence, and delighted his rural audiences with his verbal attacks. "If some of them high-collared, flyweight dudes of the East had sense enough to sit down to a big dish of turnip greens, poke salad, and hog jowls, they might sweat enough of that talcum powder off to look and smell a little like a man."

As he had only one constituency, Arkansas Democrats, and was not running for a national office, and so had nothing to gain or lose from the eastern section of the country, this strategy cost him nothing politically. Continuing in this vein, he would identify himself with the have-nots, as the majority of Arkansas farmers and laborers were in those days.

It was an essentially rural culture that fixed the limits within which Jeff Davis stayed. It was negative in that he offered little in the way of constructive and imaginative programs for the rural communities, but why struggle with that? The cleavage between city and country life was sharp enough to enable him to chart a successful course on appeals to the suspicions and prejudices of the rural mind. The average Arkansas voter, outside of Little Rock, loved his homespun handling of the contrasts, and they reacted by voting for him. I heard one of the court house politicians say, with reference to the Davis phenomenon, that in the days of his ascendancy (1898–1912) "they" (the leaders) would meet in Little Rock to plan his downfall, and, he said, "it looked as if everybody was with us. Then we would go home for the final vote, and sure enough, everybody *would* be with us—except the people."

One of Jeff's powerful drawing cards was an invitation he broadcast: "Now you all come on there to see me while I'm governor. If nobody answers the knock on the front door, just walk on through the house to the back yard—you'll find my wife back there making soap. We won't have any fancy grub to serve up, but we'll sure share what we got with you."

One of his favorite campaign slogans, a gallant but empty gesture toward his feminine adherents (who could not vote), was the emphatic assertion that "every woman is entitled to a baby and a bonnet." It shed a pathetic light on the scanty wardrobes of those days, in contrast to today where a man advocating only one bonnet per woman would be inviting the epithet "Communist."

Jeff Davis' talents and stratagems were similar to those of another southerner who was to follow a generation later—Huey P. Long of Louisiana.

One of Huey Long's most amazing exploits (and they were legion) was his single-handed advancement of Senator Hattie Caraway from a lagging position in the 1932 Senate race to an impressive victory over a number of outstandingly successful Arkansas politicians. Few of our citizens suspected that a powerful new influence was being interjected. Huey's schedule was for only one week. He entered the state near Magnolia, county seat of Columbia County, on the Louisiana line. After his first speech the Little Rock headquarters of O. L. Bodenhamer—one of her opponents, and former national commander of the American Legion—received this cryptic telegram: "A terrific wind passed through here this morning headed in your direction. Only the strongest trees are left standing."

Federal Judge Oren Harris, former congressman, relates the following: Huey Long's aides enlisted the help of an Arkansas sheriff with preparations for his first appearance. The sheriff, as an act of courtesy, assisted, but he was quite concerned about his relationship to the senator's plans, since he knew of the strained feelings between Long and Senator Joe T. Robinson, then at the height of his popularity and the strongest single influence in Arkansas politics. "Just don't give me any prominence —don't mention me," he pleaded with Long's staff. "I'll work in the background."

The senator showed up at the appointed time. A great throng stood in front of the platform on the court house lawn. The sheriff stood in an inconspicuous place, an interested but skeptical onlooker. After ten minutes of the Huey Long hypnotic performance, the sheriff turned around to look at the audience. Relating his reactions to Oren, the sheriff said, "I saw only eyeballs and open mouths—a crowd frozen in their tracks—so I said to my deputy, 'Pull Huey's coat tail and tell him if he wants to mention my name it will be all right with me.'"

Anything that I have said about the hazards of appeals to mass prejudice is not to be construed as indicating that it is not perennially open season when the two great political parties are involved. Southern Democrats, one hundred years after the end of the Civil War, still invoke its memories and emotions, while earlier in this century a candidate for office who could not claim to have fought gloriously for the Confederate cause was hardly in the running. One of Alben Barkley's stories reflects the emotion-charged atmosphere of those days.

As the custom was (and still is in many parts of the South), a political rally was being held, at which any candidate for any office could present himself and make a brief statement. On this occasion, no time was spent on the issues at stake, and no one pressed his own fitness for public office. Instead, each aspirant dwelt lovingly and eloquently on his Civil War record. One held up an empty sleeve and exclaimed, "I gave that arm at Shiloh, fighting for our Glorious Cause!" Another, on crutches, one pants leg pinned up, said promptly, "I left my other leg on the battlefield of Franklin."

Each speech followed the same pattern, until the last candidate rose. He was physically unimpressive in appearance, but was without any outward evidence of impairment, such as wounds or scars. He came to the center of the platform, and half defensively, half defiantly, as one who knew the deck was stacked against him, made his appeal. "My friends, I never lost no arms or legs fightin' for the Confederacy. In fact, I never fit in the war at all. But if physical disability qualifies anybody for an office, I want to tell you that I'm the most completely ruptured man in Simpson County."

The sympathy vote is always an important factor in an election, which would seem to indicate that many people select their candidates with their emotions rather than any cerebral activity. It might be a little difficult to follow the process that led the English woman to explain, "Oh, I voted for the Conservative. I felt sorry for him—he was such a poor speaker!" But votes for the physically handicapped, the disabled, or the victim of a recent misfortune, though perhaps to be deplored if unmatched by other claims, are to be expected.

One of the most effective antidotes for the poverty vote appeal was provided by a colorful Arkansan known and loved locally, and referred to always in his home county of Yell as Brother Vandiver. He was not an educated person, but had rare natural gifts, and was uninhibited in public speech. At Centerville the candidates were on the platform making the usual joint appeals in the biennial summer campaigns.

The county tax assessor's race was announced. Eleven hopefuls sat in a row awaiting their opportunity to appeal to the assembly. Some of them were seeking not a political career, but a salary to supplement the farmer's or laborer's income, which in that period was rather meager.

Altogether it was far from an impressive array. They were in blue denims, not adorned with cravats. Each gave his piece, and generally included were the threadbare references to hard work and the candidate's desire to better himself. But not Brother Vandiver! If he wore a necktie, it was covered by a fiery red beard, which was an appropriate adjunct for his huge frame— three hundred pounds, six feet six in height. He resembled Frederick Barbarossa, and his voice would have made Mitch Miller's bass singer sound like a high tenor. This was the substance of his modest, direct, and thoroughly honest appeal. "Mah friends, I reckon you-uns is all wondering about my candacity for 'sessor. Well, ah'm gonna tell you. I jes' looked over the field" (here he waved a long arm in a semicircle to cover his ten seated opponents) "and seein' as to how this wuz gonna be a scrub race anyhow, I wuz just as liable to be elected as aryone of them other fellers." He won!

When Henry Clay was campaigning for the legislature for the first time, he was unintentionally put in a tough spot by an exuberant well-wisher, and handled it so masterfully that his fellow Kentuckians never knew how close to embarrassment he had come.

In a county seat, one of the local political figures said, "Young Man, you want to go to the legislature, I see."

"Why, yes," replied Mr. Clay, "yes, I should like to go, as my friends have seen proper to put me up as a candidate before the people; I do not wish to be defeated."

"Are you a good shot?"

"The best in the county."

"Then you shall go, but you must first give us a specimen of your skill; we must see you shoot."

"I never shoot any rifle but my own, and that is at home."

"No matter; here is Old Bess; she never fails in the hands of a marksman; she has often sent death through a squirrel's head at one hundred yards, and daylight through many a redskin at twice that distance; if you can shoot any gun, you can shoot Old Bess."

"Well, put up your mark; put up your mark," replied Mr. Clay.

The target was placed at a distance of about eighty yards, when with all the coolness and steadiness of an old experienced marksman, he drew Old Bess to his shoulder and fired. The bullet pierced the target near the center.

"Oh, a chance shot! Just a chance shot!" exclaimed several of his political opponents. "A chance shot; he might shoot all day and not hit the mark again; let him try it over; let him try it over."

"No; beat that, beat that, and then I will," retorted Mr. Clay.

But as no one seemed disposed to make the attempt, it was considered that he had given satisfactory proof that he was the best shot in the county, and this incident gained him the vote of every hunter and marksman in the assembly. Clay, in telling about the episode said, "I had never before fired a rifle and have not since."

In campaigning, the best defense is very often a hard-hitting offense. A candidate for county commissioner in Kentucky had once spent some time as a patient in a mental hospital. He knew that the opposition was quietly trying to capitalize on this fact. To meet this disadvantage he would, in every one of his campaign experiences, exhibit a certificate signed by the mental hospital's medical director. The certificate stated that he had been completely rehabilitated. "Ladies and gentlemen," he would boast, "I am the only candidate running in this election who can produce a valid certificate of sanity."

Sometimes there is a legitimate use of sympathy that does not involve humor at all, but rather a degree of pathos that literally upsets polls. I recall as the best example the response I attempted in Charleston, Arkansas, in my first successful campaign —for Congress in 1942. My opponent was Lieutenant Governor Bob Bailey. He was from my home town of Russellville and a former neighbor of our family.

Near the campaign's close he realized that he was far behind, and he switched to drastic measures, ridiculing and attacking me. One line in his circular stimulated my memory of Bob's early struggles, so like my own (he was some ten years older). There was an allusion to my three defeats for office: "Brooks

Hays' life is a succession of failures, three times defeated by the sound-thinking people of Arkansas, and never elected to office. On the other hand, Bob Bailey has never been defeated."

This was a slip that I made the most of, for I recalled at once his defeats for county office, many years prior to 1942.

So I used the old sympathy appeal. Standing on a sidewalk with perhaps a hundred people listening, also some seated in parked cars, I did my best to offset it. Reading my opponent's statement carefully and slowly, trying to let my hurt feelings make the words tremble, I looked up after the completion of the part about me and sadly said:

"Don't you think Mr. Bailey is a bit unkind in his reference to my disappointments? It is not dishonorable to suffer defeat, is it? Particularly when we remember that in two governor's races I was battling for your best interests.

"But Mr. Bailey has a short memory. He too has had defeats. He lived close to us in Russellville when I was a growing boy. I looked up to him as an ambitious young man who was studying law at night, while he worked in a furniture store to make a living. To help advance a professional program that he had determined upon, he announced for justice of the peace. He was defeated. I was disappointed that this fine neighbor of ours had failed. A little later he ran for a county office and again he was defeated. But I was not discouraged, and seeing evidence of his pluck, I consoled myself with the thought that in this free land one may fall to rise again. Then Mr. Bailey ran for a seat in the 1918 Constitutional convention, and again he was unsuccessful. Like his other friends, I did not give up hopes for him even then, though his life was 'a succession of failures.' Finally, he was elected state senator, and I rejoiced that men may, in America, have this glorious right to keep trying till the laurels are won. My friend, Mr. Bailey, had won! So it is with me, my Franklin County friends, I am merely exercising this God-given right to persist. Won't you help me?"

I did not need to see the returns from that community to know that my response was effective. The comments of my listeners told the story.

A special election in 1933, to fill a vacancy in my own Congressional district, was typical of the anxieties that come in profusion in any tight race.

I had opposed the state organization as a candidate for governor in two races, 1928 and 1930, and further angered the group by putting through a resolution at the state Democratic convention requiring a primary to nominate a candidate for Congress, instead of having a committee handpick a candidate. This destroyed plans of the state machine to place a favorite in the office, regardless of public disfavor.

The campaign that followed was hectic. The depression was at its severest stage. The registration of voters was the lowest in our history, and because people lacked money to buy other entertainment, and also because they had hopes for help from their government, they swarmed to the political "speakings."

The climax of that campaign, however, was at Conway, county seat of Faulkner County, and it took place on a Saturday afternoon before the primary on Tuesday.

When I reached the plaza of the Missouri Pacific station, I found an enormous crowd gathered to witness the final blows struck in that unique campaign. My local manager greeted me, "Oh, boy, you'll love our arrangements here. Every preacher in town is on the platform, and they're going to run the show."

I didn't like those arrangements and said so as politely as I could. They violated my conviction that religion should never be exploited in a campaign.

"Brother Charles Campbell, the Presbyterian minister, will open the meeting with prayer," he added.

I was less polite at that point: "No, no, Guy. Please," I protested.

"No use to argue about it. Charley is at the mike ready to start," he said, and I saw that it was too late. But I was comforted by the knowledge that he was a boyhood friend and a discreet person. He proved discretion by not praying for my election. In substance he asked for divine guidance in performance of duty as voters, for "patience and tolerance and insight." It was a good beginning, and I breathed a lot easier. My adviser continued, as he escorted me to the platform, "The Baptist preacher, Brother Garrett, will introduce you and the Methodist preacher, Brother Workman, will preside."

At that moment Brother Workman spied me, and I heard his exuberant voice literally bellowing a welcome. "Here's our candidate—here's Brother Brooks. Get on up here, Brother Brooks."

My spirit soared. The atmosphere was already electric with enthusiasm, and I was borne on its invisible waves. Brother Garrett presented me with a great flourish, and with a loud "Amen" from Workman, I launched into my speech. That amen was one of many brief interruptions from the chairman, who was noted for his unconventional ways of directing a meeting. I tried to match the chairman's informality by suddenly turning to him with a request for a glass of water. Gulping it down, I turned to the audience and said, "That's more water than I ever found on a Methodist in all my life," only to hear him shout, "And I never saw a Baptist satisfied with so little!" The crowd responded happily.

I was able to compress a lot of serious talk about ending depressions and achieving justice for farmers into that political speech, and I felt elated as I brought it to an end. Again the chairman took over. I gasped as he yelled to a preacher friend in the audience, "Brother Williams, come up here and dismiss the meeting with prayer."

I had recovered from my dissatisfaction with the committee for opening the session with prayer, but this was too much! Still, there was nothing I could do about it.

Brother Williams was a gentle little person, but he had plenty of ministerial confidence and a voice like a fog horn. While Brother Campbell, in the opening prayer, had asked for a tolerant spirit and love of one's neighbor, little Brother Williams asked for the bacon. "Dear Lord," he intoned, "please send these people back to their homes to do everything in their power to elect Brother Brooks to Congress! Oh, please, dear Lord, give him the victory next Tuesday!"

I never felt that it was divine intervention that produced a surprisingly big vote in Faulkner County on Tuesday, but undoubtedly the result was influenced by the events of Saturday. A few days after the election one of the opposition leaders was asked by a Little Rock friend, "Did Brooks have a good meeting in Conway?"

The old pro replied, "Did he have a good meeting? It was so

good we had to steal one township we hadn't figured on taking, just to carry the county by a few votes!"

SPEECH WRITING: GHOST AND OTHERWISE

Political craftsmen are divided into two classes—people who write speeches they never make, and people who make speeches they never write. At the national and state level campaigning is so fast moving that it is impossible to have a newly prepared speech for every appearance.

In the pretelevision days a candidate for governor had to depend upon attracting to the county seats and large communities as many listeners as possible. He could, with impunity (for few voters heard him more than once), give substantially the same speech in every town. Of course the content changed in the course of long campaigns, but still there was a basis for the quip by Josh Lee of Oklahoma about his race for the United States Senate—A friend asked him after the election, "Is it true that you made 296 speeches?"

"No," said the famed orator, "I made one speech 296 times."

It was always an advantage to be able to speak extemporaneously. A master of the extemporaneous was Adlai Stevenson. This, even though he much preferred to have prepared texts— texts on which he himself had laboriously and lovingly worked. He quickly found out, however, that it was impossible in the heat of a campaign to be a do-it-yourselfer when it came to speeches.

An example of Governor Stevenson's ability to improvise was the time he came to Connecticut during the campaign of 1952. In a short, one-day barnstorming visit he was to appear and speak briefly in about ten Connecticut towns. Don Herzberg was assigned the task of riding with him in the motorcade and briefing the governor on the people and the towns in which he would next be speaking. Briefing was hard to do between waving at the people cheering him on his way and listening to the other candidates in the car as they competed for his ear. As the motorcade came into Bristol, Connecticut, about all Herzberg had the opportunity to tell Adlai was that Bristol made clocks, Jim Casey who owned the fish market was the Democratic mayor who would introduce him, and Senator Robert Taft had been in

Bristol a week earlier on behalf of the Republican ticket. Stevenson spoke on the town green. He thanked his good friend Mayor Jim Casey. "Jim," he said, "I know that fishy aroma I got as we drove into this beautiful town of yours does not come from your modern fish store. It's the smell left over from that Republican rally last week. I understand that Senator Taft was presented with one of Bristol's fine watches. Good! But it's not enough to give my good friend Bob Taft a watch, what you should also have given him was a calendar, because neither he nor his party knows yet that we are in the twentieth century." From this extemporizing, Adlai Stevenson then moved into his set speech, which he had given throughout the campaign, and then back to the car for the ride to the next town.

Another time during that campaign of 1952 Stevenson turned up at the Hotel Astor to appear at a luncheon of some female party workers. He had been told that the group would be small and he need not speak formally, greetings would be sufficient. When he got there he found hundreds of devoted party workers who expected some pearls from their beloved candidate. He apologized for the lack of a prepared text for this important occasion. He was, he said, "like the soldier who appeared with his girl friend before the judge on a late Friday afternoon. 'Judge,' the soldier said, 'will you marry us?' 'Certainly I will. Let's see your marriage license.' With that the lad's face fell. 'License? I don't have a license.' 'Well, in that case, son, I can't marry you until Monday, because the clerk's office is closed.' 'But, Judge, I'm being shipped out at 8:00 A.M. Monday morning.' 'I'm sorry, soldier, but I can't marry you without that marriage license.' 'Well,' said the not-to-be-downed soldier, 'could you say a few words to tide us over the weekend?'"

Speechmaking in general can be pretty hard on the campaigner. Especially if he is the kind of politician who never writes his own speeches and, worse yet, never reads the speeches prepared for him until he gets up to give them.

There was one former mayor of New York, a Democrat who had best be nameless, who consistently failed to practice his ghost written speeches before he gave them. The results, oftentimes, were deadly.

Once he was to dedicate a branch of the New York Public

Library. "Liberties is full of books," he started out. With a startled look, he said in a loud aside to himself, "That ain't right. Oh, *libraries* is full of books." This mayor wore pince nez glasses and once as he said "this reminds me of a very funny story" his eye, as sometimes happens, caught the punchline of the joke. He laughed so hard his glasses fell off the end of his nose and he was unable to read the rest of his speech.

Another time our mayor friend was giving a speech in Central Park on "I-Am-an-American Day." In what were for him eloquent phrases, he thundered, "We must go back to the days of our forefathers, back to the days of the spirit of one seven and," then unfortunately he had to turn the page, "seven six."

A final story about him involved a vacation trip which took the mayor to Denver. He had barely settled himself in his room when the telephone rang. The local Kiwanis Club wanted him to be their luncheon guest speaker two days hence. The mayor accepted and hung up the telephone only then to remember his precarious situation. A formal speech to give and eighteen hundred miles from his nearest speech writer. In desperation he called up his friend, the mayor of Denver, who assured him he'd help. Sure enough, shortly before he was to appear in the Brown Palace Ballroom, a young staff assistant for the Denver mayor appeared with a text. True to form the mayor shoved the speech into his inside pocket and went off to his luncheon. After a suitable introduction, the mayor hauled out his speech. "You don't know what it means to a boy from the sidewalks of New York to come out here and see the grandeur of the West. I never will forget coming into Denver, Colorado [we are not sure, but we think the Colorado was an ad lib—one of the few of his career], and seeing a glorious western sunset. As long as I live, I will forever see Pike's Peak,"—now a double take at his script, a frown, and then the word—"silly-hooted against the western sky."

Most United States senators work over their speeches in advance, even though a staff assistant may have blocked out a first draft. There are a few who do not change a word. There was one senator who never changed a word, but who liked to give the hardworking staff man who actually wrote the speeches the impression that the original text was inadequate. The only thing that saved the occasion, the senator would insist, was his very clever improvisations and ad libs. To make matters worse, the staff assistant was an extremely able speech writer, who since his days with this particular senator has gone on into far bigger and better things. On this particular occasion, the assignment was to prepare a speech for a labor convention. The senator was handed a thick manuscript as he left for the airport. "I hope it's better than the stuff you've been turning out lately," were his last words to the assistant. At the labor hall the speech got off to a magnificent start. Winston Churchill himself could have done no better. Eyes were wet in the audience as the senator completed the opening page, "and this, ladies and gentlemen, leads me to the five main points I wish to leave you with to-night." He turned the page. It was blank except for this hand-written note signed by the assistant, "Now you're on your own, Big Boy—I quit."

CAMPAIGN JITTERS

All is not fun and games in campaigning. The traveling, speak-ing, hand-shaking, though often tiring, have their stimulating side; but the period is subject to pressures, tensions, and anxie-ties, which are utterly enervating.

The pre-election-day jitters are at their peak just before the ticket closes, when the incumbent is waiting nervously to see whether he is "home free," without having to wrestle an op-ponent for his place on the ticket, or whether there will be an unwelcome, last-minute surprise announcement. This nervous dread is also experienced by the candidates in an open race.

One of the most delightful stories was told on Senator Tom Heflin by one of his colleagues, when Heflin's first term in the Senate was drawing to an end. He had announced that he would seek the office a second time, then waited anxiously to see whether he would have any opposition.

The day the ticket closed, the Senate was having an early session, but he was too nervous to sit still. He went to the Democratic cloakroom, where he moved restlessly about until his colleagues said, "What's the matter, Tom?"

"The ticket closes at noon," he answered shortly.

That told the whole story. He suddenly went to one of the telephones, put through a call to a party official in Montgomery, who was also a personal friend, and his colleagues heard this one-sided conversation.

"George! Has anyone filed against me? Oh, you say they haven't? Oh! They're threatening to! Well, now I hope nobody will do that! I've been a good senator and I deserve a second term. You boys try to talk 'em out of it. There's no reason for anyone to run against me! Well, I'll call you when the ticket closes at twelve. Good-bye."

Promptly at twelve, Washington time, he called George again, but he had forgotten the hour difference in time. George reported the situation was the same. Again Tom, almost dancing with tears in his eyes implored, "You boys talk 'em out of it! I oughtn't to have any opposition this year!"

Finally, one o'clock came. Tom waited a few minutes, then called Montgomery a third time, and the interested colleagues heard a suddenly valiant senator say, "Did anybody file? Oh, they didn't! Well, I just wish to hell somebody had! I'd have beat the livin' daylights out of him!"

Another filing story was told by another Alabama Congressman, George Grant. One spring a member of Congress who had taken a trip through the South ran into a colleague on his return.

"Bill, you're in trouble," he said. "I've just been in your district, and Henry Jones is going to run against you."

Bill swelled up until his face was purple, and he resembled an irate turkey cock. The friend who had brought the bad news watched the change with interest. "Well, I'm not surprised," blurted Bill. "He's a thief, a crook, and a liar. He's lucky to be out of the penitentiary!"

"That's not all," said the friend, having decided that Bill could stand a little more. "George Johnson's going to announce tomorrow."

For a minute he thought he had gone too far, and the colleague would have a stroke.

"They're two of a kind—except maybe Johnson is worse. They're just the sort that *would* run against me!" the harassed congressman was wailing, when the other took pity on him.

"Cheer up," he said laughing. "I was just kidding. I saw 'em, but they're both for you, and sent their regards."

Bill got out his handkerchief and mopped his brow. "Now see what you made me do!" he complained. "You've made me say some ugly things about two of the sweetest, finest men I've ever known."

Once the ticket has closed and the long trek has begun, all candidates are alike in one respect—they are incurable optimists. No matter how bleak the situation, the true politician normally feels he can save the situation. He will balance the budget, solve the highway mess, score an upset at the polls on election day no matter what the pollsters say. The late Senator Kefauver used to tell the story of the Senate candidate who conducted his own public opinion polls. He would get out of his car a few blocks from the hall where he was to speak. As he walked he would stop people at random and introduce himself as Senator ——. Then he would ask, "Would you mind telling me for whom you are going to vote?" Most people, when hit by a senator in those circumstances, do the polite thing, "Why, Senator, I am going to vote for you."

Upon hearing that, the senator would turn to his assistant, dutifully trailing three paces in the rear, "Mark it down, son." And the assistant would record the plus vote in a small black book. When the senator got to the hall he reported that "Victory is in the air. Why, just walking down your beautiful Main Street I stopped ten people at random. Each and every one of them said they were going to vote for me, and our glorious party in November. We cannot lose."

One day the senator was conducting his "survey" when he stopped a particularly large gentleman. He went through his routine. This time, though, the answer departed from the usual form.

"Are you really Senator ——?"

"Yes, yes, I am," he responded proudly, adjusting his tie.

"Senator, I wouldn't vote for you if you were the last man in the state. You have a lousy voting record. I don't like a thing you stand for and never have. In fact, I don't even want to stand here and be seen with you."

As he stormed away, the senator turned to his assistant, "Put him down as doubtful!"

When Governor Ed Muskie of Maine was running for re-election, he too was conducting his own survey. He asked an old-timer how it looked. "Don't know yet," the old man said, "too soon to tell."

"But," asked the Governor, "am I doing better than my opponent right now?"

"I don't know about that," the old friend said, "but if bumper stickers mean anything, this fellow Ausable Chasm is running darn strong for a newcomer."

The best illustration of the fact that a name can be a great asset comes out of Iowa. Senator Burke Hickenlooper, the impregnable Republican from that state, likes to recite the quaint situations in which his unusual name made him a target, and invariably he profits from the incidents. My favorite is the one involving the race between him and Al Loveland, his Democratic opponent for senator. Mr. Loveland approached an Iowa voter, identified himself, and said, "I am a candidate for senator, and I hope I will have your support."

He got this reply: "Nope, I'm going to vote for that other feller."

This frankness set Al on his heels, and he received another jolt when the voter added, "He's a prayin', God-fearin' man."

When he recovered his breath, the Democratic opponent of the well-known Iowa Republican Senator Hickenlooper inquired, "Yes, he is a good man, but what is it about him that impresses you to this extent?"

"Well, now," the man said, "everybody ought to know that. The papers was full of it. That airplane went down in the Pacific and a bunch of 'em was in the raft with him. He got out the Bible and read to 'em and prayed—yes, sir—he's a prayin', God-fearin' man. That's what pulled 'em through."

To this the distraught candidate replied, "Man, that wasn't Hickenlooper. That was Rickenbacker."

"I don't care what you call him . . . Hickenbacker, Rickenlooper . . . I tell you he's a prayin', God-fearin' man, and I'm fer him."

In relating the incident, Al Loveland adds with frustration, "What can you do with a handicap like that?"

Nevertheless, there comes a time when incumbents become edgy. They get edgier and edgier as it gets closer to filing time.

That's the moment of truth, when the office holder finds out if anyone has filed against him for his own party's nomination.

No chapter on humor in campaigning would be complete without some attention to the special humor that has grown up around our national conventions.

Walt Whitman, one of America's great poets, was also a newspaper reporter. He was sent by *The Brooklyn Eagle* to cover a Democratic National Convention prior to the Civil War. Here is how Whitman describes the delegates: "The members who composed it were, seven eighths of them, the meanest kind of bawling and blowing officeholders, office seekers, pimps, malignants, conspirators, murderers, funny men, customs house clerks, contractors, kept editors, spaniels well trained to carry and fetch, jobbers, infidels, disunionists, terrorists, mail riflers, slave catchers, pushers of slavery, creatures of the President, creatures of would-be Presidents, spies, bribers, compromisers, lobbyists, sponges, ruined sportsmen, expelled gamblers, policy backers, monte dealers, duelists, carriers of concealed weapons, deaf men, pimpled men—scarred inside with vile diseases, gaudy outside with gold chains made from the people's money and harlots' money twisted together—crawling, serpentine men, the lousy combinings and born freedom sellers of the earth." Now since Whitman was a Democrat, one must wonder what he would have had to say about a Republican Convention.

The 1924 Republican convention in Cleveland was the first one to be broadcast. Microphones and radio equipment were new items to be contended with, and the technical devices could be fraught with peril. At that convention there was at least one survivor of the founding group—the group that met in Ripon, Wisconsin—and he was a guest at the convention. The presiding officer introduced the old gentleman with great gusto. He was in his nineties, had a long white beard, and it was not surprising to find him deeply moved emotionally by the reception. The chairman said, "Fellow delegates, it is my great privilege to present to this convention of militant and dedicated Republicans the sole remaining survivor of that brave band that assembled in that little schoolhouse at Ripon, Wisconsin, in 1854 to inaugurate this mighty movement."

The response was tremendous. They threw their hats in the air, they stomped on the floor, they cheered for minutes. And under the spell of this profound emotion the old gentleman began his speech. No time had been reserved for this. He was expected to do no more than take a bow and then remove himself. Time was terribly limited, and the person presiding was quite aggravated that things did not go according to schedule. He walked back to the secretary's desk, leaned over to say something to him, not knowing that the microphone in front of the secretary was "hot."

This is what he said, and it went over the air in a sort of undertone, as the old gentleman's speech proceeded. "Who told the old billy goat to make a speech?"

At a New York State Convention, the business of the temporary organization was completed and the time was at hand to move to make the temporary organization into a permanent one. A delegate not up to the task of making the motion and obviously under the influence of strong stimulants shouted, "Mr. Chairman, I move that the temporary organization be made permanent." The chairman tried to gavel him down, "Sit down, sit down, sir, you're drunk, you don't even know the difference between temporary and permanent."

Before the sergeant-at-arms could assist the chairman in subduing him, the delegate shouted, "Oh, yes I do, I'm drunk—that's temporary. You're a jackass, that's permanent."

At another New York State Democratic Convention there was great agitation over the wording of the platform's liquor plank allowing Sunday sales. The Drys were adamant that the platform should support no sale on Sunday. The Wets were equally adamant that there should be such sales. As a compromise the platform makers tried this wording, "We are in favor of a law which absolutely prohibits the sale of liquor on Sunday, but we are against its enforcement."

A special kind of campaigning is required to capture delegates at national conventions. Vast systems of individual file cards on each delegate and alternate are built. These cards, containing names and addresses and candidate preference, even go so far as to render likes and dislikes "steak rare, loves to go dancing at nightclubs, a great admirer of N.Y. Yankees"—all this pertinent data is recorded in a frantic attempt to use the information in the quest for delegates.

The hoopla and excitement of a national convention make such a gathering a combination of a Roman circus and a deadly serious political operation. But humorous things still manage to occur.

In the days before the convention opens, each delegate and alternate is deluged by mail from the rival candidates. Daniel Patrick Moynihan, the distinguished young former Assistant Secretary of Labor, was an alternate to the 1960 Democratic Convention. Although known to be a staunch Kennedy supporter, his mailbox was kept full, and it included a letter addressed to Mr. Daniel Patrick Moynihan. "Dear Mr. Moynihan, I am appealing to you as a fellow Chinese-American to support the candidacy of ——."

At the 1956 Democratic Convention in Chicago, Don Herzberg was involved in the unsuccessful attempt to nominate Governor Averill Harriman of New York. Herzberg arrived a week before the convention opened and was assigned to the Morrison Hotel, where fifteen state delegations were to be housed. He had the inevitable card file containing the information on those delegates. He knew who was for Harriman, who was for Stevenson, and who the waverers were. Unfortunately, the Stevenson camp had most of the delegates sewed up tight. Tucked away in the Pennsylvania delegation, however, was the mayor of a small town not far from Pittsburgh. He and his wife, neither of whom had been farther west before than the Pennsylvania-Ohio state line, were staunch Harriman supporters. As a Harriman man, the mayor showed up dutifully in the Harriman suite at the Morrison a few days before the convention opened. Fortunately, the mayor and his wife were wonderful people, because Herzberg kept them in his sight morning, noon, and night, lest the tremendous pressures being applied by the Stevenson steamroller overwhelm his precious delegate. Finally on the Sunday evening just prior to the opening of the convention, in desperation for want of anything to do, Herzberg said proudly, "How would you like to meet Carmine de Sapio?" Carmine, the then leader of Tammany Hall, whose genius had helped to elect Harriman governor of New York, was at the height of his power and fame. Featured in national magazines, he had even given a lecture at Harvard. To have a moment with this great political leader was truly one of the finer gifts that could be bestowed on a delegate.

"O.K., where is he?" the mayor asked.

A quick phone call verified that de Sapio was in his Black-stone Hotel suite and that he would indeed be happy to meet the faithful mayor and his lady. Off they went to the Blackstone, slugged their way through the crowded lobby, jam-packed with delegates and hangers-on, anxious to spot the celebrities. Up-stairs to the suite, past the politicians gathered in de Sapio's living room—all looking on enviously as the mayor was greeted cordially by Milt Stewart, one of Governor Harriman's most trusted lawyer lieutenants—they were finally ushered into a back bedroom, where de Sapio himself extended his hand to the mayor and his wife. The Tammany leader thanked the mayor for his support, told him his confidence in Harriman was not misplaced for, after all, hadn't Harriman beaten the highly regarded Dewey machine and wasn't Harriman the one man who knew how to stand up to the Russians? In the middle of his very quiet but eloquent speech, de Sapio was interrupted by a phone call. Carmine excused himself to take the call in another bedroom.

As he left, the mayor turned to Herzberg and said, "He's an awfully nice fellow. What did you say his name was?"

Any faint hope that Herzberg might have had that the Steven-son steamroller could be stopped, faded right then. "Why, why, that's *Carmine de Sapio*," he choked out.

The mayor turned to his wife with a quizzical look on his face. "I've heard of him. What does he do?"

Adlai Stevenson was nominated on the first ballot. Later Herzberg told Governor Harriman in a remark the governor didn't think very funny, "Governor, you'll never know how many second ballot votes I had for you."

Just prior to the opening of that convention the Democratic platform committee held public hearings. These hearings, con-ducted by distinguished partisans, give the general public and the various interested groups an opportunity to appear and make statements on matters of interest in the hope that their particu-lar viewpoint will emerge as a plank in the party platform. Senator William Benton of Connecticut, one of the members of the committee, was questioning a gentleman who had expressed concern about the magnitude of federal spending. Under Benton's acute cross-examination the lobbyist became more and more uncomfortable.

Finally in desperation he shouted, "Senator, if we don't stop shearing the wool off the goose that lays the golden egg we are going to pump the well dry."

Needless to say, that splintered phrase did not find its way into a party plank.

Rumors at conventions are an important device, sometimes deliberately planted, but usually the result of delegates' desperate desire to really be in on the know. The truth is that conventions are so confused and state delegations so large that the average delegate may be the last to know that his vote in his delegation has been pledged, switched, or thrown up for grabs. In futile attempts to appear informed, people spread rumors like an uncontrolled forest fire.

On the Saturday before the 1956 Democratic Convention opened, former President Harry S Truman held a press conference and declared himself for Harriman. For a few short hours there was joy in the Harriman camp on the sixteenth floor of the Conrad Hilton Hotel and consternation in the Stevenson headquarters on the ninth floor. This lasted until the Stevenson people were able to ascertain that the damage from the Truman broadside was above the water line and no permanent damage had been done. But at the peak of the Stevenson panic a group of newspapermen, including New York *Herald Tribune* reporter Tom O'Hara, caught an elevator from the Harriman floor. At the ninth floor a group of sad, grim-faced Stevensonites got into the car. As the elevator descended, Tom O'Hara, who was tall enough to tower over everyone else in the elevator, said in a loud voice, "Too bad about Adlai. They say he was only cleaning his gun." The doors slid open and for a few brief seconds the looks on the Stevensonites' faces showed they didn't know if it were true or not true.

POST ELECTION MORNINGS AND MOURNING

Finally, there comes the time when the actual campaign comes to an end, and the candidates, in a state of combined exhaustion and exhilaration, await the fateful returns. It's difficult to describe the numbness that falls upon a candidate and his staff as the final moments of campaigning come to an end.

It is traditional in many places now for candidates to make final appeals to the voters on election eve. While the appeal is generally that all citizens should be sure to vote on the morrow, the implication is clear that those votes should be cast for a particular candidate and party.

In some statewide elections this appeal is done over television. In 1957 Governor Meyner was running for re-election in New Jersey. A twelve-hour period from noon until midnight was booked for the governor and his attractive wife, Helen, to conduct a television telethon. They would be on camera practically constantly, answering questions phoned in by viewers. In an effort to get in the last word, the Republican party booked the hour from midnight to 1:00 A.M. to present their candidate, Senator Malcolm Forbes, and allow him to have the last word. As the hour approached 11:45 P.M. Governor Meyner made his appeal for support at the polls, and then he and his wife bid everyone good night. For the next fifteen minutes all that appeared on the television screens were pictures of fluffy, white clouds, while the sound was filled with soft, dreamy bedtime music. One politician said, "Why you could hear the click of sets being turned off all over New Jersey." By 12:01 A.M. most of Senator Forbes' expected audience were in dreamland.

Election night itself is a dramatic time. The returns come trickling in. Soon a picture begins to take shape. Hopes are brightened, headquarter crowds bigger and louder, or if the trend is the other way, small bands of the faithful stand silently by, and wait for a miracle. Sometimes miracles happen. Who can forget the exuberance of Democrats in 1948 as President Truman held on to a slim lead, which failed to evaporate as the rural vote came in? Who can forget Truman's joyful take-off, months later, of H. V. Kaltenborn's doleful predictions that "the President is a million votes ahead, but when the country vote comes in, Mr. Truman will be defeated by an overwhelming majority."

More poignant was Adlai Stevenson's appearance to concede the 1952 election to General Eisenhower. Stevenson said, "Someone asked me, as I came in down on the street, how I felt, and I was reminded of a story that a fellow townsman of ours used to tell—Abraham Lincoln. They asked him how he felt after an unsuccessful election. He said he felt like a little boy who had stubbed his toe in the dark. He said that he was too old to cry but it hurt too much to laugh."

My own defeat in 1958 gave me a chance to demonstrate the importance of a sense of humor. I remember a press conference I had about a week after my defeat. It was the largest conference I ever held. One question asked was, "How did your family take it?" "Like veterans," I replied. "I was proud of all of them. There were no tears. No one was depressed. Even my eighty-six-year-old father, who always wanted to win, was unperturbed. He said, 'Son, I guess they have us licked. The governor's power was just too much for us. But we won't feel too bad. I was ready for you to quit Congress and come home, anyhow; the only thing was, I wanted you to choose the time. I feel like the old farmer whose donkey kicked him. It was a terrible blow, and when he had been carried into the house and the doctor had examined him, the results were bad. The doctor was frank, 'He can't survive this.' The old man heard and understood. He opened his eyes. 'Doctor,' he said, 'can't you keep me alive for a few weeks, and then let me go from some other cause—like pneumonia?' The surprised doctor asked, 'Why would you want it like that?' 'Because,' said the old man, 'I just don't want 'em to be able to put on my tombstone: *He was kicked to death by a jackass!*'"

I also told the press conference that I had to admit that on election night and the following morning I was pretty depressed. When my wife brought in my breakfast cereal, I said, "I can't eat this cereal."

She said, "Why?"

"It's the breakfast of champions."

Marion replied, "You eat it! Around here you're still the champ."

Later in the fall I was on a *Face the Nation* television show. The panelists, contrary to their usual assumption of hard-boiled neutrality, were both friendly and sympathetic.

Among the first questions asked was one from Howard K. Smith. "Mr. Hays, some of us did not realize how strong the feeling was in your state and how antagonistic to any moderate course, and we felt that you were sticking too near the southern shore. Would you admit the election confirmed your judgment that the situation was serious?"

I answered, "Yes, I certainly would. Few people outside Arkansas realized just how serious it was. I was like the hypochondriac who had difficulties getting any attention or sympathy. But he had the last word, after all, for he directed that there be inscribed on his tombstone: *I told you I was sick.*"

Defeat is hard enough to take without continuing to be a campaign issue on top of everything else. But it was my fate to be an issue in the 1959 gubernatorial race in Mississippi. The winner's victory statement said, "We've shown the world we'll have none of Brooks Hays' moderation."

When newsmen asked me for a comment, instead of challenging the statement, I dismissed it with a story. It was about the "sociable" sponsored by the women of a little church in Arkansas. One feature of the program was a contest on who could make the ugliest face. There was a brief wait while the committee retired to make its selection. When they returned and laid the first prize in the lap of a woman sitting on the front row, she looked up, surprised but gratified, and said, "Why thank you very much, but I wasn't in the contest."

Disappointments in politics tend to tap the resources of faith. The comfort and solace of religion often help a candidate and his family accept reverses without rancor or cynicism.

Campaign workers who "carry on" have helped the Hayses bear the inevitable frustrations. In the aftermath of the 1966 campaign for governor there was only a slight let-down. This was in my family's tradition. I saw no tears.

At dinner in the home of our son Steele on the day following the primary, there was a cheerful acceptance of defeat. Even the grandchildren were not depressed, though I presume that we elders are sometimes oblivious to their special disappointments. The mood of one came out in the short prayer, the blessing, offered by our thirteen year old grandson, "Steele the Third."

His father merely said, "Son, will you say grace?" And this is what we heard:

"Our Father, we thank you for this food, and for this nice day—although it has been a bit disappointing—Amen."

Our other grandson, Keith Bell, a Duke University senior, is

also avidly interested in politics. He visited my White House
office in 1961 on the first day of my occupancy. Observing John
Ryder's new book, *How to Get and Keep the Job You Want,*
on my desk, he said, "Granddaddy, he was about three years late
getting it to you, wasn't he?"

A gratifying expression of feeling came at the dinner my wife
and I gave for some of our workers at the end of 1966 campaign. Not many visitors to our headquarters knew that the tall
handsome young man in shirtsleeves, moving efficiently in and
out of the workshops during the campaign, was an ordained
Catholic priest, Father Bruce Streett. He devoted his vacation
and perhaps some of his parish's time to my cause. At the end
of the dinner he asked if he might offer a prayer before we departed. The spell of reverence and true thankfulness for the
friendships cemented by our struggles and sacrifices was not
broken by the quaint and unique ending of the prayer (which
followed the format used in newspaper advertisements as required by law). It went like this:

Lord, we're gathered here in the first place because we shared an
ideal. And just as we've shared this food, grant that we may always
share that ideal. And may the man that embodies the ideal have
many more years of service to his country and to his people. Lord,
he can sleep peacefully at night because he knows that the governorship wouldn't have added anything to him—but the rest of us, Lord,
we were thinking more about what he could have added to the
governorship. So find a way for us to sleep peacefully at night, too,
because we can't yet. And, Lord, this prayer is sponsored by Citizens
for Hays, Ed Lester, chairman.

2

Winds of Truth: Congress

When I was a lad of sixteen, I met a very delightful man, a former congressman from Arkansas, whose name was Colonel W. L. Terry. He was in Mineral Wells, Texas, for his health, at a time when I was there with my parents for treatments physicians had recommended for my father.

Dad was already acquainted with Colonel Terry. He remembered him as a distinguished gentleman, a popular member of the Congress, and an impressive figure at political gatherings. His appearance was striking—he had handsome features and was over six feet tall. When Dad first met him, it was in the nineties, during a campaign for re-election, and the congressman wore a garment that was frequently seen at picnics in those days, and was to become even more familiar in the first dusty years of the automobile era. It was a long linen coat in a natural color, which completely enveloped the wearer and was appropriately called a "linen duster." It became a sort of trademark for the colonel; voters were not likely to forget either the garment or its wearer.

The conversations carried on by my father and Colonel Terry were lively and interesting. They vied with each other in the relating of sparkling anecdotes and fascinating personal experiences. For a high school boy, just beginning to dream of his own political future, this was an unforgettable winter's experience. I absorbed the contents of the remarkable dialogue between these two great raconteurs as a dry sponge absorbs water. Perhaps there was an unconscious influence on me in the exciting stories told by Colonel Terry, adding to my nebulous desire to sit in Congress myself.

One thing that drew me to the great old man was his notice of me. His name for me, "Br'er Rabbit," carried the implication that I was always getting my way by outwitting Dad, whom he called "Br'er Fox." Mother was "Sis Fox," and another guest, whom he didn't like, he called "Sis Cow"—behind her back. His *sotto voce* comments on Sis Cow would usually convulse me.

It is easy to recall, even after half a century, the details of stories with which he regaled us in that little hotel lobby, sitting around a big base burner. His vivid recollections of Speaker Tom Reed of Maine fascinated all of us. The wit of this famous old Republican statesman was known even in the Democratic South. The stories seemed as fresh as if they had happened only yesterday, instead of twenty years before in the nineteenth century.

There was the time when some critical legislation was scheduled to come before the House, and Speaker Reed, anxious to secure a quorum, sent telegrams to absent members urging their immediate return.

One man, who was delayed by flood damage to a railroad, wired back to Speaker Reed:

"Wash-out on line. Can't come."

This excuse wasn't good enough for the speaker. He sent another telegram: "Buy another shirt and *come on next train*."

Colonel Terry told us of a typically acid retort, made when a congressman, with whom Reed did not agree on a matter, had made an impassioned speech on the subject, ending with Henry Clay's famous statement, "I'd rather be right than be President!"

"The gentleman need not worry," said Reed. "He will never be either."

Colonel Terry told with equal enjoyment about the time when he was the target of the speaker's barbed wit. There was some political maneuvering going on, a group of congressmen, of which Terry was one, trying to block a piece of legislation by not allowing it to come to a vote. If the speaker had to declare no quorum present, the House would have to adjourn, so when the count began Terry quickly got down behind his desk. (In the 1890's each congressman had his own desk.)

Speaker Reed favored the legislation, and wished immediate consideration. He spied Mr. Terry, who was crouched down but not invisible, as a part of his large corpus was showing. As the speaker was taking the count, he said, "And I am counting you present, Mr. Terry. I see you under your desk."

The colonel was furious. Amid the guffaws of his colleagues, he rushed down the aisle and literally shook his fist under the speaker's nose.

"It's a strange thing to me, Mr. Speaker, that when you *want* to see me, you find me under my desk, but when I want the floor and am shouting at you, you never know I'm in the room! I want you to know, sir, that I am a Democrat and a gentleman!"

The speaker merely stroked his beard and said dryly, "Well, the gentleman should not blame me for that queer combination in his makeup."

One of the colonel's best stories, I thought, was of how he had plotted against a man, whom I knew as Judge Marcellus Davis of our neighboring town of Dardanelle, but who at the time of the story was a young man with political ambitions. Said Mr. Terry:

"When I heard he was being encouraged to run against me, I was plenty disturbed, for I knew him well by reputation. He was a competent and a highly respected young man, and he might win, so I decided not to let it come to that. I would try to get him an appointment that would take him out of the country.

"So I went to the White House. Now this was a Democratic Administration. Grover Cleveland was President—and there were many new jobs. I was counting on that.

"I said, 'Mr. President, I have come to ask you for an appointment for one of my friends, who aspires to be a consul. He is young, ambitious, and thoroughly qualified to represent the government in a diplomatic post.'

" 'What is his name?' asked President Cleveland.

" 'He is a Mr. Davis of Arkansas. Marcellus L. Davis.'

"I knew the President felt kindly toward Arkansas, for by its alphabetical position it became the second state to cast its vote for him for President. He gave me the appointment, and told me I could send for my friend. I was relieved and delighted, and immediately sent a telegram to Marcellus saying, 'Come to Washington.'

"Marcellus arrived, and I acquainted him with the fact that President Cleveland had named him consul to Trinidad. He didn't know anything about Trinidad; he just wanted to be a consul, and I guess I was about the happiest congressman in Washington. I knew that I wasn't going to have opposition, with him out of the country. I saw him off on a boat and I slept late every morning, because I had nothing to worry about!

"But one morning about three weeks later something touched me on my shoulder as I was enjoying that late morning snooze, and when I rolled over there stood Marcellus.

"I just hollered, 'Marcellus! What are you doin' here?'

"He said, 'I've come home, of course.'

" 'But,' I said, 'you mean you left your post of duty?'

" 'Leave it, the devil! I never got off the boat! It's 115° in the shade down there, and there ain't no shade, and I'll bet there are not three Americans on that island.'

" 'Well, did you get permission to leave your post of duty?'

" 'No, I never got permission to leave my post of duty, because I don't consider it my post of duty. I'm not going to be the consul to Trinidad!'

" 'But Marcellus,' I said, 'what are we going to do?'

"And he said, 'What are *you* going to do? I want another post.'

"Well, I knew that wasn't going to be easy. The Democrats had had a long famine and they were a hungry lot, and the jobs had been going fast. And, of course, here I had a real complication because I had already gotten one appointment for him. But I knew I had to do something, because if I didn't he was sure going to run against me!

"Well, I did something I'm ashamed of now. But I was desperate. I went down to the White House, walked in just as if I hadn't seen the President in years, and after the amenities, I said, 'Mr. President, I have come to ask you for a favor.'

" 'Yes?' he said. 'What is it, Mr. Terry?'

"And I said, 'I would like to get a job for a friend of mine, a Mr. Davis of Arkansas.'

" 'Well, now,' he said, 'it seems like I remember giving you a job for a Mr. Davis about a month ago.'

" 'Well yes, you did, that's right, Mr. President, but you see he doesn't like his post of duty.'

" 'Well, Congressman, I can't worry about everybody that doesn't like his post of duty! I wouldn't be doing anything else if I were moving folks that wanted to get into a more desirable location.'

"I saw I was really in trouble. We didn't discuss it very long until I just threw my hands up and said, 'But, Mr. President, if I don't get him another post of duty, he is going home and run against me!'

"That did it. The President broke into a broad smile and said, 'Well, we mustn't let that happen. We'll find him another post of duty. What do you suggest?'

"And I said, 'Yucatan would be a good one, and it's close to home.'

" 'Oh, but I happen to know there's a good man there; he's very satisfactory. He's been with the service a good while, and the State Department likes him. No, we'll have to look somewhere else.'

" 'But, Mr. President, he is a *Republican*.'

" 'Yes, that's right,' the President said, 'but Republicans are capable of rendering good service, and he happens to be one of the good ones.'

" 'Maybe so, Mr. President, but what is a good Republican compared to any Arkansas Democrat that's needin' a job?'

"The President gave me the answer I wanted to hear, 'Particularly if that Democrat is threatening to run against a congressman in office!'

"Marcellus went to Yucatan, stayed long enough to relieve me of my worries, and we have been fast friends ever since."

Colonel Terry has been gone for many years, but his unerring sense of the ridiculous, and his gift for colorful communication made an indelible impression on a young boy already interested in a political career. Perhaps, too, it is owing to this association that I stored in my memory other anecdotes, which I heard or read in later years reflecting the repartee and easy give-and-take of Congressional life. A few of them which seem to me to be footnotes to history, I set down here.

Henry Clay, who had a caustic wit, served in the House of

Representatives with General Alexander Smyth of Virginia. General Smyth, a man of great ability and learning, was given to making long speeches. He interspersed these speeches with numerous and oftentimes tedious quotations, usually from the classics. He observed one day, after Clay had made a short speech on some matter, "You, sir, speak for the present generation, but I speak for posterity."

"Yes," said Clay, "and you seem to be resolved to speak until the arrival of your audience."

The House was being harangued by Congressman Enoch Lincoln, a former governor of Maine, in his usual eloquent but verbose and declamatory manner. He was considering the revolutionary pension bill, and replying to an argument which opposed it on the ground that those to whom it proposed to extend pecuniary aid might perhaps live a long time, and thus cause heavy drafts to be made upon the treasury. In one of his elevated flights of patriotic enthusiasm, he burst out with the exclamation:

"Soldiers of the Revolution! Live forever!"

Mr. Clay also spoke in favor of the humane proposition, but did not agree with Lincoln's desire relative to the length of the lives of those worthies for whose benefit it was devised; and when he closed, turning suddenly to Mr. Lincoln and with a smile upon his countenance, he observed, "I hope my worthy friend will not insist upon the very great duration of those pensions which he has suggested. Will he not consent, by way of compromise, to a term of 999 years, instead of eternity?"

One one occasion, back in the nineteenth century, when Congress was getting close to adjournment, the question arose of a Sunday session to help speed up the process. Massachusetts Congressman Benjamin Franklin Butler, a former general, had stepped over to the desk of Samuel Jackson Randall of Pennsylvania for a private consultation. Butler favored a Sunday session. Randall opposed. "Bad as I am, I have some respect for God's day," said Randall, "and I don't think it proper to hold a session of Congress on that day."

"Oh, pshaw!" responded Butler, "doesn't the Bible say that it is lawful to pull your ox or ass out of a pit on the Sabbath day? You have seventy-three asses on your side of the House that I want to get out of this ditch tomorrow, and I think I am engaged in a holy work."

"Don't do it, Butler," pleaded Sam, "I have some respect for you that I don't want to lose. I expect some day to meet you in a better world."

"You'll be there as you are here," retorted Butler, quick as thought, "a member of the lower House."

Senator Alexander H. Stevens of Georgia, who later became vice president of the Confederacy, was small and thin. He weighed under eighty pounds, stood five feet tall, and was afraid of no one. A huge western senator became enraged at Stevens in a debate on the Senate floor. He fairly spluttered out, "Why, you! You! Why I could swallow you alive and never know I'd eaten a thing."

"In that case," replied Stevens calmly and quietly, "you'd have more brains in your stomach than you ever had in your head."

Long speeches in Congress are generally not made today. In the House of Representatives there are so many members that the rules in most cases forbid speeches of more than a few minutes. In the Senate, longer speeches are allowed and are sometimes made, especially during filibusters. But generally speaking, congressmen and senators spare their colleagues long diatribes.

In the midst of a Congressional argument that had grown too heated, Representative James Johnson of Indiana called a fellow representative from Illinois a jackass. House rules forbid this kind of language, and so a point of order was made immediately. Congressman Johnson got up to apologize. "While I withdraw the unfortunate word, Mr. Speaker, I still insist that the gentleman from Illinois is out of order."

"How am I out of order?" the Illinois representative screamed.

"Probably a veterinary surgeon could tell you," was Johnson's reply.

Senator John Sharp Williams of Mississippi occasionally indulged in a few nips before coming onto the Senate floor, and it was alleged that sometimes it showed. He was once engaged in a heated dispute with Senator Tom Heflin of Alabama.

Heflin sarcastically remarked, "Well, whatever else may be said of me, when I come into the Senate chamber, I always come in full possession of my faculties."

"Well," Williams responded, "what possible difference could that make?"

While Carter Glass, the revered Virginia statesman, was serving in the House of Representatives before moving over to the Senate, he was constantly being heckled during a speech by a certain congressman. It became evident that Glass was about to lose his patience. A fellow congressman said, "Give him hell, Carter. Give him hell."

Glass paused. He glanced at his adviser and then at his heckler. "Why waste dynamite," he asked in his slow drawl, "when insect powder will do the work as well?"

Often, while to an outsider the debate on the floor appears to be acrimonious, the protagonists really are and remain good friends. Among the ready, eloquent and pungent orators in the Senate stood Judah P. Benjamin of Louisiana. One day, at the close of a set speech on the Kansas-Nebraska crisis, he made an impassioned and bitter attack on Senator William Seward of New York. As Benjamin resumed his seat, Seward rose and, turning to his assailant, said in a calm and indifferent tone, "Benjamin, give me a cigar, and when your speech is printed send me a copy." Seward then retired to the cloak room and smoked Benjamin's cigar.

Sometimes a simple figure of speech will do more than an armload of statistics to drive home a point. In a discussion of the South's need for federal aid for education a generation ago, it had been brought out that the rural South suffered a disparity, measured by the relation of per child income to that of the highest rated urban area of the Northeast, of ten to one (it is less today). The most favored area had 35 per cent of the children, the least favored 17 per cent, but the urban income was 40 per cent, while the rural South had only 2 per cent of the national income. But Congressman Luther Patrick of Alabama, with a stroke, dramatized the point that it was the larger number of children per population unit, as well as incomes, that did it. "The stork and the wolf always did pal around together—while Pop is fighting the wolf off the back steps, the stork is fluttering through the front door."

Members of Congress used to enjoy this story of how the North Dakota legislature picked one of their number to succeed a United States senator who had died. It was in the period preceding the adoption of the amendment requiring a popular election of senators. For the interim the legislative leaders in North Dakota chose a very popular, colorful, rural legislator, who, by reason of lack of education, they did not consider equipped for the full term, but as one of the beloved members was worthy of the honor. They told him that it was generally conceded that he would be elected without opposition. They had chosen the legislature's outstanding orator to put his name in nomination. The old gentleman was excited and sat silently in the back of the assembly waiting for the nominating speech. The one picked to do this stood, addressed the chair, and said, "My colleagues, I nominate for the vacancy in the United States Senate, that man among us of noble character, of outstanding ability, of unimpeachable integrity, of impressive achievements . . ." and before he could finish the sentence, the old gentleman leaned over and said to his seatmate, "Well, the dirty double-crosser! He promised to nominate me."

The Bible is often quoted (even, sometimes, misquoted) on the floor of the House.

Years ago a member named Fowler was presenting a point of view not shared by one of his colleagues, who stated to the House, "I hope that the members will reflect upon the words of the Bible: 'Beware of the snare of the fowler.'"

But Mr. Fowler was also aware of that passage from the ninety-first Psalm. "Ah, but, Mr. Speaker, the gentleman has not quoted the verse in its entirety. The Bible in that same passage goes on to assure us that we will be spared from the noisome pestilence."

Members often help each other when the one speaking makes a slip. At the height of an oratorical effort, one member exclaimed, "As Solomon lamented, 'O, Absalom, my son Absalom . . .'"

A colleague interrupted, "It was David's son."

"Thank you," the member responded, and proceeded, but in the record the parentage is correctly carried and the interruption does not appear.

The most embarrassing mistake I listened to during my years

in the House was a reference by a senior member to the words inscribed on the Liberty Bell.

As told to the House, "In the words of that grand old prophet, Leviticus, 'let liberty be proclaimed . . .'" He was not publicly put right, but the words "grand old prophet" did not appear in the printed record. Perhaps the reporter knew.

One amusing error, quite understandable, was not corrected and is probably recorded in the archives today. A member was gently rebuking his colleagues. "It seems to me," he said, "that we are going around like Sam Quixote, tilting at windmills."

I found, one time, that I was regarded by one of my colleagues as an authority on the Bible, and by a remarkable coincidence saved my standing with him at the same time.

I was having breakfast with Ernest S. Griffith, director of the Legislative Reference Service of the Library of Congress. He told me that Harry S Truman had spoken at a dinner at his church the previous evening. "He discussed his two favorite chapters in the Bible, the fifth chapter of Matthew . . ."

"The Sermon on the Mount," I interjected.

"And the twentieth chapter of Exodus," Dr. Griffith added.

"What's the twentieth chapter?" I asked.

"Why, Brooks, I'm surprised that the president of the Southern Baptist Convention doesn't know where the ten commandments are located!"

I was suitably apologetic. I walked to my office and started to read my mail. The phone rang. It was Congressman Omar Burlesen of Texas.

"Brooks, I'm trying to locate the ten commandments—where are they located in the Bible?" he inquired.

I answered quickly, "In the twentieth chapter of Exodus."

"I knew you'd know, I knew you'd know," he said, hanging up the receiver.

Tom Heflin of Alabama, that colorful member of the Senate in the twenties, has added to the lore surrounding the Congress. I think one of the most effective stories ever used to sway a vote was one he told during debate on a bill to raise the pay of senators from $7,500 a year to $10,000.

Senator Borah, the famed orator from Idaho, spoke in opposition and stated that even if the pay raise bill passed, he would not accept the increase. This placed senators who had different views in a rather delicate position. Although they might have thought the salary too low, they were reluctant to appear eager to raise their own pay. This might have side-tracked or postponed the action, had not Senator Heflin taken the floor at the conclusion of Borah's effective statement.

Former Senator Josh Lee of Oklahoma, himself a forensic artist, is my authority for the following account of Senator Heflin's performance:*

"If the Senator from Idaho does not want to take his salary on, Mr. President, he can refuse it; but I believe that when it comes due that we can induce him to take it. He will be like Private John Allen was. John Allen went home from New Orleans once after he had been down there fishing with the boys. They had treated him royally, wined and dined him, until he was a little weary and worn, and when he arrived at home he saw his doctor at the station. He said, 'My wife is a crank on the prohibition question. I haven't got a drop in my grip. I feel that I must have a little to taper off on. Won't you send a bottle up and beg her yourself to give it to me as medicine?'

"The doctor said, 'I will.'

"When John arrived at home his wife met him and said, 'How are you feeling, my dear?'

"He said, 'Very poorly. I have never felt quite so weak. I feel like I need a stimulant, but I am not going to take it. I will never touch another drop of it; never, never.'

"She said, 'Well, now, John, you must not be cranky on the subject.'

"He said, 'No; I have made up my mind.'

"He lay down on the bed, and the phone rang, and Doctor Jones said, 'Mrs. Allen, I am sending up a quart. You make a nice mint julep and make your husband drink it. I saw him at the station. He is weak and worn to a frazzle. You give him this mint julep.'

"The brilliant John Allen was lying there on the bed, and he heard the ice chunks clinking in the glass. His wife bore the mint julep into his bedroom in graceful, queenly fashion, with

* Taken from Senator Lee's book *How to Hold an Audience Without Using a Rope.*

frost on the sides of the glass, a band of sugar an inch deep at the bottom, and three strawberries nestling thereon like so many eggs in a bird's nest, while the mint leaned over the rim of the glass.

"His wife took it up to the bedside and she said, 'Now, I want you to take this.'

"He said, 'I can't do it. I have said I will not do it.'

"She said, 'But John, you must drink it. The doctor says for you to take it. The doctor has prescribed it.' . . .

"As we are about to prescribe a dose for the Senator from Idaho [Laughter].

"She said, 'You must take it.'

"He said, 'I can't, and I won't.'

"She said, 'Won't you take it for me?'

"He said, 'If you put it that way, I will.' "

Then Senator Heflin lifted the mint julep to his lips and the amber-colored fluid fell into the velvet folds of his stomach like dew drops fall into the petals of a rose. (Here the Congressional Record notes that there was laughter on the floor and in the galleries.)

"He looked up at his wife, said, 'I believe I am going to sleep now, but before I fall into a deep sweet sleep, let me ask you a question. When did the doctor tell you to give me another mint julep?' [Laughter]

"She said, 'In two hours.'

" 'Well,' he said, 'if I am asleep, wake me [Laughter], and if I won't take it, make me.' [Laughter]

Senator Heflin concluded:

"So Mr. President, I do not think it will be very hard to make the able senator from Idaho [Mr. Borah]—and we all love him, or did before this [Laughter], and of course we do now; we are even going to forgive him for the wrong that he has done in this instance, even in the face of the fact that he brought it all upon himself." (Again the mystic word appears in the record, "Laughter.")

The touchy question regarding salaries—to raise or not to raise—has given congressmen more pause than Hamlet's dilemma gave him, and of course it has inspired some gibes at the lawmakers' expense.

One I used to enjoy telling concerns a conversation overheard on a bus. The newspapers that morning carried the news across the country: Congress had raised its own salary. Two passengers were discussing it.

"What do you think of it?" asked one.

"I don't approve of it," said the other. "I think they are over-paid now."

"Why, what do we pay them?"

"I don't know."

Another incident, which I enjoyed sharing with my colleagues, though I was the victim, had to do with a forum in Arkansas. I had devoted considerable time to defending the action of Congress in boosting the salary for members. I had anticipated violent opposition to this increase, and consequently was not prepared for the comment of one little lady in a Perry County audience. She said, when the chairman called for questions, "Mr. Hays, I agree that the salary should have been increased. Tell me now, please, since it's up where it ought to be, do you think it will encourage better men to run for Congress?"

Of course, I had an answer for her—entirely extemporaneous. "No, I don't think so—but it will be an encouragement to those who are there to continue in the public service."

On many occasions humorous stories illustrating or under-scoring points have been extremely useful. Senator Everett Dirk-sen, the loquacious and likable Senate minority leader from Illinois, is a past master of this art. A perfect illustration of the senator's skill took place recently in a Senate debate over the ceiling on the debt limit of the United States Government.

"I think it is wonderful. There has not been anything in the Treasury that has not been appropriated for so long that the memory of man runneth not to the contrary. So up the expendi-tures and up the debt; then when we catch up with the debt ceiling, we raise it again. Then we spend more to catch up with the new ceiling.

"It is a great little business. I am reminded of a man who had a balky mule that lay down on the pavement. He would not budge. Any amount of punishment made no difference. At long last the fellow built a fire under the mule but that did not seem to help.

"A veterinarian came along and said, 'What is the matter, Sam? Can't you do anything with this mule?'

"The man said, 'No.'

"So the veterinarian took his syringe and gave that mule a squirt in the hind quarters. Up the mule got and bounded down the road lickety split. The owner looked at the vet, looked at the departing mule, and said, 'Doc, how much was that?'

"The veterinarian replied, 'Ten cents.'

"The owner said, 'Here is twenty cents. Give me two shots so I can catch that mule.'

"So up goes the debt, and expenditures come up to meet it. Up goes the debt and expenditures come up."

From this it is easy to understand how a colleague listening to Dirksen when he was still in the House could whisper in my ear, "If a bowl of ripe Elberta peaches could talk—that's what it would sound like."

On some occasions, the senators take advantage of their liberal rules and indulge in long speeches. After the late Senator Robert Kerr from Oklahoma had been subjected to a colleague's endless speech, he told this story:

"A Baptist church called a new pastor, one of these long-winded brothers. One Sunday morning he was really wound up, and for an hour and a half he had preached away and was still going strong. In this church was an old, dusty clock that had hung on the wall for years and years, without running and without striking a single time. All of a sudden, right in the middle of the sermon, the old clock started striking—one—two—three—four, and on up to twelve, but it didn't stop there, just kept right on striking—thirteen—fourteen—fifteen—until finally it struck twenty-two times without stopping.

"One old gentleman sitting on the second row from the front got up and started up the aisle. The preacher called to him, 'Wait a minute, Brother Jones, I'm not through preaching yet.'

" 'Well, maybe you're not,' the brother replied, 'but let me tell you something. I'm eighty-two years old, and never in my whole life have I stayed out this late before, and I'm going home.' "

Inevitably, there have been some very funny practical jokes perpetrated by the members of Congress on each other. Two of these, which happened only a little before my time, I have enjoyed telling. The details were supplied by Donald O'Toole of New York, one of the great practical jokers of Congress.

One day, John Sparkman, then a young House member from Alabama, was explaining a farm measure, Will Bankhead presiding.

Mr. O'Toole and Congressman Henry Ellenbogen of Pennsylvania were sitting on the back seat studying the daily racing forms, and paying no attention to the floor debate.

John Sparkman was putting his best into the explanation of an Agriculture Committee bill, explaining that there were certain alternatives before the House. He used the expression "if you choose" in introducing the alternatives. "If you choose" showed up in the speech quite often.

This phrase suddenly caught Ellenbogen's attention: "If you choose . . ."

He said, "Don, what's he saying, what's he saying?"

O'Toole got the point. He recognized that Henry thought that he had made a reference to the Jewish people.

"Well," Don said, "he's just kicking the pants off of your people."

Henry threw his papers aside and raced down the aisle, shouting, "Mr. Speaker, Mr. Speaker."

"For what purpose does the gentleman from Pennsylvania rise?" Mr. Bankhead asked.

"A point of high personal privilege, sir. A point of high personal privilege."

"The gentleman will state it."

Before the speaker could stop him, Ellenbogen picked up the children of Israel in the land of Egypt, carried them across the Red Sea, through forty years of wilderness wanderings, finally to establish a new home in Canaan, described their being carried into captivity by the Babylonians, brought them back for the restoration, referred to the dispersion, the final agonies connected with the building of the temple, the destruction of the temple. Having described in detail Solomon's exertions in this respect, he brought the Jews across the ocean establishing a new home in the United States; had them save the Republic with Chaim Soloman's money, and referred to the Jewish veterans marching down Fifth Avenue in triumph following the First World War!

Finally Mr. Bankhead gaveled him down. "The chair will state to the gentleman from Pennsylvania that what he has said is all very true and all very interesting, but it hasn't the remotest connection with what the gentleman from Alabama has said about the farm bill!"

"But, Mr. Speaker, he was attacking my people."

Sparkman was flabbergasted. He hadn't the faintest idea what had set off the tirade, and he stood in bewilderment.

The chair said, "The gentleman from Alabama will take his seat." This, of course, is in accordance with the rules of the House, requiring that the words objected to be written out by the clerk and reported to the House. If found to be an infringement, then the member guilty of the infraction loses the privileges of the floor for a full day.

John sat in silence. Ellenbogen grew suspicious. O'Toole sat on the back seat with a deadpan expression, looking straight ahead, with no indication of interest in the proceedings. Finally the words were reported.

It was evident then what had happened. Mr. Sparkman of Alabama was reported as saying, "Now, if you choose . . . ; on the other hand, if you choose . . ." A great light dawned. Ellenbogen pointed his finger at O'Toole, and shouted (they said loud enough to be heard at the Senate end of the Capitol), "O'Toole, you dirty Irish scoundrel!"

Another practical joke attempted by the press was suggested by the elaborate but temporary steel supports for the House chamber ceiling. This framework was put up during the war because the old supports, which had not been strengthened since the wing was built one hundred years earlier, showed signs of sagging. To do a real job, too much strategic material needed in the war effort would be required, so beauty had to be sacrificed for safety, as the lovely ceiling was crisscrossed by the unsightly steel bars. That wasn't quite all. In addition, for some reason never explained to me the loud-speaker system required the use of a large metal contraption, which also was just below ceiling level, and it was in the exact center of the chamber. It always looked like the bottom of a boat to me, but to another it might have suggested a coffin or a bathtub.

On a dull day, when nothing was happening, two bored veterans of the press were sitting in the press gallery. With them was a third member, a young fellow who was still new to the Washington scene. One of the veterans, looking idly up at the loud speaker apparatus, said to the other, "I wonder when they are going to take Speaker Bankhead's body back to Alabama?" Mr. Bankhead had died some years before, and the older newsmen knew that his body had long since been interred in his home state. But the act proceeded.

"Very soon now, I think," said the other, without batting an eye. "I heard a rumor the other day that it was soon going to be taken to Jasper, Alabama, for final burial."

"It ought to make a good story when it breaks," said the first conspirator.

Blandly, they watched their young colleague breathlessly excuse himself and rush to a gallery door, his coattails almost quivering. Then they looked at each other and smiled contentedly.

The victim of this satanic hoax, thinking he had the makings of a scoop if he could just get a definite detail or two, saw Majority Leader John McCormack. He rushed up and asked bluntly, "Mr. McCormack, when are they going to remove Speaker Bankhead's body from the House chamber?"

The horrified expression on the majority leader's face was really enough. It didn't need the explosive "What!" which followed, to enlighten the tyro newsman. He knew he had been had, and good.

Usually, I managed to avoid being the victim of the practical jokes of the cloakroom, but one day the boys got me good. It was in that famous election year of 1948. Henry Wallace had just been nominated for President by the ill-fated Progressive party, meeting in Philadelphia.

One day soon after the House had convened, a page appeared at my elbow and whispered that I was wanted on the phone in the cloakroom. I went through the swinging doors and picked up the receiver. A voice said, "Mr. Hays, this is George Reedy of the United Press. Henry Wallace's headquarters has just issued a statement in which your name is mentioned. Would you like to hear it?"

I gulped. No matter what it said, I couldn't imagine the release being other than bad news. "Yes, yes, I would."

Mr. Reedy then quoted: "Mr. Wallace's managers say that Mr. Marcantonio of New York will not be the only member of Congress who is supporting their candidate. Among his many friends in the House is Mr. Hays of Arkansas, who was assisted in his race for Congress in 1942 by Mr. Wallace's friends. He will either openly espouse the cause of the former Secretary of Agriculture, or let it be known privately where his sympathies are. That is the end of the paragraph that pertains to you. Do you wish to comment?"

This was a shocker, worse even than I had imagined, and so paralyzing that it took a few moments for me to pull myself together.

While I was struggling, Mr. Reedy prompted me with another question. "Did Henry Wallace support you when you ran for Congress?"

This question brought a little relief. "He couldn't! He was not a resident of Arkansas."

"Then did you support him when he made his bid for the Vice Presidency?"

Feeling like a drowning man grabbing at straws, I answered, "No, I couldn't. I was under the Hatch Act. I couldn't actively support anyone."

"Oh!" said my tormentor. "Then you were an employee of the federal government?"

"Yes." This came feebly. Even the straws were being withdrawn.

"Which department?"

"Agriculture," I moaned.

"While Mr. Wallace was Secretary?"

"Yes."

"Who appointed you?"

I was about to say, "Dr. Rexford G. Tugwell," when I realized that wouldn't help me any, as Tugwell was as controversial a character as Wallace. Suddenly I found another straw—my boss, and the man who had really recommended me. "Dr. Will Alexander," I said firmly.

The newsman gave up that scent (to change the metaphor from water to woods), and tried a new one. "What kind of Secretary of Agriculture do you think Henry Wallace made?"

The feeling that I had emerged from the encounter fairly intact restored some of my self-assurance, and I was able to answer honestly and without stuttering, "A very fine one. He knew agriculture. He was a good administrator, both from the production and distribution side, and he was a dedicated man, one of the best we have ever had."

"Are you willing to be quoted on that?" asked Mr. Reedy in some surprise.

"Certainly. Provided you add this addendum: I think his left wing captivity is a tragic aftermath to a distinguished career, and just about the saddest spectacle we have seen in American politics."

He thanked me and hung up.

I was limp. I began to pace the cloakroom corridor, growing more frantic by the moment as I realized what the repercussions of the news release might be. I could see the Arkansas papers spelling my doom with their headlines alone, "Hays for Wallace." I called my legislative assistant, Claud Curlin, a former newspaperman, but got small comfort, as he too was horrified.

"Prepare a statement for the press," I told him, "and I'll get to work on a one-minute speech, for I think I'd better make a statement to the House."

Back I went into the chamber, but I was so nervous I could hardly sit still. My colleagues, who sat by or near me, had no trouble perceiving my state of mind.

Finally, Wilbur Mills came over, and said, "Brooks, Mr. Reedy of the United Press is outside and wants to meet you."

Out to the hall I went and looked around for a stranger, but saw none. Wilbur, grinning broadly, said, "Shake hands with Mr. Reedy." And there with his hand out was Marcantonio of New York!

They went off into howls of laughter. In fact, the whole House had a wonderful afternoon, passing the story around and laughing about it. As for me I was too relieved to be mad at anyone.

Not all of the relaxation was in the House cloakroom. When the legislative schedule permitted I would slip back to my office for lunch with my staff, which I modestly regarded as "the finest team on Capitol Hill." Occasionally my wife would join us for the pleasant interlude, and more rarely Dick Emerson, who was in charge of the Little Rock office, participated.

Heading the office was the popular John McLees. Ably assisting him were Lurlene Wilbert of Alabama (not related to the other Lurleen), Kitty Johnson, and Warren Cikins. The last named was a Harvard graduate and at first he exhibited the characteristic New England reserve. Lurlene called him "The Brain" because of his cerebral efficiency. If he laughed at my efforts to amuse, it was because he really was amused. He conceded nothing to either politeness or apple polishing. At one of the noon sessions I related a story only to find no visible sign of amusement on his countenance. "Laugh, Brain!" Lurlene cried, but he said, "I give Mr. Hays's efforts what I think they deserve." To this Lurlene said, "Then you aren't going to be around here very long!" But he was, as all of them were, until the 1958 retirement from Congress.

Congressman Howard W. Smith of Virginia and I once collaborated in a little joke on the House with the pleasing result of giving them a good laugh.

In the years immediately following World War II, one of the big problems facing the Congress was enacting legislation to aid Great Britain as she recovered from the devastating effects of the war. The Mutual Aid Program, at that stage called the Marshall Plan, was devised. At the same time, in northern and eastern sections of our country, where many people of Irish descent live, there has always been strong sentiment for consolidation of all Ireland under the Dublin Government. So their representatives in Congress would each year, when Mutual Aid was debated, try to put Congress on record on "the Irish question" by means of an amendment to the aid bill to provide that aid to Britain be conditional upon the release of the six northern counties comprising Ulster, which could then, after a plebiscite, be joined with southern Ireland under one government.

As a member of the House Foreign Affairs Committee (incidentally, it has always been a source of some amusement that the comparable Senate Committee is known as the Senate Foreign Relations Committee, and Congressional wags allow this is because "senators can only have relations, they are too old to have affairs"), I took the position that this was a British internal affair and that to include the Irish amendment would be to defeat the purpose of the bill. As a tactical move, which hopefully would shut off debate, I suggested to Representative Howard Smith, who shared my views, that he offer an amendment to the amendment, stipulating that the Irish union should take place only after West Virginia had been restored to Virginia.

Congressman Smith, of course, saw the possibilities. He got the floor and with a perfect deadpan expression and in the most solemn fashion offered his amendment. He explained that while his loyal forebears were fighting the Yankees honorably on their borders, some of the enemy had sneaked around to their rear and stolen fifty-five of their counties.

"So," he concluded, "only when this great injustice has been righted should we try to solve a similar problem in another country." As the House roared in laughter, he ended, "Mr. Speaker, I move the adoption of this amendment." Needless to say both his and the Irish amendments were defeated.

On one memorable occasion, in debate over some farm matters, I was involved in an exchange with Congressman Chester Gross of Pennsylvania. He said: "Mr. Speaker, I have a question I would like to direct to the gentleman from Arkansas, who was just speaking for the agricultural people in the country. I would like him to tell me whether this statement is correct or not— The Arkansas farmer gets up in the morning at the alarm of a Connecticut clock, buttons his Chicago suspenders to Detroit overalls, washes his face with Cincinnati soap in a Pennsylvania pan, sits down to a Grand Rapids table, eats his Chicago meat, sprinkled with Tennessee flour cooked with Kansas lard on a St. Louis stove. He puts a New York bridle on a Kansas mule fed with Iowa corn. He plows a farm, covered by an Ohio mortgage, with a Chattanooga plow. At the end of the day he says a prayer written in Jerusalem, crawls under a blanket made in New Hampshire, only to be kept awake by an Arkansas hound dog that howls all night—the only home product on his place."

At this point Oren Harris slipped over to me and said, "Give him your speech on the Arkansas domestic animals." It called for a little paraphrasing, and with the help of some of my colleagues we quickly put it in shape as a response. I said:

"Mr. Speaker, the people of Pennsylvania, represented by Mr. Gross and other distinguished men of the Congress, should love Arkansas, because we are among the best customers of the industrial state of Pennsylvania, but when the gentleman speaks disparagingly of an Arkansas hound dog, my hackles are up. Mr. Speaker, if all the cows in Arkansas were one cow she could stand with her front feet in the great plains of the West, her hind feet in the Dominion of Canada, and with her mighty tail could swish the icicles off the North Pole. If all the hogs in Arkansas were one hog, he could stand with his front feet in the Caribbean, his hind feet in the Atlantic Ocean, and with his tremendous snout could dig another Panama Canal. And if all the dogs in Arkansas were one dog, he could stand on top of the loftiest peak of the Alleghenies and raise a howl that would blow the rings off the planet Saturn. Not all the groundhogs in Pennsylvania could cast a shadow across his left hind leg."

To remain in Congress, obviously the congressman must maintain a good relationship with his constituents. The old adage, however, to vote as your district expects, has had to be modified somewhat, as the United States has grown as a world power. Probably as this power has grown, more and more congressmen have reached for Edmund Burke's quotation on the subject, "A representative owes the people not his energy alone, but his judgment as well. He betrays their best interests if he yields his considered judgment to their passing opinion."

Right after my election as president of the Southern Baptist Convention, Ross Bass, who was then congressman from Tennessee, felt that there should be some formal recognition made of the high honor that had come to me. It was right at the time that the Aga Kahn was receiving his weight in diamonds from his Moslem constituents, and much was being made of this in the press. Ross began his conversation with me, about holding a little ceremony in my honor, by saying that obviously diamonds were out of the question in my case, but he felt something of that kind might be arranged. Some gift approximating my weight on the scales could be selected. We could have a little ceremony of our own.

"What," he asked, "would you suggest?"

I responded, "Watermelons."

Oren Harris was in on the conversation and he said, "All right, then, two of our average Arkansas melons will do it."

I then told them about my Uncle Will Lyle, who countered, when a neighbor came over to borrow his cross-saw in order to cut a watermelon, "Well, I'd be glad to let you have the saw, except that we got it hung in a cantaloupe this morning."

With the House of Representatives comprising (not compromising as one school boy once wrote on an exam paper) 435 members, it is not always possible for every member to know every other member. Even after eight terms in Congress, there were a few representatives I knew only by sight. In any event it takes a while for the older members to get to know the freshmen congressmen. This can occasionally lead to some embarrassment.

Joe Hendricks of Florida, the baby member of the Seventy-seventh Congress, was one who didn't look his age. He was sometimes mistaken for a page. One time, according to Hendricks, a revered member of the House, an elder statesman, Will Whittington of Mississippi, walked up to him in the cloakroom and said, "Son, get my secretary on the phone." Hendricks complied; he stepped into the phone booth, got Mr. Whittington's office, and handed the receiver to him, just as the pages customarily do when a member asks that kind of service.

Mr. Whittington said to him, "Now, tell him to take that stack of papers in the big blue envelope lying right in front of my chair, and bring it over here at once."

This was a little too much for the new member. He handed the receiver back to him and said, "Tell him yourself, I'm not paid to do this kind of thing."

Mr. Whittington looked startled, and when he'd finished the conversation with his secretary, went up to the chief page and said, "You've got the most impudent page here I have ever run into. You ought to fire him."

The chief page said, "But Mr. Whittington, that's the new member from Florida, Mr. Hendricks."

Another episode involving mistaken identity is equally amusing. It came about because of the remarkable physical similarity between General Lewis Cass and a Washington hotel owner named Guy. A newly elected southern congressman, who had put up in Guy's hostelry, did not like his room. He went downstairs to complain about it. On the way he met General Cass and, taking him for the landlord, treated him to some very emphatic comments on the indignity he felt he had received.

"Sir," the general sternly replied, as soon as he could get a word in, "you have made a mistake. I am General Cass of Michigan."

"General Cass," the congressman stammered, "I beg a thousand pardons! I took you for Mr. Guy, who is an old friend of mine. Pray excuse me, sir."

The general bowed stiffly and went out, but immediately returned and happened again to meet the southerner. The latter had seen General Cass go out and felt sure of his man this time.

He came up, slapped him heartily on the shoulder, and said with a laugh, "Say, Guy, I've got a good joke to tell you. I met that stupid old Cass just now and thought it was you, and began to berate him about my room."

"Young man," replied the general, drawing himself up more sternly than ever, "you've met that stupid old Cass again."

Patronage plays an important part in a congressman's life. Particularly the patronage that accrues to a congressman which enables him to make appointments of young men to maintenance positions, such as elevator operators, or even members of the capitol police force. These jobs normally are given to young men who are attending one of the many colleges in the District of Columbia. If a congressman can get a boy from his district onto the Congressional payroll while he is going to school, it obviously can be politically useful back home.

One time I received a request from Congressman Burr Harrison of Virginia for a patronage job for a theological student. (I was one of three members of the Patronage Committee at that time.) Burr brought the young man to my office. "I assume," I began, "that being from Virginia, you are a Baptist?"

"No, Mr. Hays," the student said. "I am in the Episcopal Seminary."

"Then you are not of my faith. You have come at a bad time,"

I told him with mock seriousness, which the congressman recognized, but which perplexed the young man. "You see," I added, "I have just been reading a volume of church history and I find that three hundred years ago you Episcopalians were putting Baptists in jail in Virginia. I have seen a copy of the warrant signed by an Episcopal magistrate, committing a Baptist preacher named Jeremy Moore to jail for being 'a Baptist minister and stroller'—that's pretty humiliating. Before giving you the job I want your assurance that this practice has ended, and that Episcopalians will not persecute Baptists any more in your state." By this time he had caught the spirit of my comments.

A few days later Congressman Harrison received a letter from the student saying, "I am very grateful to you and Mr. Hays, but am worried about his story of Baptist persecution. So far I have covered only the first seven centuries of the Christian era in my history studies, and I find no record of persecution of Baptists, but my professor tells me that what Mr. Hays said is true, that there has been some persecution of Baptists in Virginia."

Harrison replied, "Young man, I fear if you didn't find Baptist persecution by Episcopalians in those first seven centuries, you wasted some time. Mr. Hays insists that Herod was an Episcopalian."

This experience produced a warm friendship. The young man went on to graduation and now has a parish in Virginia. I occasionally hear from him.

Debate at times can be confusing. Especially to our friends who may not always understand the vernacular, which occasionally slips into that debate. Such was the case with my good friend General Carlos Romulo. He served as the Philippines' resident commissioner to the Seventy-eighth Congress back in the days before Philippine independence. The Philippines were entitled, just as Alaska and Hawaii were, before statehood, to send to Congress a nonvoting representative, who had most of the rights of a congressman except the right to vote on bills.

One day the general sat down beside me and asked a question about the legislation being debated. I said, very simply, "General, I'm afraid you're leaning on a broken reed."

"How's that?" he said.

My fellow Arkansan, Congressman Jim Trimble, sitting on my

other side, said, "General, he means you have brought your bucket to a dry cistern."

"I don't understand," the general persisted. Jim made another attempt. "He's trying to say, you fetched your ducks to a poor market."

With that the General stood up and said, "I've got to find somebody who will speak the English language to me!"

In the cloakroom the harshness that often creeps into official debates is abandoned, ribbing is good-natured, and the laughter that follows personal thrusts is untinged with malice. Even when the philosophical cleavages are sharp, such as those between the Virginia Conservative, Judge Howard Smith, and hard-hitting left-winger, the late Vito Marcantonio of New York, the off-the-floor give and take is pleasant and often witty. Marcantonio could always get a chuckle from colleagues by his threat to go into Virginia to campaign for Judge Smith by saying nice things about him at every stop.

Judge Smith would get into the spirit of the game and say coaxingly, "You wouldn't treat me like that, now would you, Marc? You're much too kind a man!"

Underneath the badinage, there was considerable respect for each other, despite the vast difference in their political philosophies.

Judge Smith told me once that in the fight over repeal of the prohibition amendment he commented to Senator Claude Swanson that he might have trouble in his district, since he had so many constituents of the Baptist and Methodist denominations, who opposed repeal, and on the other hand a lot of city dwellers who felt they were unjustly deprived of their privileges.

"Well now, Howard," the senator replied, "you can't straddle this one; you'll have to get off the fence. Just remember that there are only three men in the history of Virginia who could straddle the fence and survive: George Washington, Robert E. Lee, and Claude A. Swanson."

After the election, in which the judge had managed both to survive and to avoid being deeply involved, he approached the senator and said, "Claude, add the name of Howard W. Smith to that immortal list."

This calls to mind a story involving two former Arkansas congressmen who were caught in the same dilemma, Judge John E. Miller and David D. Glover, who served in the thirties. "Uncle Dave," as he was affectionately called, was a conscientious churchman and went regularly to the Metropolitan Baptist Church in northern Washington. The pastor was John Compton Ball, a highly respected minister and a crusading prohibitionist.

The bill calling for repeal of the prohibition amendment was to be submitted to the House on a certain Tuesday. During the preceding week, the Democrats held a caucus.

After personal feelings had been registered in a poll at the caucus, the members were expected to abide by the majority view, and on Tuesday vote, not their personal convictions, but the sentiment of the Democratic caucus. This procedure was not unprecedented, but was embarrassing to those who represented districts that were overwhelmingly dry, because the caucus voted *for* repeal. Uncle Dave was from such a district.

To make matters worse, Dr. Ball, in his sermon on Sunday, included a strong condemnation of the bill to repeal, and climaxed it with a paean of praise, as yet unearned, for his own parishioner, "I know not how 434 members of the House will vote on this iniquitous measure. But I *do* know how one member of the House and this congregation will vote. The Honorable David Glover of Arkansas will vote *no!*"

Uncle Dave squirmed. The caucus, with its unit rule provison, was not publicized; but even if it had been, a *yea* vote on Tuesday would be hard to defend or explain at home.

On Monday the news was heard on the Hill that Uncle Dave was sick.

Congressman Miller, thinking he smelled a rat, promptly made a "sick" call on Monday afternoon. Unannounced, he went up the stairs to Uncle Dave's bedroom. The door was slightly ajar, and he could see the invalid sitting up in bed reading a newspaper. He tapped lightly, pushed the door open and went in, looking very grave, although he had seen Uncle Dave in one convulsive movement flatten himself in bed.

"Well, Dave, how are you feeling?"

"Oh, I feel terrible, John. Just terrible." To prove it, Mr.

Glover gave a heart-rending groan. "It's my leg. Ouch! It hurts to move it an inch. I couldn't walk from here to the door."

"Just your leg? We could get a wheel chair . . ."

"Oh, no! I've got a congestion in my lungs, too . . ." He paused to give a rasping cough. "I may be coming down with pneumonia!"

"Well, move over, Dave. I'm getting in with you. I'm just as afraid of that vote as you are, and pneumonia of the leg is a good enough excuse for anybody!"

Sometimes the cloakroom incidents have a character-revealing aspect that is impressive. One Monday morning, in a mischievous mood, I told a handful of listeners in the cloakroom about the experience at the eleven o'clock service the day before, at Luther Rice Baptist Church in Washington. It involved my good friend the very popular congressman from Nashville, Percy Priest, the majority whip at that time. I made sure that Percy was present and listening, and began with the assertion that I had confirmed his faith in our friendship.

"You see, Saturday afternoon I found a note on my desk. I did not even get a telephone call from the congressman, just a hastily scribbled note saying, 'Brooks, I am scheduled to speak at the Luther Rice Church in the morning. Something has come up that makes it impossible. I am counting on you filling this engagement for me. Thanks, Percy.'

"Now, Gentlemen, you can't disappoint faith like that. He didn't say let me know if you can, he just said please do it. And I went.

"Obviously there was no advance notice. Percy had been advertised to speak, and frankly I think because of that there was a little larger congregation than usual. The pastor was disappointed, and I am sure the parishioners were, but everyone was trying to be considerate. I had had no time to make special preparation, I just had to dish up something in a hurry to occupy the sermon period. I felt pretty bad about my performance, but when it was over a sweet little lady came up to me and said, 'Mr. Priest, I heard you over the radio three weeks ago, and now I have the great pleasure of hearing you in person. I will say this, however, I never knew a man to improve so much in such a short length of time in all my life.'"

With Percy present, enjoying the story, it was repeated by request during the day. As Percy and I returned to our offices after the House adjourned late in the afternoon, he was still chuckling over it, and finally, with a straight face and sincerity in his voice, he said, "Brooks, please tell me, what did you say to that lady?"

In utter amazement I said, "Percy, you don't think that really *happened* do you?"

He said, "Didn't it?"

My comment on that was, "Well, Percy, it couldn't have happened, but I will say you're not only equipped with a fine sense of humor, but with a very beautiful modesty."

I remember the time I made my maiden speech in the House. There is a tradition in Congress that new members should be seen and not heard, but after several months I finally got up enough courage to address the speaker, and I spoke for five minutes. The next morning I was too impatient to wait for the *Congressional Record* to be delivered, so I hurried down to the basement of the Capitol to the record clerk's office to pick up a copy. To my great disappointment and utter disgust I found my speech attributed to my good friend, Congressman Oren Harris, also of Arkansas. There it was, just as I had delivered it, but Mr. Harris got the credit! I raced into the Record Clerk's office and told him what I thought of that kind of mistake. I was disappointed and irritated, and could not avoid showing it. Then I suddenly realized that I was completely out of character, and making too much of what was really an unimportant matter. I had gotten along well with the staff and wanted the happy relationship to continue. So I apologized and said, "Forgive me. Why, of course, I shouldn't have said anything about it. We all make mistakes. It was understandable."

He said cheerfully, "Oh, that's all right, Mr. Hays. You should have heard Mr. Harris."

Often seen in Congressional gatherings is Theodore McKeldin, who "commutes" between the governorship of Maryland and the mayor's office in Baltimore, being the biggest Republican vote gatherer in that state. He has a choice response to an elaborate welcome to speaking engagements. He is reminded, he tells audiences, of an incident in Baltimore when he returned as governor for an important event, shortly after taking office.

Near the city limits, a little hitchhiker, a ten- or twelve-year-old lad, asked for a ride into the city. The governor, perhaps unconsiously thinking in terms of goodwill with a pay-off a decade later, welcomed him to the back seat to sit beside him. The identity of his benefactor was unknown to the new passenger.

They rode into the city in grand style. At the edge of Baltimore, a welcoming committee met them with a police escort and band, and they rode toward the center of the city with all the pomp and pageantry that accompanies a popular governor.

Sitting back in the huge limousine, the lad, with two big eyes bulging, recognized that something big was taking place. Governor McKeldin decided the moment had come to relieve his little friend's curiosity.

"Son, do you know who all of this is for?" he inquired.

"Well," replied the lad, "it must be for one of us."

I recommend this to any speaker wanting an appropriate acknowledment to a warm welcome.

One of the new senators, Mr. Percy of Illinois, has a good story, one carried over from his 1964 race for governor. The incident, which produces much laughter now, gave him a sinking feeling at the time, and his auditors can understand his reaction. He tells it like this:

"My opponents, for some reason, made headway with the charge that I was really not interested in the governorship nor in Illinois. It was charged that I was aiming at the Presidency and only sought the state office as a stepping stone. My friends were worried. When one of my advisers was invited to appear on a statewide question and answer television program, near the end of the campaign, he was eager to reassure me that this question would be put to rest. 'Don't worry any more,' he said to me, 'I'll clobber 'em. I've got just the right answer—a good, short, convincing statement when the question comes.'

"I was in his audience feeling rather calm after his confident expressions. Sure enough, the question was asked—almost the first one, and my friend jumped at it.

"'I'm glad you asked that,' he began, his voice and manner exuding confidence that he was wrapping up one campaign question. 'I want to give you the facts, and My Friends, I know the facts, for I am among Chuck Percy's closest friends. I know his innermost thoughts and purposes. I can guarantee that he has only one interest and one purpose in mind, and his sole ambition is to be Governor of the United States!'

"I doubled up in anguish at that. It is funny now, but for days after that slip in November 1964, I took plenty of kidding over my friend's bobble."

Charles Percy has probably learned by this time, from his cloakroom conversations in Washington, that few of his fellow senators have enjoyed immunity from such hazards.

There is little occasion for newsmen or others to publicize the pleasant and often significant social influences that congressmen find essential for relieving the tensions of their strenuous lives. The cloakroom facilities, the breakfasts, luncheons, and dinners, and the corridor conversations provide opportunities for exchange of ideas on legislation as well as the light talk which adds to the conviviality of men who must always take seriously their official responsibility to a demanding public.

An afternoon nap is relished by some. In fact, during my tenure, there was one member who was loath to rise at the end of his nap and generally remained prone on his comfortable couch till adjournment. When a colleague failed to recognize him one day, an apology was immediately offered.

"You see, this is the first time I have ever seen you vertical."

One of the common complaints voiced by tourists when they visit either the Senate or the House gallery is the small number of congressmen or senators who are actually on the floor listening to the proceedings. Of course what most of these citizens do not realize is that floor attendance is only a small part of the job of being a Congressman. Attending to constituent problems will often take a congressman or senator off of Capitol Hill to one of the Executive departments downtown. It is also quite likely that the representative is involved with some of his committee responsibilities. It is in the Congressional committees and their sub-committees that the hardest work is done, preparing the way for legislation. Often debate on the floors of Congress is anti-climactic. All the hard decisions have been made by the committees. The work of Congress and the problems they deal with today are so complex that there is a tendency for most legislators to accept the work of the committees without question. This job then, of committee participation, is the heart of Congressional activity. It is also another place where humor may have a role.

Back in the early days of World War II, President Roosevelt appointed Mr. William Knudsen, the Norwegian-born president of General Motors, to be the head of the Office of Production Management. One of the first efforts was to get mobilized for the gigantic war effort to be undertaken. Mr. Knudsen, already a man of great skill and prestige with a reputation as a skilled administrator, was given the rank of brigadier general. He was summoned by a Senate committee to discuss with them the work of his new agency. Knudsen, who spoke with an accent, read a prepared statement, and then it became time for the senators to ask questions. The question period is one of the most important parts of a Congressional hearing, and many a man's reputation has been shattered by the way he handles his responses. One of the senators asked General Knudsen why some particular administrative plan was not being used in his agency.

"Yentlemen," he said, "it von't vork."

Senators normally prefer fuller answers than that, and so Knudsen was pursued by follow-up questions. To each he persisted that it "yust vouldn't vork." Finally, in some anger and exasperation, General Knudsen slammed shut his notes, pulled his papers together, stood up in his imposing fashion and said, "Yentlemen, Yeneral Motors pays me two hundred sixty thousand dollars a year. Ven I tell them something von't vork, they know damn vell it von't work. Good day."

And out he stalked, trailed by an awed group of military and civilian aides who had never in their bureaucratic lives seen a Senate committee spoken to like that.

The senators were startled, too, but it wasn't until weeks later, and after General Knudsen had developed a warm working relationship with the group, that he confessed to the senators that on the ride back to the Pentagon after his performance, he had slumped down in his seat and said to his aide, "You know, I yust plain couldn't remember vhy it vouldn't vork."

The Foreign Affairs Committee has had many long arduous sessions around their curved table, Chairman James P. Richards of South Carolina (known affectionately as Dick) in the central chair, and the late Chairmen Charles Eaton of New Jersey and John Kee of West Virginia, looking benevolently down from their portraits on the wall.

Toward the end of the day, which seemed more tiring and frustrating than usual, with tempers fraying, the chairman said, "We're not going to adjourn until we have a story from the gentleman from Arkansas. Come on, Brooks, put us in a good humor with one of your Arkansas tales."

"Well, Mr. Chairman, it just happens that I've been thinking of a man my father once encountered when he was a young country school teacher, and had a summer job taking the census. It took him way back into the hinterland. The man I mentioned, a big black-bearded fellow, was sitting on the porch of his mountain cabin when Dad paused at the steps and said, 'Good morning. I'm taking a census, and I need some information. What is your name, please?'

"The mountaineer hawked, spat, wiped his mouth on the back of his hand, and after these elaborate preparations, declaimed in a deep and at the same time nasal voice, which could be heard down the road a piece, 'Hearn's the name,' (he pronounced the *H* like a Cockney making a superhuman effort to be elegant) 'Randall J. Hearn.'

"My father's pencil, poised to write, paused a moment, 'How do you spell it?'

"The bearded one leaned back as if to indicate the interview was over, an expression of supreme indifference on his face. 'Spell it yourself, stranger, I'm a nonscholar.'"

Mr. Richards joined in the laughter, and then said, "I see why our afternoon's mish-mash made you think of Randall Hearn. Now all you nonscholars are adjourned, but let's do better tomorrow."

The chairman never forgot Randall Hearn. In fact, he seemed to develop something like a fondness for him, and would occasionally turn to me in the midst of a serious debate and say, "I wonder what Randall Hearn would say to that?"

One day a representative of the State Department appeared

before the committee to answer questions about some American soldiers who had been arrested and detained in a foreign country.

One of the soldiers was an Arkansas boy, and I was asking for details about him.

"Is he Randall Hearn's son, by any chance?" asked Mr. Richards, with a deadpan expression.

"No," I said. "This lad was not a nonscholar. You see, he went to school *to me.*"

There was never any explanation offered to newsmen or visitors of these little exchanges, which always left the partipants amused.

Another time, when the committee was considering the appointment of a special subcommittee, the chairman turned to me, catching me off guard, and asked, "What would Randall Hearn think of this idea?"

I remembered an old gag I could turn to account.

"Randall would be against it. He always said of his church committees that they were a group of the uninformed appointed by the unwilling to do the unnecessary."

"Well," said Mr. Richards, "perhaps that makes a scholar out of him."

One day in 1951 General George C. Marshall appeared before the Foreign Affairs Committee. This happened to be my first day on that committee, as I had just come over to the committee from eight years with the Banking and Currency Committee.

The chairman, Mr. Richards, knew me well, however, and was well acquainted with the strongly idealistic streak in my character. And so, with a touch of the sly humor that was characteristic of him he said, "General Marshall, may I introduce our new member, Mr. Hays of Arkansas. He rode to work on a six-cylinder cloud this morning."

General Marshall's face was an interesting study as the other members laughed, but he got the point, and his eyes twinkled as I, not at all disconcerted by the sudden thrust of my chairman, responded smoothly, "Well, you see, General, I take the position that this committee and its chairman, like your army, need reconnaissance."

During the period when I was taking kidding about my cloud-riding, Congressman Henderson Lanham of Georgia addressed the House on the subject of civil rights, and he spoke approvingly of my "Arkansas Plan" for a compromise that would produce some immediate progress. Included in his speech was the following paragraph:

"Mr. Speaker, a few days ago, I heard one of our colleagues gently chide the gentleman from Arkansas, Mr. Hays, for always floating around on a cloud. He admitted that Mr. Hays occasionally parks his cloud and comes down to earth.

"In this age of materialism and cynicism, I am sure that we need more cloud-riders, for 'where there is no vision the people perish.' Mr. Hays' head may be in the clouds where the winds of God's truth can reach him, but his feet are firmly planted upon the ground. He possesses that rare combination of vision and practicality."

My enjoyment of this beautiful speech by Mr. Lanham was doubled because I happened to be sitting by my chairman, whom I knew, of course, to be the author of the witticism.

I was about to murmur, "Now maybe that will keep you quiet!" when Mr. Richards spoke up, "Not on the ground—in the water."

This addendum, an obvious reference to my Baptist affiliation, gave Chairman Richards the last laugh.

Some of the long committee meetings were enlivened a trifle by my inveterate habit of doodling, combined with a certain facility in drawing. There was one weary session where it seemed that every member present wanted to do some carpentering on the bill, which apparently pleased no one as it stood. Amendment after amendment was proposed, chewed over, and pulled to pieces, as the hour grew late and agreement seemed further off than ever.

A paper was passed along the table till it reached Chairman Richards. He expelled his breath in a sigh of resignation, then opened it. What met his eyes was a monkey with a bland expression, hanging from the chandelier and saying, "Mr. Chairman, I offer an amendment."

Mr. Richards tapped the gavel for dismissal, and the members departed laughing.

There are occasions when committee members, for one reason

or another, cast votes that displease the leadership. I remember once when Chairman Richards and Speaker Rayburn were irritated with me—angered might be a better word for it—because of a vote I had cast in committee. After several days the speaker was satisfied with my explanation of my vote, but there still were strained feelings between Richards and me. I told him this story that Governor Battle of Virginia gave me about an aged doorkeeper and general handyman, affectionately called "Mosley," who had served several governors. He was a wonderful person, a great helper, faithful and loyal, but he had one weakness—on occasion he would get drunk. He would go off on a real binge, and not only be incapacitated, but bring some humiliation to the office. Finally the inevitable happened. Mosley was fired by Governor Battle. Some days after his dismissal, Mosley came very humbly into the governor's office and asked if he might see the governor. The governor said, "Yes, of course; come in, Mosley. I'm glad to see you."

The old man said "Governor, I don't want to say anything to you, but I want your permission to offer a prayer."

This the governor could hardly deny.

The old gentleman got down on his knees and in the governor's presence offered this petition: "Oh Lord, this old man is no good. He is undependable and unreliable. He has sinned against you and against his governor. You, oh God, have forgiven him. Put it into the heart of this great governor to forgive him, too."

Of course Governor Battle forgave him, and Mr. Mosley went back to work. I wound up this story by saying to Chairman Richards, "The speaker has forgiven me, and I am praying that you, Mr. Chairman, will forgive me too."

He smiled and added, "But I'll bet he got drunk the next week."

I said, "I'm going to check with Governor Battle and see."

I pretended I had, although Richards knew it was tongue in cheek as I told him the next day, "I asked Governor Battle about old Mosley, and he said, 'He never touched another drop.'"

One of the most important functions of a congressional committee is fact gathering. With the executive branch of government grown so large and so complex, Congress is compelled to call in expert witnesses to report to committees and give them guidance and knowledge. Members of the specialized committees like Agriculture or Finance or Armed Services are looked to by other members of Congress for leadership in specific fields.

If the congressional committees are the heart of congressional activities, the camaraderie of the cloakroom must be the soul. The cloakroom is the one place where the congressional brethren may gather, away from the public eye. These are actual rooms. Each chamber has two spacious clublike lounges, one for the Republicans and one for Democrats, immediately off the actual formal chambers, where they can let their hair down. The easy informality of the cloakroom exchanges mitigates the personal and sometimes bitter clashes on the floor. One might even be jerked out of mental depression by the frolicsome talk of statesmen who are first of all human beings, and almost invariably these humans are universally articulate. The cloakroom invariably leads to relaxation, and relaxation ultimately has to lead to horseplay and humor.

When I came to the House, I wanted to be a member of the "Lodge" and I didn't want to pretend to be a member until I had really been admitted. Somewhere along the line I apparently acquired a reputation as a good storyteller. Deserved or undeserved, it was pretty firm, and this was a great advantage. Something just naturally sounds funnier when it is related by one who has that reputation than by one who doesn't have it, and if I did deserve it, it was because in the probationary period of congressional service, I had exploited as effectively as possible the natural humor of the rural counties I represented. This is partly a legacy of my father, and partly an acquisition of my public service.

The House has many legends. I think House members enjoy imputing various qualities and characteristics to their respective members. The crowning example was Carl Vinson's reputation as a master strategist. Everyone felt if "the Admiral" decided that a certain course was wise and proper, every barrier would fall. These examples could be multiplied. I was glad to be the beneficiary of this practice.

The most eloquent statement with reference to my having benefited from it came from Representative Burr Harrison of

Virginia. Once in the cloakroom, after one of my little stories, which at the time I deemed relevant, Burr exclaimed after the laughter subsided, "That burns me up! I told that same story yesterday and not a one of you birds laughed! Now Brooks tells it, and you give him a good hand. And, moreover, it isn't even funny." He knew that I would regard this as a supreme accolade. We were warm friends.

The story I had just told had to do with the old gentleman in eastern North Carolina (it's always a good idea to establish the locale and provide the necessary details), who had passed the century mark. When the new preacher came to town, and they told him about "Uncle Johnny Thompson" and his remarkable life, one of his first pastoral calls was, of course, to visit the centenarian. After the introduction the minister said, "And they tell me, Brother Thompson, that you are over a hundred years old."

"Yep," he answered. "I was one hundred three last Sat'day."

"Would you tell me to what you attribute your long life?"

"Of course I will," said the old man. "I sleep eight hours every night. I walk a mile every morning, and I drink one glassful of straight whiskey every day."

The parishioner who had accompanied the preacher spoke up, "Hold on, Uncle Johnny, you know this man is a preacher."

"I don't care if he is a preacher, he oughtn't to drink more than one glassful of straight whiskey every day."

No chapter on congressional "folklore" would be complete without tapping the resources of humor built up around the famous gallery shooting by a group of Puerto Ricans, during the Eighty-third Congress. This startling episode had grave consequences for some, and set all Washington in a buzz that lasted for days. For once, even the Senate would admit it was overshadowed in importance by the House!

When it was over, and the worst had become known and accepted—there were no fatalities and the injured would recover—I felt a touch of compassion for those who had not been on the floor that day. I saw the pitiful efforts of some to explain their absence, and to indicate they had been just offstage, as it were, in the wings. It made no difference. Those who had not

been onstage during the big scene of the session might as well
have been in Limbo.

Whenever an avid Washingtonian asked eagerly, "Were you
in a dangerous spot, Congressman?" and the unfortunate public
servant was obliged to stutter, "No—you see, I wasn't there at
the moment—I had an important constituent—" or a phone
call, or even a summons from the President; no matter what, he
was dropped like a cold potato, as the siren voice of one who
had been there at that precise moment lured his audience away.

The House had been considering the "Wetback" bill, to allow
agricultural workers from Mexico to enter this country on a
temporary basis. Someone had made a point of no quorum, so
Speaker Martin had a count made, and announced there were
247 members in the Chamber therefore, a quorum being present,
they would proceed with the bill.

Suddenly the sound of gunfire rang out, a series of loud pops.
Afterward, when some member said he thought it was firecrackers, Congressman Cooley of North Carolina answered (or
so it was reported), "Oh, I knew it wasn't firecrackers! It's
against the rules to shoot off firecrackers in the House."

Most, if not all, of the august body did not wait to figure it
out, but made a reflexive dive for whatever cover there was. I
was sitting between Congressman Mills and Congressman
Trimble, and when it started, I ducked down on my knees between the seats, and hoped my rear had cover. Mr. Trimble
confessed later that he found himself at the committee table,
fifty feet away, and had no recollection of moving out of his
seat.

It was all over in a few seconds. Gallery guards, at first
paralyzed by the unprecedented and staggering event, located
the source and closed in on the perpetrators, five Puerto Rican
revolutionaries who had smuggled in guns (that is against the
rules, too!), and fired them from the gallery, in order to
dramatize their movement.

All the members except five were very, very lucky. The five
who were hit were Bentley of Michigan, Davis of Tennessee,
Fallon of Maryland, Jensen of Iowa, and Roberts of Alabama.
Mr. Bentley's injury was the worst, but Mr. Roberts and Mr.
Davis were also hospitalized, and all the wounds were painful.

Dr. Calver was summoned, and he and his aides appeared quickly and took charge of the victims, while the House, totally uninterested in the Wetback bill or anything else for the rest of that day, quickly adjourned.

By the next day, their aplomb sufficiently recovered and the reaction of relief having set in, they began to see the humorous side of even such a serious situation as the one of the day before. Many small incidents were told about, and made much of, stretched and enhanced by the alchemy of one of the American male's most persistent characteristics, a keen sense of humor.

One such incident concerned Congressman Frank Boykin of Alabama. Someone met him as he rushed out of the chamber and headed south. "Where are you going, Frank?" the newcomer on the scene asked.

"To get my gun!"

"Where is it?"

"In Alabama," he called back over his shoulder.

Another reaction that caused chuckles later was that of Congressman Lou Graham of Pennsylvania, who was a little more than five feet tall, but weighed two hundred pounds. Someone asked, "What did you do, Lou?"

He said, "I just stood there."

"You just stood there! Couldn't you have lain down?"

"Yes, I could have, but I'd a been as high lying down as standing up."

Congressman Forrester of Georgia was not on the floor, but managed to get into the act, as he was "wounded" in the aftermath of the explosions. Mr. Forrester is short in stature, and he has a precise, clipped way of speaking. His claim to fame was that he was injured by Martin Dies, a six foot, three inch Texan, and the largest man in Congress.

"I was in the cloakroom," complained the little congressman, carefully enunciating each syllable, "when I heard a commotion in the chamber. I said to myself, 'I'd better see what's going on.' I started through a door just as Martin Dies rushed out—he knocked me twenty feet! I was hurt worse than any of those who were shot."

It was a newsman who got off the *coup de grâce* and repaid

at one stroke any grudges he may have held against congress-men, either individually or collectively. He said that of the two hundred newsletters sent by the members to their home districts each week, and which he scanned regularly for possible tidbits of news, 117 of them started their next missive with the fateful statement, "I was sitting next to Congressman Bentley when. . . ."

The informal decision made in the cloakrooms the next day was that members' pay would be increased as follows:

"Combat pay for those who stood up; flight pay for those who ran; and submarine pay for those who lay down on the floor."

I easily qualified for submarine pay.

3

Humor in High Places:
Executive Department

I FIRST LOOKED upon the city of Washington in July, 1919, shortly after the first World War, when the city with its environs had about a fourth of its present population. Horse-drawn vehicles were still a common sight, and a row of carriages would be drawn up before the theaters to pick up their passengers after a performance. Although relatively quiet, it was even then a wonderfully attractive and exciting place. I loved it.

In recent years, it has become "the entertaining city," and I should add "the entertained city." We Washingtonians should be entertainers, for the city belongs to the American people. One of my constituents, an Arkansas farmer who saved his money to pay a visit to the city his taxes had helped build, wanted to see the Capitol and the White House. In the Capitol he got into a restricted zone, and an insensitive guard, probably new and uninstructed, waved him back rather abruptly.

"Get back there! Who do you think you are anyway?"

My friend from Arkansas controlled his feelings. "Nobody," he answered mildly. "Nobody much. Just one of the owners."

In 1919 my attitude toward my capital city was one of awe, not brashness; I had none of the proprietary feeling that the perceptive Arkansas farmer had. Rather, the city overwhelmed me. I had no such feeling about Chicago, where I had spent June of 1918 in training at Fort Sheridan. I felt toward Washington as Samuel Johnson felt toward London. "Who does not love

89

the City does not love life, for the City has all that life can afford.'"

Some of the excitement Washington held for me was of the conventional movie and stage play kind. The National Theater was going strong in 1919, in its present location, but it had keen competition from Belasco's, The Garrick, Poli's, and others, and Keith's was on the Orpheum vaudeville circuit. For fifty or seventy-five cents—which was a lot of money to us government clerks, struggling on one hundred dollars a month to get through law school—we could enjoy hearing Will Rogers make targets of Presidents and congressmen with his gentle humor.

With an apparent artlessness which is the height of art, Will twirled his rope, while he talked of his visits to the White House and the Capitol. "Dropped over to see President Harding today, but he wasn't home. Gone on his yacht for the weekend.

" 'But it's only Thursday,' I said.

" 'Yep,' the man at the door admitted. 'He'll be back Tuesday.'

" 'Then I'll come in to see him next Wednesday.'

" 'Better not. That's the day he plays golf.'

"I tell you," said Will, with mock seriousness, "We'll never get this government headed right till we have a President that gets seasick and can't hit a golf ball!"

Having paid his respects to the White House, he would turn to the Senate.

"Yes, sir, I sat up there in the balcony the other day. It was a real busy day—as many as four of them senators was there at their desks at one time. And Jim Reed [this was an acid-tongued senator from Missouri], he's got a specially good act this year."

In addition to the immortal Will Rogers, we could watch Pat Rooney and Fred Stone and Fanny Brice perform with fine supporting casts in the musicals. I recall also the performance of William Gillette in *Dear Brutus,* Julia Marlowe as Juliet, and David Warfield in *The Auctioneer.*

One was more apt to see notables on the streets of Washington, in casual movements through the stores or on the sidewalks. I was excited once when I found myself walking a few feet behind William Jennings Bryan along Fifteenth Street. Also, when seated near Secretary of State Lansing in the Covenant Church (now the National Presbyterian), or watching Charles Evans

Hughes take communion at Calvary Baptist, his church home
and in later years our own. I was proud to walk into a bank
right behind Chief Justice Edward Douglas White.

I recall how excited my bride was one April Sunday in 1922
when we attended National Baptist Church at Sixteenth and
Columbia Road and found ourselves being escorted down the
aisle right behind President and Mrs. Harding. The usher
thought we were in his party, and obviously expected us to follow
him into the pew. It was our blank expressions, I have always
believed, that made him realize his mistake. It caught him a little
off balance, but he did recover quickly enough to seat us just
across the aisle.

One can never entirely lose the feeling of awe in the presence
of an American President. Even in later years—beginning with
Mr. Roosevelt's administration in 1933, when my service on
the Democratic National Committee and in the Congress produced invitations to many social events in the White House—
I had a self-consciousness that fortunately operated as a brake
on my conversational proclivities. I have an embarrassing recollection of an occasion when President Roosevelt invited seventy
freshmen congressmen of both parties to the White House. Afterward Joe Martin told Charlie Halleck, the President shed so
much charm it would take a month for the Republicans to come
out of the ether.

As we gathered around President Roosevelt, Speaker Sam
Rayburn gave me a push toward a chair on the President's left,
and whispered. "You sit down there, Brooks." Taking thank-
fully what the gods provided, I slid into the vacant chair, just as
the President began to speak.

It was an informal occasion, and when presently he said
something I agreed with, I said, "That's right."

He whizzed around, leaning slightly forward in his chair. His
eyes, only about a foot away, looked right into mine. "How's
that?" he said.

My self-consciousness, forgotten for a moment, returned in a
rush. "That's right," I repeated feebly. He looked pleased,
jerked his head up and down twice, and ejaculated, "Yeh!"

The next day I was the butt of the badinage that normally
goes on in the cloakroom. Those who weren't there were regaled

with the story of how the greatest living man turned to their colleague with a question, gave him the floor, and paused along with a waiting world for words of wisdom to issue from his lips! And what happened? In a tone so low it was hardly above a whisper, like a fizzling fuse, their colleague from Arkansas had murmured, "That's right."

Reflecting on my Washington experiences, beginning with three law school years which ended in 1922, I suddenly realized that I had seen every President elected in this century, have listened to conversations participated in by all of them since Teddy Roosevelt, except Woodrow Wilson, and (I hope this does not sound immodest) have heard myself called by my first name by all since Mr. Hoover. I have received commissions from all since President Truman, and have had executive office quarters in the White House under Presidents Kennedy and Johnson.

The conversation with Mr. Coolidge was, I must concede, very brief. It happened during his service as Vice President. I greeted him one morning when, at the Senate door, he glanced toward me. I said, "Good morning, Mr. President."

In the distinctive nasal voice the country came to associate with him, he answered, "How'd ya do?"

The Coolidge legend has a fascination for me, which I can account for only by the similarity of Plymouth, Vermont, life to the hill country patterns in Arkansas (though there are substantial differences, too). Living now only seven miles from his Northampton, Massachusetts, home, I find myself interested in the Coolidge stories that originated before he went to Washington.

My theory that he possessed a quiet but deep and wholesome sense of humor is held by others, who have studied his record and personality more closely. And I do not include in this category a public official of my state who had to deliver a document to him, and who spent some time in his White House office in the company of one of our senators. Telling about it later, this Arkansan, who was both uneducated and uninhibited, and whose language bore all the evidences of educational neglect, reveled in the colloquialisms of the backwoods. "Well, sir, I'd allus heerd that President Coolidge was a serious solemnlike sort of feller. You know, I never found him that way a'tall. He laughed the whole time I wuz in thar."

Some of my contemporaries in Washington were surprised to learn that among his classmates at Amherst College, Calvin Coolidge had earned a reputation as a campus wit.

The frugality of Vermonters I could understand. Our hill people have the same trait, and the story told by one newsman claiming to be an eye witness might have happened to an Ozark inhabitant. Mr. Coolidge, as we remember, was thrust into the Vice Presidency and then into the Presidency with great suddenness. Prior to the changes wrought by the Washington environment (and no one is so sturdy as to resist them entirely), Mr. Coolidge was visiting his old home in Plymouth. A reporter, whose identity escapes me, sat on the front porch of his father's home with him. One other newsman was in the company. Mr. Coolidge suggested that they walk over to the store to get a cold drink. There was quick acceptance, and the three walked together right up to the counter. I remember that according to this story, which had the earmarks of authenticity, the host ordered a moxie, a popular nickel drink in New England.

As they were finishing, the teller of this tale saw Mr. Coolidge draw from his pocket a snap purse, extract a single nickel, lay it in front of his empty bottle, and start toward the door. The reporter quickly placed a dime in front of his bottle, and the three returned to the modest Coolidge home.

My good friend former Speaker Joe Martin, whose defeat in 1966 grieved a lot of us, is my authority for another Coolidge story. I don't recall that Mr. Martin, who is one of Coolidge's great admirers, vouched for it, but he enjoyed relating it. Mr. Coolidge was receiving a small committee to discuss a matter of state. One of the number arrived early, and while they waited for the others, the President poured a glass of sherry for his guest and one for himself.

When the other two arrived, Mrs. Coolidge escorted them into the office, and brought out the sherry for them. Having filled their glasses, she turned to the first guest, whose glass was empty by that time, but the President forestalled her. "He's had his," he said.

It was ironic that the only one of the Presidents whose voice I never heard was one of my greatest heroes—Woodrow Wilson. I did hear the cheers of the crowd as he and Mrs. Wilson rode along Pennsylvania Avenue in the Harding inaugural parade on March 4, 1921, and I have a vague recollection of how he looked that day in his silk hat. As a college student I had plenty of company in my adoration of Mr. Wilson. I was an ardent member of the George Washington University student organization dedicated to perpetuating his principles.

I recall that on one occasion our group's plans for an evening devoted to oratory and acclaim went awry, but the event gave us a lot of amusement. We had secured a United States senator as the principal speaker, and true to his word this eloquent legislator showed up at the appointed hour. He was appropriately introduced, but had scarcely uttered a word before his audience became aware of his condition. It was obvious he had had access to the contraband liquid that flowed rather freely in the prohibition era. His tongue thickened, and he swayed rather alarmingly from one side of the podium to the other. But he admired Woodrow Wilson and was determined not to give up the effort.

The little "put and take top" was a toy top used in a game which enjoyed great popularity that year, and the senator wanted to use the phrase figuratively. His effort was one of the funniest things I ever heard on a platform! It threw him—almost literally. He swayed and tottered, as he tried to wind up the reference.

"Woodrow Wilson was as high above his detractors as the Washington monument is higher than a p-p-p-put nam t-t-t-take nem t-t-t-top!" he finished triumphantly.

Even though amused, we sighed with relief when his stuttering ceased, but the evening wasn't over yet. Pointing to Sarah Tilghman, a brilliant law student (currently a federal judge in Dallas—the Judge Sarah Hughes who later administered the oath of office to President Johnson), he asked, "What was the greatest thing Woodrow Wilson ever did?"

She promptly said, "He inspired the League of Nations."

"No, not that; it was not the League of Nations. It was not the Federal Reserve System. It was not the reform bills he put through Congress. The greatest thing that Woodrow Wilson ever did . . ." he was deadly serious, "wash to veto the Volshtead Act!"

His heart was in that stirring tribute.

We learned later that this senator's weakness was well known to his colleagues. If they had shared this information with us, some monitoring might have been done and an embarrassing performance avoided.

Each year on April 6, anniversary of the World War I declaration, during my service in the Congress, I went to the library just adjoining the House chamber to read his message to the joint session of the House and Senate. There are some incidents involving Woodrow Wilson recorded in this volume, but the March 4 parade on the day he went out of office is the extent of my personal contact.

In later years I became a close friend of his grandson, Francis Sayre, Dean of the Washington cathedral, but my talks with him regarding his grandfather never penetrated the surface of general knowledge. He told me that actually he was not aware during Mr. Wilson's lifetime of his prominent place in history. "He was my grandpapa—I just loved and enjoyed him."

Later, of course, he came to appreciate him as a tremendous figure in American life.

I did not meet Herbert Hoover until near the end of my Congressional service, and then only because a longtime mutual friend, Raymond Miller of California, was eager to bring us together. He knew that I admired Mr. Hoover; and he knew also that I had been interested in Hoover's brief residence in Arkansas, when, in the early 1890's he spent a summer vacation helping John C. Branner conduct his famous geological survey of Arkansas mineral resources. One of my associates at the state house, while rummaging through some old documents in 1925, ran across a canceled state warrant for one month's pay amounting to sixty dollars. It was made out to and endorsed by "Bert Hoover."

In the talk I had with him in New York, when Mr. Miller brought us together, he spoke affectionately of the people with whom he became acquainted in the Arkansas Ozarks during that summer's employment.

I would like to record, too, that Mr. Hoover, with all of his solemnity in political addresses, knew how to use a self-depreciating incident to get a laugh. He told the following one so naturally that he convinced a small audience of which I was a part that it really happened.

He said a small lad came up to him once and asked for his autograph. When the former President graciously complied, the little fellow said, "Would you mind signing it again, further down?"

"All right," said Mr. Hoover, and did so. Then he asked, "But why twice?"

"Because," was the young businessman's answer, "with two of yours I can get one of Babe Ruth's."

As a boy I had heard Theodore Roosevelt campaigning from the rear platform of a train. Later I told Mrs. Alice Longworth about it, though it was worth only passing mention. I did, however, get an appreciative laugh from her when I related an incident I picked up in northeast Ohio, "where there are more Republicans and Methodists per square mile (it is said) than in any place in the world."

In a little church service, according to the story, a devout layman of strong convictions was called on to lead in prayer. He offered this petition, "Oh, Lord, we thank you for this great land we love so much, and for the wonderful men of the past who have made it what it is. Men like Lincoln and Grant and Garfield and McKinley and Roosevelt—*Theodore*, that is!"

Being able to pass on to members of the families of some prominent leaders, anecdotes involving their forebears has given me pleasure on several occasions. I recently told Mrs. William Gossett of Detroit, daughter of Chief Justice Hughes, about something that happened when her father was associate justice, and Chief Justice White presided over the Court.

A young and inexperienced Arkansas lawyer was making an oral argument before the Court. Justice Hughes interrupted him to ask a question, and the young lawyer went into a long and boring dissertation. After some minutes of this the chief justice stopped him.

"Just a minute, Mr. Rector. The Court appreciates this, but it doesn't appear to have the remotest bearing upon this case."

"That's right, your Honor, it doesn't," my friend cheerfully acknowledged, "but Justice Hughes asked me."

When the whole Court laughed, the Arkansas barrister realized that this bordered on contempt, and his face flushed with embarrassment, until he noticed the benevolent countenance of the great elder statesman and judge, Mr. Hughes. He was laughing with the rest. Mr. Rector relaxed.

Warren G. Harding loved to make people happy by joining their clubs and lodges and fraternities. During my junior year in law school, he accepted membership in my law fraternity, Phi Alpha Delta. It was a great occasion, when the active chapters at George Washington and Georgetown Universities were invited to the White House for the induction ceremony and to have the traditional picture taken on the White House lawn.

It was a delightful spring day, and there was an atmosphere of gaiety befitting the weather. General Pershing and Chief Justice Taft were there as members to welcome the distinguished new brother. We students stood as close as possible to the great trio, so as not to miss a word. I was glad I was within hearing when the chief justice, with his inimitable chuckle, inquired of the President, "Mr. President, did you see what Abe Martin said about me yesterday?"

We boys listened alertly to hear the rest of the story, for Bolon Turner, Joe Barrett, and I (the three Arkansas members of PAD) had seen it, and I had expressed the hope that Mr. Taft had seen and enjoyed it. Here—to our surprise—we were learning that he had indeed seen it! So we were all ears when Harding answered, "No, I didn't, Mr. Chief Justice. What did he say?"

Taft chuckled again. "Well, Mr. President, Abe said, 'I thought when Mr. Taft got to be chief justice, he would put on a little dignity, but he always looks like a fellow who's just looked in an old vest and found a dime.'"

Three years later, when I was admitted to the United States Supreme Court (still meeting in the old Senate chamber in the

Capitol), Mr. Taft seemed to have that same marvelous expression, as he said, "Mr. Hays, you may step to the clerk's desk and take the oath."

Speaking of admissions to the Court, I recall something that the late Chief Justice Fred Vinson, one of the most popular public servants ever to grace the Capitol, had to say about my appearances. I was among the guests at a White House luncheon, and while we waited for the President to appear, there was a chance for a little conversation. Mr. Vinson and I were old friends. I had not reached Congress when he resigned his seat to become a judge, but he had often appeared before the Banking and Currency Committee during his tenure as Secretary of the Treasury.

"Don't see you often, Brooks, to 'howdy' with you," he said, "but I look over at you when you bring a lawyer to introduce to the Court, and I say to myself, 'Well, there's old Brooks with another twenty-five dollars for the kitty.'"

I told Chief Justice Warren of that conversation one Saturday night at a dinner honoring our highly respected former member of the House, Judge Marvin Jones, and on the following Monday morning I was in the Supreme Court chamber to introduce not one, but two, lawyers.

When the chief justice called on me to present them, his broad smile was almost audibly announcing, "Another fifty dollars for the kitty."

The infectious smile and splendid conversational ability of Chief Justice Warren had something to do with his political success. I first comprehended this when I met him in Sacramento in 1949, while he was governor. I was in his state to help with a survey of housing conditions. Bart Kavanaugh, a housing expert, brought us together at a luncheon, and in the course of that talk, mention was made of the continuing movement of Arkansans to California. They were going from other states too—in great numbers, "a thousand a day," the governor said, and "we need help to house and find employment for them."

"Yes," I added, "it will cost Arkansas a congressman."

"What will you do if it is you who loses out in the redistricting?" the governor asked me—not seriously—just pursuing the problem of relocations.

"I'll come out here and ask you to help me get a gerrymandered district with only ex-Arkansans in it. It would be possible—you know. I have found them in droves all the way from San Diego to Sacramento."

"It's a deal," he said. He remembered that talk and referred to it at the Marvin Jones' dinner, good naturedly. He apologized "for leaving [me] in the lurch" when something really did happen to me ten years later.

A building foreman's directions to four workmen, employed on a construction job, demonstrates California's cosmopolitan character better than anything I have heard.

Congressman Chet Holifield, a former Arkansan himself told me that he overheard this: "Hey, Arkie, you and Tex help Missou, and Okie move that lumber."

Finally, among stories of notables passed on to their families, is the threadbare one (familiar at least to all Philadelphians—or so I thought) about the Biddles.

Seated next to Mrs. Anthony Biddle one night at our embassy in Madrid, when her husband was our ambassador to Spain, I just mentioned it, saying I had always thought it very funny. To my surprise, she said she had never heard it, so I got to tell her.

It is a simple little story about the British visitor, who, upon returning from an American tour, was besieged by his friends with questions. One asked, "And did you visit Philadelphia?"

The traveler paused a moment to consider. Then he said, "Ah, yes, Philadelphia—that's where everyone is named Scrapple, and they eat biddle for breakfast."

Franklin Delano Roosevelt was probably the most noted of our Presidents for his love of laughter, his high spirits, and his enjoyment of a good joke, even when it was at his own expense. Like Lincoln, who had carried the same kind of terrific burdens, humor was a respite and a moment of laughter was a release from tension. Lincoln once told a congressman, who had come to see him about a disaster that had befallen the Union Army, "with the fearful strain of war upon me, if I did not laugh I should die."

In 1942 Walter Karig, the Newark *News* Washington correspondent, presented President Franklin Roosevelt with a book by Max Herzberg called *Insults*. This book was, as its title would indicate, a collection of the best of the breed from all over the world. As F.D.R. accepted the book, he said, "Does this gentleman think I need any lessons in giving insults or in taking them?" Then he laughed and said he would read the book with interest because actually "my stock of insults is low."

On another occasion Roosevelt decided the time had come to lower the boom on H. L. Mencken. Brilliant and witty as he was, in his later years Mencken had become extremely violent in his opposition to the New Deal and to F.D.R. personally. In December of 1934 the Gridiron Dinner, the annual gathering of the fifty top Washington correspondents and their guests, was the scene of battle. First Mr. Mencken spoke. He began "Mr. President . . . and fellow subjects of the Reich." He described in Menckenian terms a country that had been transformed by the New Deal into a place where every aspect of the Bill of Rights had been desecrated.

Then it was F.D.R.'s turn. He spoke gently of his "old friend, Henry Mencken." Next he turned to his text and unleashed a withering attack on American journalism. "There are managing editors in the United States, and scores of them, who have never heard of Kant or Johannes Müller, have never read the Constitution of the United States; there are city editors who do not know what a symphony is or a streptococcus, or the Statute of Frauds; there are reporters by the thousands who could not pass the entrance examination for Harvard or Tuskegee, or even Yale."

The newsmen, shocked by the attack, stirred, as F.D.R. spoke. Then as they watched Mencken himself, they suddenly knew what F.D.R. was doing. The words he spoke were not his, but a quote from H. L. Mencken.

During his second term F.D.R. came to Syracuse University to speak at a medical school commencement and dedicate a medical building. He was to be introduced by the distinguished dean of the Syracuse University Law School, Paul Shipman Andrews. The two were seated together on the platform as the proceedings continued. The taking of the Hippocratic oath by all the new doctors was an impressive sight and an emotional experience.

Dean Andrews was much touched by it. He turned to F.D.R. "Isn't that something, Mr. President? Don't you think it would be a great thing if all new lawyers had to take some similar kind of an oath?"

"Paul," the President responded, "don't make me laugh. I've got a split lip."

It is said that among Roosevelt's favorite stories about himself was one he used to tell about the Westchester County, New York commuter. Westchester in those days was the heartland of Republicanism, and the mention of the name F.D.R. was an act of sheer infamy. Every day this Republican commuter, according to F.D.R., would go up to the newspaper stand, hand the newsboy a quarter, take a copy of the New York *Herald Tribune,* glance at the headlines, shake his head sadly and hand the paper back to the boy. Then he would rush for his train. After years of this the newsboy asked him why he did this every morning.

"I'm interested in the obituary items," he replied.

"But the obituaries are in the back of the paper, not on the front page."

"Son, the——I'm interested in will be on the front page."

One of my cherished recollections about President Roosevelt is of a trip in his special train from Washington to Little Rock. He had accepted an invitation, extended by Senator Joe T. Robinson on behalf of the state, to speak at the centennial celebration of Arkansas's entrance into the Union, and I was included in the party because I was Democratic National Committeeman from our state.

The President invited Senator Robinson, Jessie Jones, Marshall Diggs, and me, and maybe one or two others to dinner in his private dining room. While the rest of us had steaks, the President had a simple dinner of scrambled eggs.

The talk had turned to tax reform and how hard it is to interest voters in any tax program, and as the rest were expressing themselves, Mr. Roosevelt turned to me. I was again on his left—maybe there is some significance in that!

"You have run for governor. Didn't you find it so?" he asked.

"Mr. President, I have a perfect example," I said. "I was the first candidate ever to advocate an income tax in Arkansas, and I had rough going trying to sell it to the voters in 1928. You will recall the Scopes trial was held in Dayton, Tennessee, in 1927, and the young school teacher, John Thomas Scopes, was convicted of the sin of teaching the Darwinian theory of evolution.

"Well, I was doing my best to make my program sound simple and sensible. One day I was speaking in a small community forty miles from a railroad called Big Flat. I was standing under a large tree in front of a blacksmith shop, surrounded by a small crowd, and pouring out my heart on taxation, when a big brawny fellow, leaning against the door of his shop, said, 'Hold on a minute. Can I ast you a question?'

" 'Certainly,' I said, mopping my forehead.

" 'Well, that talk about taxes is all right, I reckon, but what we folks here at Big Flat want to know is—How do you stand on evolution.'

Everybody about the table joined in the President's laughter, as he threw his head back in his familiar gesture.

A few minutes later he came back to the story. "What did you tell that fellow?"

Not wanting to bore him with any part of my old speech, I said, "Well, Mr. President, after I had gone, one of my listeners is reported to have said, 'If Brooks is as good a two-stepper as he is a side-stepper, I'll bet he's popular at them Little Rock dances.' "

One of the favorite stories circulating in Washington half a century ago had to do with President Wilson's habit of reaching for the phone to call someone himself, without going through the front office. One of his military friends happened to be in Walter Reed Hospital, and the President wanted to talk with him, so he put in the call himself. When he heard the voice of the hospital receptionist, he said, "This is President Wilson. I want to speak with . . ."

That was as far as he got. He was interrupted by a cheerful greeting, "Well, hi, Woody! This is Queen Wilhelmina. How's it goin'?"

Bill Clark of USIA tells me that something like this occurred during the tenure of President Roosevelt. Franklin, Jr. was his classmate at Harvard, and Bill was invited to have lunch with Franklin, his fiancée and the President at the White House.

They had hardly entered the family dining room when Frank's fiancée had a sudden illness and had to go to the hospital. Frank made a quick exit with her after apologizing to Bill, and hurried off to the hospital.

Bill reached for his hat, and began his good-bye to the President, but Mr. Roosevelt vigorously protested. "No, no," he said. "Don't leave me here to eat lunch by myself."

He prevailed on Bill, a boy scarcely out of his teens, to eat with him. The subject of books came up and the President related the following: The President having decided to get help from the Library of Congress in cataloguing his naval library, simply reached for the phone and called the Library of Congress. As in Mr. Wilson's case, someone came to the phone who let his skepticism get the best of him. When the President said, "This is Franklin D. Roosevelt," the reply came quickly, "Well, well! The hay fever's got you down, hasn't it?" and then there was a click.

The President laughed, hung up, and waited a few minutes before trying again.

He began with the same salutation, only to hear, "Oh, it's you again," and another click.

The President enjoyed it immensely. He decided to give it a third try. This time he began a little differently. "Young man, please don't hang up on me! This really is Franklin D. Roosevelt, and I am calling for assistance with my book catalogue."

This time the library official was convinced. In just the time it took for him to come from the Library, an embarrassed Library official showed up with abject and multiple apologies.

It was a great day for Bill Clark, of course, and he has enjoyed regaling private audiences all over the world with his tale of what happened the day he had lunch with the President.

Mr. Truman had a good sense of humor, too, and a forthright charm with which he was not always credited by those who had no personal contact with him. I never quite understood the intensity of feeling of some of his opposition, though I could, of course, understand their differing on policies. His natural friendliness and easy manner of establishing rapport was evident to all of us who served with him.

I am indebted to Congressman Jim Trimble for a fine illustration of his disarming ways.

Jim represented a district with a thriving poultry business, and when a committee asked him to make a White House appointment for them, he promptly did it. The purpose was to extend to the President a personal invitation to attend a great "Chicken Festival."

Prior to the appointed hour for meeting the President, the group came to Jim's office to get instructions. While there, they drifted into a discussion of the President, and it was obvious that most of the group were decidedly hostile to him. Hardly anyone defended him. But in spite of this attitude, he was "the President," and they wanted to get him to attend the festival if they could.

Jim ushered them into the President's office, and after the introductions Mr. Truman flashed his famous smile, and said, "Jim tells me you're in the chicken business." And then in the friendliest possible tone, "What kind do you raise?"

One or two poultry strains were mentioned. Then the President referred to his boyhood at Grand View, Missouri. "Now Mama liked Rhode Island Reds. I like them but I like the Domineckers, too. We had a lot of chickens, and I used to enjoy helping Mama take care of them."

Jim could see his committee melting like butter in the sun. They became so absorbed in the talk about chickens, they almost forgot to extend the formal invitation! They didn't seem to mind too much when the President turned it down, they were so pleased to have had such a man-to-man down-to-earth talk with the President of the United States.

One day my friend Claud Byrd of Kansas City got on an elevator in an office building of that city. At the next stop, another Arkansas friend, Joe Culpepper, hopped on the elevator and was promptly greeted by Claud. "Where were you last night? We waited till eleven o'clock for you."

Joe shot back, "Well, where were you?"

A voice from the rear of the elevator, with a nice calculation of timing, said incisively, "He asked you first!"

Both looked around, and their jaws dropped. The "umpire" was Harry S Truman.

Mr. Truman had an unusually devoted staff while he was President, but once even they failed to brief the President properly. Truman was speaking in a town where there were a great many railroad workers, and railroad repair shops; railroading was the town's biggest industry. Truman somehow got off talking on how much his administration had done for highway construction, and what this meant in the way of advantages for truck transportation. He pointed dramatically to the railroad depot and said, "These big railroad magnates have got to get used to this competition. We may have to jolt them a little to make them understand highway competition is here to stay and it's good for the farmers." The President didn't know until he left that town and read the petitions that everyone in the town had signed and given to him, that the people in the town were deeply concerned about the loss of railroad revenues, which were their greatest source of income.

Speaking of staff work reminds me of my interesting year in the State Department, when I was Assistant Secretary for Congressional Relations. One morning at staff meeting, Mr. Rusk turned to me and asked me to make a contact with a senator concerning a certain bill.

As discreetly as possible I suggested that this particular matter would require a personal call from the Secretary himself; this task I felt could not be delegated. I had known Dean Rusk a long time, and so I went further than I would have done otherwise, when he started to veto my suggestion. I said, "But Mr. Secretary, I have the Bible on my side—it says in Hebrews, 'Jacob leaned on his staff and died.'"

Mr. Rusk folded up, laughing with the others. He made the call.

I had an unusually pleasant relationship with President Eisenhower. His aide, General Wilton Persons (usually known as Jerry), a favorite on Capitol Hill where he did liaison work for the Pentagon, brought the general and me together more than once before the 1952 election. I recall a visit with him in Paris in 1951, when I went out to his headquarters primarily to see General Persons and other staff members.

As Jerry led me down the hall to pay my respects to General

Eisenhower, he suggested that I repeat some of the stories with which I had been regaling him and his office staff. "He's under pressure," Jerry said, "and it would relax him a bit."

Just as Jerry had predicted, the general seemed to get a lift from my line of chatter. He told me, on my departure, that by actual count sixty congressmen had been to see him that summer, and that only two (Keogh of New York and myself) had refrained from asking, "Are you going to run for President?"

We had been there forty minutes when he asked me to stay to lunch. Jerry explained that he and Mrs. Persons had already prepared for me, so we departed.

As we left, I was already anticipating meeting the newsmen. I would say I had had a highly pleasant visit with him, but would refuse any comment on the general's election plans, or indeed on news of any kind. I would give my interview an air of mystery. That thought had inspired the last story I gave him, just before I went out the door. It went like this:

A group of Protestant preachers were discussing the desirability of finding a Protestant version of the Catholic confession. "It would help us all if we could only tell someone else of our misdeeds," one said. The group of four was in agreement. Another suggested that they give the plan a trial by revealing to each other their weaknesses or sins.

The first confession had to do with drinking. "My big temptation is liquor. My congregation doesn't know it, but I secretly imbibe, and sometimes I slip away and go on a binge."

The second minister said, "Well, mine is gambling. I go away during the racing season to lose money on the horses, and I can't resist casino gambling if I get to a place where it goes on."

The third man spoke delicately of his temptation which involved the fair sex. "A pretty face or a pretty hat takes my mind off my sermon. My people would be shocked," he said sadly.

They turned to the fourth minister. His confession was quickly concluded even as he picked up his hat. "My sin is gossiping, and I can hardly wait to get out of here!"

"And General Eisenhower," I said, after a word of thanks and farewell, "I can hardly wait to get out of here to see those newsmen."

My latest visit with General Eisenhower was on the evening

of November 13, 1966, at a dinner in Washington at which he was given the Charles Evans Hughes award, by the National Conference of Christians and Jews. I was asked to present a gift to Mrs. Eisenhower. It was an ideal time for reminiscing briefly, and for conveying to the general my appreciation for the TVA appointment he had given me in 1959. Also, I had a chance in the presence of a sympathetic and important group to identify both of us with an historic event, and to draw a lesson or two from it for the cause of brotherhood, which had brought us together.

I was sent to the podium not only to speak for the conference in appreciation of Mrs. Eisenhower, but, according to the program committee, to supply a light touch. So, turning to Mrs. Eisenhower, I assured her that while I wanted to speak to her, if her distinguished husband wanted to listen that would be all right. "I have talked to him before, you see—indeed, I had quite a talk with him at Newport on September 13, 1957. Some others were present. . . ." Then in an aside to the general, "We never did wind that one up like we wanted to, did we, Mr. President?"

I referred to my appreciation of the President's statement when I was given my commission as TVA director. Jerry Persons had said, "Maybe we can make a Republican out of Brooks."

But, smiling, the President had said, "Why Jerry, you couldn't do anything with a good old Democrat like Brooks. But maybe they can soften him up down in Tennessee."

"Mrs. Eisenhower," I added, "he doesn't know what I'm about to tell you. I didn't see a Democrat for weeks. I was on a Republican island in a Democratic state. Finally, a good old Baptist preacher friend said to me, 'You know I'm a Democrat,' and I thought well now, I can talk a little politics. But he added, 'This year I'm going to vote for the Republicans—they've been so nice to you!' "

It was a perfect evening for bipartisan goodwill, following by less than a week the 1966 fall elections. I referred to the fact that as early as 1938 I had gone on record as favoring a two-party system in the South. "Of course, I think they're sort of overdoing it," I said, and got a surge of laughter from my friendly audience.

Then I told of the incident at Park Seminary, a liberal arts college in Chicago, maintained by the Covenanters. One of the political science professors told me that a theme on the subject of the Abolitionists contained this statement, "The feelings of hatred and bitterness between the Abolitionists and slave holders were severe, so much so that Senator Charles Sumner of Massachusetts was attacked on the floor of the Senate and severely injured by Congressman Brooks Hays."*

Simulating hurt feelings, I said one of my reasons for accepting my present assignment in Massachusetts was to dissipate any impression that I had anything to do with that attack. When I walked into the Boston Public Gardens recently and came to the bronze figure of Charles Sumner, I paused and said, "Senator, tell them it isn't so."

Then I had second thoughts about what I was doing, and self-consciously hurried away: I would rather have them think I assaulted a senator, than to believe a new professor of government at the University of Massachusetts goes around mumbling to statues.

Finally, I told General and Mrs. Eisenhower of the little lady in Little Rock who proclaimed after the 1952 election, when asked how she voted, "I voted for Ike and Brooks. I never split a ticket."

I had another example of a humorous nature on that happy evening. My friend Robert Murphy, an eminent career diplomat, presided, and before I spoke he told of an incident involving Major John Eisenhower, who had prepared to use a parachute over Africa when two of their four motors had gone out. Fortunately, this was averted, but Bob Murphy made a good story of it anyway.

They were ready for my story, proving what I declared to be a fact, that Arkansas lads are pretty rugged. The sergeant in charge of training had a group in the plane for their first jump. "Now we will jump at seven hundred feet," he told them.

"Aw Sergeant," the Arkansas rookie protested, "that's too high —Let's jump at three hundred feet."

"Why you fool," he replied, "your parachute wouldn't open at three hundred feet."

* The perpetrator was actually Congressman Preston Brooks of South Carolina.

"Oh," the Arkansas youth said, "we're going to get a parachute?"

After I accepted the Rutgers professorship and title, my White House title became officially "consultant"—no longer "special assistant to the President," but most of my friends paid no attention to that. I was referred to in introduction as Assistant to the President. At the Democratic National Convention in Atlantic City, my longtime friend, Bruce Price of Virginia, pastor of the Newport News First Baptist Church, invited me to eat lunch with him. As we sat down, Bruce said to the waitress, "Mr. Hays is Assistant to President Johnson."

My self-esteem suffered a great blow just then as she asked, "The wax company or the baby talcum people?"

It developed however, when Bruce cleared it up, that she was *with* us not against us.

Our American history is replete with humorous anecdotes, many of which have been preserved only because Presidents or other notables were involved in them. Of all our Presidents, Lincoln is the richest source of anecdotal material. He was also the target for the most criticism.

He told a group of friends once that he had about taken all he could. He said he was being bothered to death by those persons who boisterously demanded that the war be pushed vigorously; also, those who shouted their advice and opinions into his weary ears, but who never suggested anything practical. These fellows were not in the Army, nor did they ever take any interest, in a personal way, in military affairs, except when engaged in dodging the draft.

"They remind me," Lincoln said, "of a farmer who lost his way on the western frontier. Night came on, and the embarrassments of his position were increased by a furious tempest which suddenly burst upon him. To add to his discomfort, his horse had given out, leaving him exposed to all the dangers of the pitiless storm.

"The peals of thunder were terrific, the frequent flashes of lightning affording the only guide on the road, as he resolutely trudged onward, leading his jaded steed. The earth seemed fairly to tremble beneath him in the war of the elements. One bolt threw him suddenly on his knees.

"Our traveler was not a prayerful man, but finding himself involuntarily brought to an attitude of devotion, he addressed himself to the Throne of Grace in the following prayer for his deliverance:

"'O God! Hear my prayer this time, for Thou knowest it is not often that I call upon Thee. And, O lord! if it is all the same to Thee, give us a little more light and little less noise.'

"I wish," the President said sadly, "there was a stronger disposition manifested on the part of our civilian warriors to unite in suppressing the rebellion, and a little less noise as to how and by whom the Chief Executive Office shall be administered."

Part of the legend of humorless Presidents is doubtless a result of catering to what many feel is the proper view—that our top officials should be somber, to befit the gravity of the office. Adlai Stevenson, of course, was advised by some not to be funny in his campaigns for President. That he could not restrain himself is part of the public record, which is all the richer for Stevenson witticisms. As one who believes it had nothing to do with his defeats and that his wit was of high quality, I am glad he did not follow the advice.

Not all Presidents are good at expressing warmth, and some, while good at oratory, have difficulty after they finish the inevitable handshaking that must be done. President Benjamin Harrison had a great reputation as an orator, but was known as a horribly cold fish in meeting people. One contemporary United States senator said, "If Harrison were to address an audience of ten thousand men, he would capture them all. But if each were presented to him in private, he would make him his enemy."

On a campaign tour through Indiana, President Harrison was having a great success with his speeches. In community after community he would stir the crowd with his brilliant oratory. Then he would hold a reception in his private railroad car, and people, after shaking the President's hand, would leave depressed and quiet. In one town, where it was particularly important for Harrison to make a good impression, a Presidential assistant pulled the cord to tell the engineer to start the train. He did this just as Harrison finished talking, and before the inevitable, cold reception. When bawled out for this he said, "Never mind, I know what I'm doing. Ben Harrison had the crowd red hot. I did not want him to freeze it out of them with his handshaking."

Making appointments to jobs and all the problems of patronage have been a continuing concern to all Chief Executives. Office seekers plagued Washington, and they plague President Johnson. The problem is, at least, two-fold: too many unqualified people seeking jobs and the really qualified candidates being unwilling to accept positions.

There was a wonderful cartoon in the *New Yorker* magazine some years ago right at national convention time. It showed a little man slumped in a big chair with ten or so cigar-chewing politician types crowded around him in an obviously smoked-filled hotel room. "But, I don't want to be Minister to Guatemala," the little man is saying.

At the beginning of his extraordinary career, Al Smith was elected president of the New York City Board of Aldermen. He was approached by a man with whom he had gone to school. The man asked Smith for a job as an elevator operator in one of the city buildings. Smith told his school friend that the job was covered by civil service, and in order to qualify there was an examination.

"Examination in what?" he asked.

Smith replied, "Hydraulics, for instance, and a lot of other subjects you don't know anything about."

"Now look here, Al," the would-be elevator operator said, "save that baloney for the Eyetalians and the Poles. Remember, I went to school with you."

After Andrew Jackson retired from the Presidency, he still tried to keep a weather eye on his successors. The old general became seriously concerned when, in 1845, President Polk chose James Buchanan to be his Secretary of State.

Jackson complained bitterly only to be told by Polk, "But after all, General, you yourself appointed him minister to Russia, while you were President."

"Yes, I did," Jackson reported, "it was as far away as I could find to send him and where I figured he could do the least harm.

I would have sent him to the North Pole if we had kept a minister there."

President Jackson was running true to form and his reputation for positiveness survived. After his death someone said to one of his Tennessee neighbors, "Do you think he went to Heaven?"

"He did if he was a mind to!"

Lincoln, too, had his difficulties with office seekers. He once told a whole group of them, who had waylaid him in his office, a story about an ancient king. "This king," Lincoln said, "asked the court minister if it was going to rain." The minister, a fore-runner of our own weather bureau, told him that the weather would be fair. That forecast pleased the king because it allowed him to set out on a hunting trip he had planned. As they rode along, the king and his party met a farmer riding a jackass. He warned the king it was going to rain. The king laughed at this prediction, for after all, he had the word of authority from his court minister that it would be fair. The king rode on, and no sooner had he unsheathed his bow and arrow than a torrential downpour thoroughly soaked him. He managed to get back to the palace where he fired his minister and sent for the farmer.

" 'Tell me how you knew it would rain,' he demanded.

" 'I did not know, Your Majesty. It's not me. It's my jackass. He puts his ears forward when it is going to be rainy.'

The king sent the farmer off and commanded that the jackass be brought to the palace to replace the fallen minister.

"It was here," said President Lincoln, "that the king made a great mistake."

"What was that?" asked one of the would-be officeholders, fall-ing into Lincoln's trap.

"Because, ever since that time," said Lincoln, "every jackass wants an office."

Another time Lincoln had to make an appointment for com-missioner to the Hawaiian Islands. Eight candidates had filed their papers. A delegation from Congress appeared one morning in Lincoln's office on behalf of a ninth applicant. The delegation was adamant. They cited all their man's fine qualifications for the position. Then they played what they thought would be their trump card. Not only was their candidate fully fitted for the job, he also was in bad health and a residence in Hawaii would be of great help to him.

Lincoln listened with typical Lincolnesque patience, but he finally grew impatient and broke in with the remark, "Gentlemen, I am sorry to tell you, but there are eight other applicants for the commissionership, all fully backed by equally creditable delegations. And, furthermore, gentlemen, each of those eight applicants is sicker than your man."

Ulysses S. Grant was not a spectacularly successful President but he was a man of definite likes and dislikes when it came to people and the making of important appointments to his government. While he was still President-elect he was considering various appointments to his Cabinet. Senator Charles Sumner of Massachusetts was extremely anxious for Grant to appoint the distinguished American historian Motley as Secretary of State. Motley had been our minister to Vienna but had been removed by President Johnson for being too critical of Johnson's reconstruction policies. Motley was interested in the job, and Grant, after reading some of the historian's speeches, was interested in Motley. Grant made a visit to Boston where Motley lived. They met. Grant did not appoint him. When asked why, Grant replied, "He parts his hair in the middle and wears a single eyeglass."

In pursuit of positions, job seekers seem to be prepared to go to any lengths to get attention. Woodrow Wilson's daughter insists that a story told about a job seeker and Wilson while he was governor of New Jersey is absolutely true. Governor Wilson's highway commissioner passed away. Early in the morning of the next day, around 2 or 3 A.M., the governor's phone rang by his bed. Sleepily, Wilson picked up the phone. The voice at the other end of the line identified itself, and Wilson recognized the name of a second echelon New Jersey Democrat. "Governor," the voice said, "I understand the highway commissioner has passed away. I would like to take his place."

Governor Wilson with quiet disdain retorted, "If it is all right with the undertaker, I am sure that it is quite all right with me." He then hung up the phone and tried to get back to sleep, probably by counting disappointed office seekers jumping over a pork barrel.

The Chief Executive's choice of Cabinet members is an ex-

tremely important factor in the success or failure of an administration. A President is not always free to make the choice he
wants. For instance, in 1864 when Lincoln accepted the resignation of his Attorney General, a man named Bates, his Cabinet
lost its only southern member. All of Lincoln's advisers insisted
that he must replace Bates with another southerner. Lincoln
reluctantly agreed to that proposition, but unhappily said, "I
suppose if the twelve apostles were to be chosen today, the interests of locality would have to be heeded."

There are other stories of Lincoln's problems with his Cabinet.
Once, after a bitter dispute on a policy matter, Lincoln called for
a vote of the Cabinet. All five members voted *aye*. Lincoln
voted *nay*. Lincoln announced, "The *noes* have it."

President Grant was not quite as polished in his dealings with
his Cabinet, and his administration suffered for it. One of Grant's
difficulties was in reprimanding his Cabinet officers or displacing
them. In one attempt he did prove to be successful. He was trying to get rid of Postmaster General Jewell. After pondering the
problem of how to do it, he finally called Jewell into the White
House. Grant discussed several postal matters with him and
then casually asked, "Jewell, how do you think your resignation
would look written out?"

Jewell, not suspecting a plot, went along. He took a piece of
paper and scribbled out his resignation. "How does that look,
Mr. President?"

Grant replied, "Jewell, that looks just fine, I accept your
resignation." Nothing Jewell or his friends could say or do could
force Grant to change his mind.

In modern times there have been many cracks about Cabinets.
Will Rogers commented in 1933, after F.D.R. made his appointments, "They've found the common man. There's nine of them
and one woman."

In those hectic first days of Roosevelt's administration, there
was inevitably much confusion, as F.D.R. and his colleagues attempted to set the country back on an even keel. Paul Appleby
recounted that during those first, fast-moving days a little old
lady, a retired employee of the Agriculture Department kept
appearing at Henry Wallace's office. Repeatedly she was told
that the Secretary of Agriculture was just too involved to see

her. Finally she agreed to see Appleby, who then was serving as assistant to the Secretary of Agriculture. Appleby asked her in a kindly way why she wanted to see Mr. Wallace. "Well," she said, "my hobby is making hooked rugs from the pants of Cabinet officers, and I want to ask Mr. Wallace for a pair of his old pants."

Appleby, struggling to maintain a straight face, asked her if she had had much luck pursuing her hobby.

"Oh, yes," she insisted, "many Cabinet officers have already given me a pair of their pants."

"Well," Appleby retorted, "when you have gotten a pair of pants from every other member of this Cabinet, you come back and see me, and I promise you that I'll get you a pair of Mr. Wallace's."

The lady was delighted with this promise and departed never to be seen by Appleby again. Musing over this, Appleby figured that what finally stopped her getting pants from all the Cabinet officers was Madame Perkins—Secretary of Labor.

Of all the aspects of the Presidential job, probably none are as delicate as executive-legislative relationships. Congressmen and senators tend to become quite suspicious of the executive. The growth of executive power has not helped to assuage those suspicions. Sooner or later all Presidents and all governors have their problems with the legislative branch of government.

Abraham Lincoln once confessed to a friend, who had found him in a particularly depressed state of mind, "I have just made Senator Ben Wade my enemy for life." "How?" his friend asked.

"Wade was here just a while ago, and he was trying to get me to get rid of General Grant, and in response to something he said, I remarked, 'Senator, that reminds me of a story.'

"Wade then kind of lost his temper and he said, 'Mr. Lincoln, it is with you all story, story, story! You are the father of every military blunder that has been made during the war. You are on the road to hell, sir, with this government, by your stubbornness, and you are not a mile off this minute.' "

"What did you say to him then?"

"I said, 'Senator, that is just about the distance from here to the capitol.' He was very angry, took his hat and cane and left."

It is related that George Washington suggested, on hearing

that some members of Congress wanted to constitutionally limit the standing Army to three thousand men, "Perhaps there should be an additional amendment providing that no enemy should ever invade the country with more than two thousand soldiers."

In dealing with Congress, members of the executive branch try many devices, including wining and dining. Lincoln's Secretary of State William Henry Seward knew that some congressmen were coming to see him to persuade him to change his views on some matter. Seward invited them for late in the day, listened to them, and then invited them to stay on for dinner. As he threw open the doors leading to the dining room, he said to the congressmen, "Gentlemen, let us table your motion for the present."

A contemporary of Seward, Senator Charles Sumner was particularly a thorn in the side of the executive branch. Someone remarked about him that Sumner did not believe in the Bible. President Grant, who heard the remark, commented somewhat bitterly, "Why should he? He didn't write it."

In modern times, Douglas Dillon, a very successful and wealthy investment banker, ably served Presidents Eisenhower, Kennedy, and Johnson in a variety of capacities. It was while he was serving as Secretary of the Treasury that the United States debt ceiling needed to be raised, or the government would illegally be exceeding the debt limit. On June 30, the last day of the fiscal year, Dillon's staff tried to get him to make some phone calls to key senators to get the Senate to act by midnight. They warned the Secretary that if Congress did not raise the debt ceiling by midnight, the law would be violated, and he, the Secretary of the Treasury, was personally liable for the excess debt. Theoretically if he did not pay it, he could go to jail, they warned. "How much are we going to owe?" Dillon queried. "Over 462 million dollars," he was told. Dillon clapped his hand to his forehead, "Boys, it will almost wipe me out!" Nevertheless the calls were made and the disaster averted.

Another well-to-do political leader is former Governor W. Averell Harriman of New York. One of his friends was asked, "How much is the governor reputed to be worth?"

The answer sounded impressively high, but another friend supplied this addendum. "Oh, I think you have vastly overestimated Averell's poverty."

One of the questions my Arkansas friend, Winthrop Rocke-feller, would prefer not to hear, particularly during campaigns is this one. "Would you mind giving an estimate of your worth?"

His usual answer is accompanied by a smile. "Well, let us say that I am solvent."

The late Robert Kerr, senator from Oklahoma, never seemed to mind references to his wealth. A newsman asked him for a figure and got a reply in specific figures. "But," the reporter continued, "the statement of the Kerr McGee Oil Company of which you are half owner, shows a net worth more than double your figure, and you have other property, haven't you?"

With typical good humor, the senator answered, "Oh, yes, a fellow ought to be more accurate—add five million to that figure I gave you."

Mrs. Betty Hughes, the wife of the governor of New Jersey, Richard Hughes, has constantly demonstrated wit and good humor during her husband's governorship. Both Mr. and Mrs. Hughes had been widowed, and when they married, she brought four children to the marriage and Governor Hughes, who was then a judge, had three. Subsequently they had three more chil-dren. After his election in 1953, Mrs. Hughes was being given a tour of Morven, a prerevolutionary war home which serves as the governor's mansion, by Mrs. Helen Meyner, the outgoing first lady. Morven, while extremely beautiful, is actually rather small when it comes to living quarters and there are very few bed-rooms. After the tour the reporters asked Mrs. Hughes if she didn't think she'd find it difficult living at Morven with ten children. "I don't think so," she retorted, "after all we took seven on our honeymoon."

The changing of the guard, one government taking over from another, is never easy. It is a great tribute to our system that we do see governments change hands, and that it is done in orderly fashion without violence. No matter how bitter the campaign has been, American sportsmanship and our political tradition de-mand that the transition be orderly.

In West Virginia, some years ago, the Democrats took back the governorship, which they had not held for many years. As soon as the new governor was installed, a party worker came to see him. He said, "Governor, you remember Jim Williamson from Johnson County?"

"Yes."

"Well, you know he's in the penitentiary."

"Yes."

"Well, Governor, Jim ain't happy."

"Yes."

"Well, you can pardon him."

"But, I'll have to have reasons."

"Reasons, hell! If we'd a had any reasons one of them Republican governors would a pardoned him."

On December 1, 1961, I took the oath of office as Special Assistant to President Kennedy in the Cabinet room of the White House.

Those of my family who were in Washington and a few friends were present. After the oath was administered, the President welcomed me to his official family, and I acknowledged the honor. I began with this comment:

"Mr. President, it is a great honor to serve under and with you. I would like to mention the fact that my wife's mother, Mrs. Prather, is present. She is ninety-five years old, and her presence is a tribute to you as well as to me. You are familiar with the expression that back of every achievement is a proud wife and a surprised mother-in-law. Well, mine really is surprised—she thought I would be the President!"

President Kennedy laughed with our little audience.

Later in the day, my wife asked her mother, "Did you enjoy the ceremony, and meeting the President?"

"Of course I did," Mrs. Prather said, and added complacently, "He shook hands with me twice!"

My feeling for President Kennedy was not only one of admiration but of affection. Our friendship ripened before he became President, and when I went to the White House as one of his special assistants we had established a congeniality that made it one of the most pleasant assignments my long political service had ever provided.

He was understandably interested in my church life, particularly since he knew of my friendship with Billy Graham, and was also familiar with my activities in behalf of interfaith goodwill and understanding. When he saw Billy Graham and me pass his office one day, he came out to greet the famous preacher, and turning to me he said, "Brooks, I'm going to South America a month ahead of Dr. Graham. I will be his John the Baptist."

Once Mr. Kennedy said to me, "What kind of Baptist are you, Brooks?"

Knowing he was joking, I answered in the same spirit, "I'm an ecumenical Baptist."

"You're what?" he asked, laughing, but puzzled, too.

"You can just call me a catholic Baptist, Mr. President, but be sure to spell it with a little *c*." Then I thought of something else, and added, "And I hope, Mr. President, that you are a *protest'-ant* Catholic, spelled with a little *p*."

I wish I could have taken time to tell him of the legends regarding Bishop Fitzgerald of Arkansas and his famous dissents, for they compose a little footnote to history with which even so scholarly a student of history as Mr. Kennedy might not have been familiar.

The Bishop cast one of the two votes against the dogma of infallibility in 1871. (The other negative vote was that of the Bishop of Ajaccio.) The Pope is said to have commented, when he heard of this action, "Oh well! The Big Rock rolled over the Little Rock," which indicates that even in the nineteenth century a sense of humor was displayed at the Vatican.

President Kennedy's keen sense of humor is too well known to call for further documentation by me. One comment of his, however, had a special appeal for me. A friend of mine, C. E. Bryant, asked him to designate his first choice among my Arkansas anecdotes and political yarns. He gave not only his first choice, but included the runner-up. Here they are:

I asked an Arkansas voter early in an election year, "How do you think you will vote in the governor's race?"

I got this reply, "I ain't decided yet, Brooks, but I'll tell you one thing—whichever side I come up on, I'm goin' to be awful bitter!"

The second choice went like this:

A prospective candidate for state office went to a friend who was given to very frank expressions of opinion. "Earl," he said,

"I'm figuring on running for land commissioner against Uncle Bob Hawkins. Which one of us do you reckon has the best chance?"

Earl replied, "Well, Jim, it depends on which one of you gets out and sees the most people."

"That's how I figure it, too."

"Yes," Earl said, "if Uncle Bob sees the most, you'll win; if you see the most, Uncle Bob will win."

During Mr. Kennedy's occupancy of the White House, his desire to have the privacy of his family protected was known and observed by the staff. However, I believe at this time there could be no objection to my telling of one incident in which Caroline participated.

I was in the White House reception room one morning waiting to talk to the President, and found that his secretary, Mrs. Lincoln, was trying to entertain Caroline and at the same time proceed with her own duties. I took it upon myself to occupy the little girl's attention, partly to release Mrs. Lincoln for her work. I sat down and began to draw some pictures for her. She became interested immediately. I went through my repertoire and was able to produce pictures of animals that Caroline could recognize. The exercise was dragging out, and finally I had to resort to drawing legendary animals. This had an advantage for me, as she had to take my word for what they were. Having described the willipus-wallipus, who lived in the Ozark forest, I was about to do a portrait of him, when the door of the President's private office swung open and out he came.

"Caroline, come here. I want you to meet a prime minister."

He took her hand and led her into his office. Just before the door closed, I heard him say, "Now, please be a good girl."

He used a tone that would be familiar to all fathers.

In a few minutes she was back. She came at once to me, and said, "Now let me see the willipus-wallipus."

I didn't have the time to draw the other legendary Arkansas animals that day, but later I gave her a reproduction of the others, which I had drawn for my grandchildren. This sketch included the kingdoodle, the gowrow, the jimplicute, and the side-hill hoofer, as well as the willipus-wallipus.

The reproduction of this collection by some of the newspapers inspired some interesting correspondence regarding the legends in other states. One Maryland lad wrote that he wanted to start a willipus-wallipus farm, and could I procure one animal for him? Then, probably recalling Noah's experience, he indicated, before concluding the letter, that on second thought I should send two.

Another letter I received stated that a willipus-wallipus is not an animal at all, but a carpenter's gadget.

Still another made the point that maybe these animals had once actually existed centuries ago. "Sure, nobody ever seen 'em. I never seen a panther, either, but my grandpappy seen one, and I believe they were here. He told me that he never seen a willipus-wallipus, but *his* grandpappy seen one once, so he believed it really lived in them deep woods!" Pretty good logic, at that.

In every talk I had with President Kennedy, from the day we met in 1947 till his death, there was generally an interval for a smile or perhaps a good laugh inspired by one or the other of us. One exception is notable, for it was my last talk with him, and it was a long-distance phone conversation.

Shortly before the fateful Dallas trip I called him from the University of Arkansas, where I had a speaking engagement, to ask approval of my acceptance of the National Brotherhood Week chairmanship. I talked to Mrs. Lincoln first. "Miss Evelyn, I would appreciate your saying to the President that the National Conference of Christians and Jews has asked me to be chairman of Brotherhood Week. Would he mind if I accept?"

Her answer was, "Mr. Hays, I think you should ask him yourself. I will hand him a card saying you are on long distance. He is in a Cabinet meeting, but the phone is at his elbow, and I'm confident he will talk to you."

My ego had a big bulge when I heard his voice, "Brooks, where are you?"

He knew how I was jumping around and that to make a speech, I might go to Patagonia. I gave him all the information he needed—my location and the reason for the call. If I had known on that fall day that I would never hear the familiar voice again, I would have it indelibly in my memory now. But I do recall that in substance he said this: "I think that's wonderful. That's a good work, and you are a good one for it."

Maybe there was another word of commendation for my exertions in the fields of interfaith and interracial understanding and justice. There was enough in his affirmation to remind me of the beautiful passage in his inaugural address—"With a good conscience our only sure reward, with history the final judge of our deeds, let us go forth to lead the land we love, asking His blessing and His help, but known that here on earth God's work must truly be our own."

4

Covered Wagons: Frontier

I GREW UP in the foothills of the Ozarks. Mountain people have often demonstrated to me that they possess a love of humor that is distinctive. The frontier disregard of conventional rules of conduct and speech produced a great many stories in which rural people still delight. Variations of these stories may circulate in urban centers, but the origins are clear. Yet there is great diversity. They may have a lusty quality born of the frontier and shocking to the more fastidious plainsmen, or they may reveal a gentleness and subtlety that would do credit to an Oxford man.

Each area has its distinctive types, its differing forms and terminology, reflecting the morals and thought habits of the section, yet they are alike in essential characteristics. One often finds the same stories, differing only in detail, cropping up in New England, the South, the West. They seem to have followed the migrations with amazing faithfulness.

One of my good friends in the Congress, Senator Ralph Flanders of Vermont, always smiled tolerantly at my reference to his Green Mountains as "Merely the Ozarks, which have gone underground and emerged east of the Hudson." And a story of mine about a backwoods Arkansas woman which seemed to amuse him could, he said, have just as logically taken place in Vermont.

According to this tale a mountain lad went to a doctor with this complaint, "Doctor, something's got to be done about grandma."

"And what's the matter with your grandmother?" the doctor inquired.

"She's gone to smokin'!" the youngster exclaimed.

"Well, I wouldn't worry about that. Most woman are smoking now-a-days."

"Doctor, she's smokin' cigarettes. . . ."

"That's normal enough," the doctor interrupted.

"But, Doctor, you don't understand," the boy persisted. "Grandma inhales. . . ."

"Don't worry about it! They all inhale these days."

"But, Doctor, grandma *don't exhale!*"

In Congress, the distinguished Vermonter and I sponsored a bill known as the "Rural Industries Bill," a sort of forerunner of the Area Redevelopment Administration Bill. I followed him at a committee hearing one day in support of the bill, and in order not to take the committee's time, but also to indicate that I embraced his ideas, I told about the tenant farmer and the landlord whose farm was not far from my home.

My father and I were going down the road and saw Mr. Carr and his tenant having what appeared to be a heated controversy. Whereupon the tenant departed and reached the gate just as we approached it. My father, interested in everything that concerned his neighbors, said, "Eph, I hope you and Mr. Carr weren't having a falling out."

"Oh, no, Mr. Hays. The Big Boss said to me, 'Eph, I think the watermelons grow best in the sandy land.' I said to him, 'That's what I think, too.' And we argued it out right there."

The folklore of the Appalachians has an interesting counterpart in the Ozarks and in the piney woods (as we say) of the mid-South. The stories were carried overland by the settlers and then acquired a local flavor. Sectional rivalries developed and the stories reflected this. I recall an introduction to a western Kentucky audience in Bowling Green thirty years ago, which contained this comment: "We're always glad to have Arkansas in the Union. We know we won't be last in education."

I made answer, "Well thanks, Mr. Chairman, for wanting us in the Union. But whatever our deficiencies in education, you can take credit for them. All the teachers I had were Kentuckians, and when the family that lived down the road from us moved from eastern Kentucky, the old man said as they loaded their belongings in the wagon, 'Well Sarah, we'll just move to Arkansas. We can't worst ourselves none.' "

American folklore abounds in such tales. A choice sentence in *The Way West,* A. B. Guthrie's story of the Oregon Trail, is the answer of the old man in a Midwest village to the question, "How do you know so much about it [Oregon]? Have you been there?" asked another. "No," was the reply, "I haven't been there but been here."

One would have to know the piney woods of Arkansas, which are remarkably like the piney woods of Mississippi and Louisiana, to appreciate the unique way of life this isolated but interesting rural population has developed.

Its lack of sophistication is well illustrated by the story of a young farm lad who had courted an attractive neighborhood girl for a long time. They could not marry, for he had never possessed the price of a marriage license. Neither of them suspected that more than a few hundred dollars circulated throughout the United States. Neither had ever been outside their native county.

Suddenly, like a thunderbolt out of a clear sky, oil was struck on the young man's land, a development that radically altered the lives of this young couple. The young man accepted with bewilderment the news that he was a very rich man. It conveyed little to him beyond the fact that now, at last, he could get married. He mounted his little pestle-tailed mule, which made the speediest trip of its life to the girl's home in a clearing two miles away.

At this point I digress with a nod to a south Arkansas orator whose fluid language adds a certain pungency to the account. (This friend once said to me, "Ah, Brooks, you should have heard me at the Grapevine picnic yesterday—I grasped a few shining shafts from the panorama of truth.") If related by him, the rest of the story would go something like this:

She accepted his awkwardly stated offer of marriage without ceremony but with a betrothed's usual misgivings. He mounted his patient mule and turned toward home, no saddle to soften the irregular vertical movements of the animal. Still, no discomfort could diminish the unutterable joy that filled his soul.

They would marry next week and then the honeymoon trip to New Orleans. His heart was buoyant as he rode through the fragrant woodland. Elfin notes seemed to float on the zephyrs that gently stirred the branches of the evergreens. A full moon cast a thrilling golden glow around him. He stopped long enough to breathe a prayer of thanks for the goodness toward him that the whole universe was displaying. "Thank you, Lord, thank you very much." And as a sort of afterthought his lips transmitted this simple sentiment, "I don't have nothing agin' nobody, Lord, —not a thing agin' nobody."

The oil company representatives bought the couple's tickets, and put them on the nearest train with money and travelers' checks in the groom's pockets. His sentiments were summed up in the unuttered paean of praise that reverberated in his mind, "I aint got nothin' agin' nobody!"

In the swanky restaurant in New Orleans, where the management had been alerted to give them special attention, they were helplessly confused. The elegant maitre d'hotel, bowing reverently to wealth, handed them a menu in French. The waiter, pencil poised over pad, stood waiting their order.

The bride, unwilling to appear stupid, looked over at her new husband and said, "Honey, I don't see nothin' on here that I keer fer."

The maitre d' spoke quickly. "Madam, if it isn't there, we will get it for you. You can have anything you want."

A look of great relief chased the anxious frown from her face. "In that case," she said, "I'll have some new-ground turnips and a slice of cold possum."

Former Congressman Robert Hale of Maine is the source of this incident: A "city man" from Portland was looking for an isolated rural community in the backwoods, which we will call Johnson's Corner. Finding scant signs of human habitation, he was about to give up when he came to a cabin in a clearing. The traveler called a good-day to a man sitting on the step, and then said, "I am trying to get to Johnson's Corner. Can you help me?"

With an authoritative ring in his voice, the local man said, "Don't move another damn foot!"

My residence in Knoxville for two years, while serving as a director of the Tennessee Valley Authority, gave me an excellent opportunity to enjoy the rare type of humor the Southern Appalachians produce.

I discovered, however, that the Tennesseans, migrating to Arkansas in an earlier period, had transported much of the folklore and choice anecdotal material the mountaineer preserved as part of his heritage.

One of my favorite Tennessee expressions came out in a telephone conversation with Adlai Stevenson on the memorable day when Khrushchev pounded on his United Nations Assembly desk with his shoe.

Adlai asked me, "What did you think of Khrushchev's performance today?"

I promptly answered, "He over-egged his puddin'."

This brought a chuckle, and another question. "Where did you get that expression?"

I said, "Oh, it's an old Tennessee saying."

Later, something a bit mystifying happened: That very night Harold Macmillan, who was at that time in attendance at the General Assembly of the United Nations, said in a radio address, "In the language of an old British saying, "Mr. Khrushchev 'over-egged his pudding.'"

I wrote to Adlai immediately to say, "I don't mind Mr. Macmillan giving the British credit for the wonderful expression. It only shows how deeply the life of the southern Appalachians is rooted in Elizabethan culture!"

In former days, even as recently as 1942, standards of propriety might seem to the new generation to be a bit lower than good taste would dictate. However, those old standards permitted some really funny utterances, such as that of a very popular Methodist minister, Dr. James Workman of North Little Rock. My friends in northern Pulaski County gave a watermelon party in my honor some twenty-five years ago, and Jim was called on after the scheduled speeches to say a few words. It was a spontaneous action by the chairman. Sensing that the audience was ready to disperse and that everyone was full of melon and friendship for the honoree, he rose and without going to the front merely announced in stentorian tones, "Mr. Chairman, we have heard enough praise of Brooks. I suggest that we all stand, give a hearty belch, and go home."

When the audience recovered from its surprise, a roar spread over the landscape that could be heard a mile away. Then they *did* go home.

The country or crossroads store is a wonderful breeding place for yarns and conversations. They are told around the big stove in the winter and are redolent of folklore and local color.

A typical chat in one such gathering place turned on inventions and their creators. "Who's the greatest inventor that ever lived, in your opinion?"

One farmer proposed Edison. "On account of that there graphiphone and that 'lectric light, not to mention all them there other things he done. I think he wuz the greatest."

There were other nominees. One thought Eli Whitney's cotton gin had done so much for the cotton country that he should get the nod. Another put in a word for "that Eyetalian" and the wireless.

Finally, one old Nestor, after putting the sawdust box to its appropriate use, looked challengingly around and said, "Well, now, Levi Garrett wasn't so bad, hisself."

To his companions around the stove, Levi Garrett's name was better known than Shakespeare's. His claim to fame was the popularity of his snuff.

I have heard two yarns about this inelegant commodity which I think are among the funniest I know, but they really need to be seen to be completely savored.

One of them is a fragment of a courtroom scene, where a hearing was being held to determine the cause of an automobile accident. The presiding judge turned to the witness, whose protruding lower lip testified mutely that it was loaded with some foreign substance. (When I tell it, my tongue fills the vacuum very satisfactorily.) "The plaintiff says that at the time of this collision he yelled at you, 'Watch where you're going, you stupid snuff-dipper.' What did you say to that?"

With his upper lip drawn down to meet the lower one, and the lower one taut to hold its contents, the witness mumbled, "I did'n say nuthin', Judge, I could'n."

One of my Smoky Mountain friends from North Carolina relates this incident: He was talking with a rustic acquaintance whose lower lip protruded in a tell-tale fashion; it was obviously filled with Levi Garrett's product.

"Do you smoke?" my friend asked curiously.

"Nope." The man tipped up his chair a mite, and tightened his lower lip. "Nope, I never smoke."

"Not at all?"

"No, sir."

"That's kind of surprising. Here you are living in the greatest tobacco state in the union, and you don't smoke. Why don't you?"

The answer came slowly, due to the difficulty of articulation. "An'thing that tastes this good shouldn't be burned."

One excellent source of Arkansas folklore was my father. In a way, he was a product of one of America's last frontiers, western Arkansas, and his stories of the life of that area in the last two decades of the nineteenth century are fascinating. He was just seven years old when his father brought the family to settle in Arkansas, and he grew up in the period when blanketed Indians were a common sight, there were bears in the mountains, and brush arbor religious meetings, which were a regular feature of the long hot summers, were frequently broken up by drunken rowdies in search of excitement.

Dad had no formal schooling beyond the eighth grade (except for a term at Washington and Lee University studying law), but he was the son of an old-fashioned schoolmaster, and he had the advantage of good home training. He loved above everything to read, and a book seldom left his hands or his pocket. When plowing he would whip open his book and read a few lines at the end of each row. He made good use, too, of McGuffy's *Readers* and the *Blue Back Speller*, with the result that, though he had never been to high school, he was offered the position of principal of the high school at Atkins, and accepted. Earlier, in our elementary rural school, the board of directors, who had been so impressed by my father's love of books, was composed of three Baptist deacons; and while I think their confidence in this case was not misplaced, I do think their qualifications for running a public school system were open to grave doubt. Further evidence is a well-nigh incredible incident which actually happened, and which throws a light on the antiquated views and the lack of scientific knowledge of the section and period. One Sunday, one of the three deacons, Mr. Lindsey, joined my father after church, and they walked away together. This gave Dad an opportunity to bring up something that had amused and at the same time horrified him.

Thinking he would get a sympathetic response from the deacon, he said, "Brother Lindsey, I was amazed to find out the other day that Brother Taylor thinks the world is flat, and he expects me to teach it like that!"

Dad was in for another shock. Mr. Lindsey stopped in his tracks, and with his brows reaching for his hair line, turned on his young employee.

"But Brother Hays, it is well known that the world is flat. The Bible says so! Surely you are not teaching anything else?"

Here was a majority of the school board against what Dad knew to be the truth, and probably the third would be in agreement with them. While he had no idea of teaching anything so erroneous, he hastily decided that discretion was the better part of valor, bade Brother Lindsey a polite good-day, and went home to dinner, fervently hoping that he would prove to be a skillful tightrope walker.

I never tired of hearing (when I was a boy) of his exploits on the farm and in the woods; of the Thanksgiving when the family had wild turkey for dinner, because Dad made a lucky shot with a rock when the turkey's head bobbed up from behind a stump; of the tragedy of his first store-bought suit, which as Dad retold it came out at least half comedy. When he and a younger brother named Fred saved up enough money earned doing farm work to order a suit of clothes apiece from a mail order catalogue, their excitement at the arrival of the big package was probably seldom surpassed in later life. Feeling like a couple of Beau Brummels, they set out for preaching, accompanied by their dog.

On the way, Hector (named for President Cleveland's dog), "treed" a skunk and set up a furious barking. The skunk, equally furious and also frightened, defended himself in his traditional fashion—and what a defense! Dad and my Uncle Fred went running up just in time to be in the direct line of fire as the skunk let go.

Not realizing the extent of the disaster, they went on to church. As soon as they sat down near the potbellied stove, which on this frosty morning was red hot, they began to steam. In seconds they had the unwelcome attention of the entire congregation, including the choir and the minister. With crimson faces, not even waiting for the next hymn, they beat a strategic retreat to the sound of windows being hastily opened.

At this point, pathos always outweighed humor, as Dad would tell how the two boys tried to save their wonderful and dearly bought suits. They were told that running water would remove the odor, so they weighted the clothes down in a stream and left them for twenty-four hours. When taken out, they were changed in other ways, but the fragrance was the same. Another suggestion they followed was to bury them for several days. The two heroic measures did not improve their looks, shape, or fit; everything about them suffered a sea or land change, except the smell. It was indestructible.

Finally, the boys gave up. They resigned themselves to the gruesome reality they would never be able to wear those suits.

I often called for Dad's story about how he met a bear, because that was pure comedy. I have a shortened account of it in his own words, written only a few years ago:

Dear Mr. Editor,

I saw that bear. I was interested in the account of the killing of a bear near Prairie View about 60 years ago as related to you by Leslie Gray and George Hampton in the *Progress* of March 24.

I saw that bear very briefly the day before he was killed. I was plowing on my father's farm nearly a quarter [of a mile] from our home. I was then about fourteen years old. The first thing that attracted my attention was the falling down on the north side of the hog lot fence, the whole fence, and the hogs running wild into the field. I was about 200 yards to the north of the lot. I stopped my plowing (not a hard thing to do). Then I saw a bear. He was headed just a little to the west of where I was.

The bear saw the horse at the same time the horse saw the bear. I had already seen enough to know I had no further business there.

The bear and the horse, as well as myself, seemed to have agreed on leaving that location, and the bear having elected to continue his journey north, I chose the southern route toward home. The horse seemed to prefer my society rather than the bear's and followed me. He was not more than a hundred yards behind me when I passed the barn lot.

About a week later my father told me the bear had been killed near Prairie View. I thought that was his story to get me to the plowing again. I am glad to know now that my father's story of the killing of the bear was true, as both Gray and Hampton say the bear was killed.

The account in the *Progress* says "They agree that the bear was extra large." Mr. Editor, I have seen many bears in circuses and in zoos in various cities since that year of 1886 but the biggest bear I ever saw at the zoo looked like a "little bitsy" cub to the side of that bear that made his way from Rich Mountain through my father's field at Ellsworth on his way to Prairie View and his untimely death.

From the Letters column—*The Paris* (Ark.) *Progress*, April 2, 1947

My father was a very positive person, with a vast capacity to inspire and impress others, particularly those rural young people. One of his pupils became a college president; another an outstanding lawyer; others, businessmen and teachers.

Although he himself deserted the schoolroom for the courtroom, he never doubted that any Hays would make a good teacher, so one summer he procured for me the summer session at Sunny Point, a rural school between Russellville and Dardanelle.

I had eighty-two pupils, and I was just seventeen years old. Anyone more unsuited than I at that age it would have been hard to find. It stands out in my memories as the worst summer of my entire life.

A few years ago when I was visiting in Russellville, a very elderly little lady came up to me. "Mr. Hays," she asked, "didn't you teach at Sunny Point?" I answered in the affirmative.

"I told my granddaughter you did."

"Oh, your granddaughter went to school to me?"

"No," she said. "I did."

This humbling encounter was no doubt good for me, but it did nothing to add glamour to my brief sashay into academia.

One of my favorite raconteurs is Bolon B. Turner, who was my George Washington Law School roommate and Little Rock law partner from 1928 to 1934. He later served with distinction as presiding judge of the Tax Court of the United States.

Bolon grew up in a rural community near Little Rock, known as Zion Hill. He and I used to swap stories about the interesting events that made up the fabric of a family's life in the hill country. His father was the local magistrate, a deacon in the little Baptist church, and the area's leading citizen and sympathetic counselor for all who needed help and advice.

With a remarkable alertness, Bolon as a boy observed his father and his other seniors guiding the destinies of Zion Hill. We both used to draw upon the resources of humor supplied by our interesting and numerous relatives. One of Bolon's relatives, a beloved uncle, had a quaint way of repeating his metaphors interminably, and consequently often illogically. This example was cited by Bolon:

His father was listening to the tale told by the uncle, who was explaining how he had subdued a mule he had purchased the preceding day. "Yes sir, Graves, I tell you that mule was a wild one—wild as a buck—just as wild as a buck! I gave him the works. Had to tame him, you know, and would you believe me, when I went out to the barn next morning, he was as tame—as tame as a buck, as tame as a buck?"

Another story told by Bolon with a tinge of pathos, but with full appreciation of its humor had to do with a Christmas dinner, which he and a cousin were invited to help consume. These were the circumstances. Bolon and his cousin were making deliveries of milk from his father's dairy. At the home of a regular customer, one of their hospitable friends, they found that dinner was on the table when they stepped into the kitchen with the milk. It was a "groaning table" loaded not only with a magnificent baked turkey and trimmings but with myriad delectable dishes. The friend, a gracious lady, said with a convincing tone, "Now we want you two young men to come on in and eat Christmas dinner with us."

Bolon was forming these words, "Thank you, yes—this was our last delivery and it'll be a wonderful way to wind up the day."

He never got to say it, for the cousin with an emphatic negative, so emphatic that it left no alternative, declined on the spot. They climbed onto the delivery wagon and slowly began the trek homeward.

Bolon finally broke the silence. He was utterly perplexed. "Bill," he said, "why did you do it—turkey and everything was on that table. You saw it, why in the world did you?"

This was the amazing reply. "Wanted to eat at home—we got good old navies—good old navies."

Some delightful additions to the folklore of the South, which Bolon and I have taken pleasure in preserving, were made by our mutual friend and college classmate, Dean Davis, from Tennile, Georgia. His father, like our own fathers, was a benevolent patriarch. He was a positive character with managerial gifts.

Among the stories Dean told for our enjoyment was one about helping his father "slop the hogs." The elder Davis gave minute instructions at each step of this prosaic and familiar task.

"Now, son, take this bucket inside the pen. Be sure to latch the gate after you. Be careful when you pour this in the trough. Do this. Mind that. Look out. . . ."

Dean followed each step of his father's instruction without comment, though he knew what to do as well as his father.

Finally satisfied that the job had been completed, Mr. Davis said, "Now, come on out."

At this point, Dean exploded. "Thank you, Papa!" he exclaimed. "Thank you for not leaving me in here with the pigs!"

Legends abound in the rural areas. Many of them grew out of the sufferings of the Civil War and later the experiences of the frontier. Here is a rather typical story, perhaps apocryphal. I am indebted to Lee Shippey of the Los Angeles *Times* for it.

"I'm surprised," says Lee, "by the numerous echoes to last week's column about Ozark simplicity. Jack Wilkinson Smith, noted artist, who hails from Kentucky, gives me this corroborative incident told him by a mountaineer:

"Shucks," he said, "I traveled clean across Arkansaw with nothin' but a bridle. It cost me nary a cent. I always had good vittles, a fine corn husk bed to sleep on almost every night and plenty of good corn likker. First I got me a middlin fair bridle and started out. Come sundown I'd go to a cabin and holler. (In the hill country you don't knock on the door, you hail and then you are invited in.) When they answered I ast them if they had seed anything of a flea-bitten white mare, I tole them I was camped about four miles down the road along the crick. The mare's tracks led thisaway and I was mighty put out to get her. No, they ain't seed nary sign of her, but it's getting right dark, you better lite and come in and have some vittles and hunt her in the morning. After a good night's rest I would pick up the bridle and mosey on."

One of my favorite entertainers is John Henry Faulk who emerged from his recent bitter experience carrying new laurels. Everyone familiar with his background knew that he was not a Communist sympathizer and that the charges were cruel and unjust. He had a good story from his Army experience. His bunk mate was a colorful young man from the hills of Alabama.

John introduced himself. "I am John Henry Faulk from Texas."

"Well I'm sure glad to meet you, John," came the drawling reply. "I'm Verban C. Lee from Calhoun County, Alabama. And do you know what, John? I can tell right off I'm not going to like the Army. They're rude to you."

At roll call the next morning before dawn the strong, rough top sergeant called the names Faulk, John Henry.

Answer "Here."

Lee, Verban C., no answer. Lee, Verban C., still no answer.

On the third call, a voice came drifting through the darkness from the barracks. "Ah'm in here, Sergeant."

The Sergeant raced into the barracks and with language fitting the situation and quite appropriate for a sergeant gave him the works.

When he could make himself heard the recruit said, "I wouldn't get so excited about it, Sergeant, I always been a slow dresser." John and his friend Verban Lee went into different units overseas and did not see each other until the war had ended. In the meantime Verban had won some honors for heroism. John greeted him at the reunion with words of praise, "I'm awfully proud of you, Verban."

He got only this answer. "I really don't deserve it, John, you see I was advancin' and all the time I thought I was retreatin'."

The humor that comes out of the life of the people is always the best kind. It has the quality of naturalness not produced by artificial exertions or a Broadway format. The chances are it will have the quality I have termed, for want of a better word, universality. If it amuses farmers in Arkansas the chances are that it will amuse farmers in Liberia, though perhaps not sophisticated city dwellers anywhere. I can illustrate. In Liberia in 1963 while on a special mission for President Kennedy, I had some difficulties establishing rapport with the people of Monrovia, but two hundred miles inland at an Institute for Farm Youth, I reverted to Arkansas methods and manners, knowing that I was addressing students who had mastered the English language and who, as the products of the very attractive hill country of northern Liberia, would understand my efforts to entertain them with Arkansas hill country folklore. Having identified myself as an Ozark mountaineer, I related a story that I felt sure would bolster pride in a rural man's native wit and his capacity for survival in a competitive world. It went like this:

A farmer who had had a good year was traveling on a bus to Memphis to visit some relatives. He seldom went out of his farm community, and this was quite an event to him. He found himself sitting by a stranger, a salesman, who engaged him in conversation.

"Would you like to make a little money playing quiz games?"

To this the Arkansan said, "Well, I don't know nothing about them, what are they?"

"Well," the city man said, "if you can answer questions, you can make money."

The farmer was interested.

The city man continued, "See, if I ask you something you don't know, you give me a dollar. If you ask me something I don't know I give you a dollar."

"No," the farmer said, "I'd lose money at that. I'm not educated, I'm not traveled, and I can see you are, so I wouldn't be interested."

"Well, I guess you would be entitled to a little advantage," the salesman said, "just make it fifty cents if you can't answer my questions but I've got a dollar for you if you ask me something I can't answer."

The farmer was interested again.

"All right, let's just play the game once, I think that's all right."

"Okay," said the city man, "you start."

The farmer said, "What is it that's got two heads, six wings, two tails, and it can't fly a foot?"

The city man pondered this one a long time, finally gave up and said, "Well, I declare, I don't know; here's your dollar, what is it?"

The farmer answered, "I don't know either, here's your fifty cents."

When I told that yarn to the students at Zor Zor in Liberia, I detected the same kind of response one would find in Arkansas.

An illustration of this sense of triumph is an actual experience of the late George Mitchell, one of Dr. Rex Tugwell's assistants. On a short field trip he was accompanied by a Ph.D. from a distant college, a researcher without an adequate briefing on the southern mores. The visiting professor had some questions for a housewife in one of the Farm Security communities but phrased them very unfortunately, using one and two syllable words, obviously "talking down" to her.

When they departed, George thought he should counsel with his companion about future interviews and tactfully suggested that his friend had failed to appraise the high native intelligence of the local farm people. He was rebuffed. "Oh no," the visitor said, "they are far down the scale. One must use simple language with those who have only second rate minds."

A few days later George was again in the community after the professor had departed, and when he saw the housewife who had been interrogated, she said, "Mister Mitchell, that man who wuz out here with you the other day—he aint real bright, is he?"

In those days the lack of educational standards was often reflected in the pathetic grammar used even by men in public positions. I recall hearing two members of the Arkansas General Assembly conversing in a Capital corridor about noon just after the morning legislative session.

"Howdy, Lige, have you et yet?"

"Yep, Lem, I've et, have you et?"

"Nope, haven't et yet—just wonderin' if you'd et."

"Yep, I've et." Thus Lige and Lem ended the conversation.

I had always assumed that the use of "et" for the past tense of eat was a regional distortion, but David Grayson's *Countryman's Year* having to do with New England life put me right. A diary entry contains this paragraph, "I know a man who reads as many books as any other in this town, good books, too, but they seem to do nothing for him. Reminds me of one of my neighbor's comment on a common acquaintance who died—as cadaverous a human being as ever I saw—'he et and he et but it didn't do him no good, he didn't get no fatter.' "

Another past tense colloquialism—"hope" for helped was introduced to me by an unlettered Sunday School teacher. "The little boy Samuel hope the priest Eli in the temple." Later I understood more quickly what he meant in saying: "What can't be hope has to be bore."

The coming of the automobile brought some unexpected problems, one of which was a new relationship to time and space. The Model T Fords, which were the most prominent and the most numerous of the early cars, were made to move over the unpaved and often rough roads, and transportation was so much speedier than our horse-drawn population was used to that we had to accustom ourselves.

The county seat of Yell County, which adjoins my home county, was Danville, twenty-six miles from our home of Russellville. One of our venerated lawyers, whose law business was so extensive that frequent trips to Danville were necessary, had one weakness. He loved what he called his "little nip." His practice was known to the Bar but tolerantly accepted because he never allowed it to interfere with his duties. However, he had not calculated on the changes produced by the introduction of the automobile. Soon after, one of his fellow barristers acquired a car, it was time to go to Danville for the summer session of court, and the fellow lawyer invited the elder to ride with him. As usual, he carried his supply of liquor. The car functioned well. Everything moved on schedule. The roads were dusty but passable, and the little car made the normal speed.

At Mosley's store, our friend said, "Now wait a minute. Stop here. I always have a little nip in front of this store." Then they drove on.

At Chicalah, he asked again that the car come to a stop. "I always take a little drink right here." Again they proceeded.

Another four stops—at Ranger, Petit Jean bridge, "the foot of the mountain," and at "the big oak tree"—he asked his friend to stop for his usual "little nip." What he had overlooked was the fact that the car was covering a distance in thirty minutes that with horse and buggy had required three hours. His consumption of liquor had been stepped up accordingly. He had drunk as much in half an hour as he ordinarily drank in three hours.

At Danville he was in a state of collapse. They had to carry him into the hotel. His case was continued a whole day, and it required that twenty-four hours for him to sober up.

In the backwoods of every area, quaint expressions get into the political exchanges both in the conversations and public addresses.

One of the most colorful political figures of north Arkansas was a rural minister who enjoyed serving as a member of the Arkansas legislature, to which he was elected several times. He was not an educated man but possessed enormous native ability and an uninhibited eloquence, both in the pulpit and on the stump. This made him a legendary hero in his section of the state.

Apocryphal stories spring up around men of this type, and I cannot resist passing on one of the oft-repeated stories about this remarkable person, Judge Boyle (the title was acquired by his election as county judge).

According to this particular legend, the judge had angered a group of local politicians who decided to file charges against him, seeking to prevent his being seated as a member of the House of Representatives. When his opposition abandoned their plan, Judge Boyle made the most of it in his campaign for re-election.

His stirring appeal to the voters allegedly went like this:

"Ah, yes, my friends, where was thet committee my enemies sent to Little Rock to file them nefarious charges agin' my character? When I heard they wuz there, I sent for 'em to invite 'em before the bar of the House, to have a full and a free

discussion thereof. But they had a deadly fear of meeting me—
They would not come. The only place I ever seen 'em was walking pro and con in the conundrum of the Capitol."

It is with pained reluctance that I close this chapter on rural
people, their fun-making and quaint ways. It is obvious, I trust,
that their humor has a special kind of flavor and that this writer
has a special kind of feeling for them.

Underlying the quaintness which is featured in this chapter
is a rugged character, which has both individual and social expression. There is an essential neighborliness in most families of
the groups I have mentioned. For their part in the evolving faith
which has an outcropping in these passages I must express my
own profoundest appreciation. I was pleased when I found that
the first mention of my name which I ever saw in a book identified me with the rural South. The author, recognizing my lifelong devotion to its people, indicated that I had never ceased to
love the region which nurtured me.

5

Country Lawyer: Courtroom Wit

SOME OF MY favorite courtroom stories center around my father, who was a notable trial lawyer and at one time a district prosecuting attorney in western Arkansas.

While teaching school he began reading law, and in 1901 he went to Washington and Lee University Law School for one term. Since he had a family to support, and little money, this was all he could afford, and all he ever had. He had natural gifts, however, which many a young man today who has spent three years in law school might well envy. One of these was a powerful resonant voice, which owed none of its carrying power to a public address system.

One summer day, when the court house windows were open wide and the whittlers' bench on Main Street had its usual quota of senior citizens enjoying the outdoors, another man came along.

"Where you goin'?" one of the loungers asked.

"Over to the courthouse to hear Steele Hays plead a case."

"No need to do that. The court house is only two blocks away. Set down here with us—you'll be able to hear him all right when he gets started!"

Dad was an impressive figure in the courtroom, or indeed anywhere. His hair was white by the time he was forty, and with his clear ruddy complexion, and wearing the white linen suit that used to be the trademark of a southern gentleman in the

141

summer, he looked as imposing as the original Kentucky colonel, even without the traditional goatee.

To make things more difficult for his opponents, he was not just facade and little else; he had an exceptionally facile mind, he reasoned like a logician, and he had a memory like a steel trap. As if to make him completely unbelievable, but without exaggerating a trifle, I must complete the picture by saying that he had charm of manner and a sense of humor that were unexcelled.

One who knew his skill in human relations could pity the opposition lawyer who once implored the jury not to be swayed by Dad's winning manner.

"Your Honor," he almost whimpered, "he sits over there by the jury during the recess where he can nod, and smile, and ask them about their folks. They don't realize it, Your Honor, but he's making it hard for them to be objective."

Like any prosecuting attorney, he sometimes had to press the state's case when his heart wasn't in it.

It was with divided sympathies that he prosecuted an old man known as "Uncle Ben Hawkins" for making and selling whiskey.

Uncle Ben lived in the Ozark Mountains, forty miles from the county seat. He was respected by his neighbors, and had once been elected to the state legislature, but never ran for a second term, because (it was said) he didn't care for Little Rock. One reason he gave, according to rumor, was that the corn pones they served there "jest didn't have the print of Sarey's hands on 'em," and therefore didn't seem to have the proper flavor.

Mr. Hawkins was charged with selling only a small amount of whiskey, one quart, but this was in the prohibition days when known violations were prosecuted. He was a solemn, not to say pompous, old gentleman with a voice like a foghorn, and he kept his dignity to the last. Clad in his Sunday suit of rather rusty black, he took the stand to plead "Not Guilty."

Dad, the prosecuting lawyer, asked the following question on cross-examination, "Now, Mr. Hawkins, you say you did not sell the whiskey as charged in the indictment?"

With immense dignity, Mr. Hawkins inclined his head. "That is correct, no, sir, no, sir."

"Then I'll ask you," said Dad, "if you have sold any whiskey in any amount, to anybody, for any price, at any time, in the last twelve months?"

A moment of silence. Then Uncle Ben, on a great intake of breath, boomed with his deep voice, "Repeat the question."

Dad obliged. "I'll ask you if you have sold any whiskey, in any amount, to anybody, for any price, at any time, in the last twelve months?"

Mr. Hawkins had not changed expression. Now he turned to the judge.

"Your Honor, do I have to answer that?"

"Yes, Mr. Hawkins. Mr. Hays has the right to ask you that question, and you'll have to answer."

Again Uncle Ben took a deep breath. "Repeat the question."

His patience still unimpaired, Dad said, "I'll ask you if you have sold any whiskey, in any amount, for any price, to anybody, at any time, in the last twelve months."

Mr. Hawkins took a breath to end all breaths. As he exhaled, he let Dad have it: "The answer is *NO!* That is, not that I recollects."

It was patently clear to judge and jury that Uncle Ben was fighting a rear-guard action in a lost cause, but the judge took all the circumstances into consideration in pronouncing sentence, and Mr. Hawkins was not disgraced in the eyes of his community.

This was all right with the prosecuting attorney.

During Dad's term as prosecuting attorney, he had to prosecute some other colorful characters. One was self-confident enough to defend himself (a course permitted by Arkansas law for minor offenses.) After Dad's plea to the jury for conviction, the judge addressed the defendant.

"Mr. Allenby, you may now address the jury in your defense."

The tall and eloquent mountaineer rose from his seat and without waiting for the court's permission, dropped to his knees and offered this audible prayer, "Oh, Lord, you know I'm not guilty. Put it in the hearts of this jury to vindicate me. Thank you, Lord, for giving me a judge to try this case who wants to do right. [This dissolved any chance that the judge would stop the unusual procedure.] And please forgive this good man, Steele

Hays, for persecuting me—he thinks he's doing his duty, but you and I know he's persecuting an innocent man. Amen."

Dad then announced to court and jury, "Your Honor, I ask that the charge be dismissed. I can't prevail over divine intervention."

Walking close to the judge he added in a whisper, "And if you ever let a fellow do me that way again, I'll ask for your impeachment."

My own career at the bar was undistinguished. Dad took me into his firm when I proudly came home with an LL.B. after my name, but there was no immediate demand for my services. In fact, it wasn't long till I was wondering if there would ever be any. My father already had a law partner of his own generation, Judge Arthur Priddy, and they were known to be two of the ablest lawyers in western Arkansas.

One day when I was in my small office, I heard a man come into the reception room and say to Miss Ivy, our secretary, "Is Judge Hays in?"

"No, he's in court," said Miss Ivy.

"Judge Priddy in?"

"No. He's out of town."

The man had started toward the door when Miss Ivy said suggestively, "Mr. Brooks Hays is here."

But the prospective client didn't take the bait.

"I'll just wait for one of the lawyers," he said.

Even more dampening to my self-esteem was the fellow who hoped to get a little free advice. Instead of presenting himself at the office and asking for "one of the lawyers," he accosted me on the street.

"Say," he said, "you're a sort of a lawyer, aren't you? Let me ask you a question!"

And then he got about five dollars' worth of free advice.

On rare occasions courtroom episodes can produce some father-son humor. Once in Paris, Arkansas, a lawyer was prosecuting a case against his son, who was the attorney for the defense. The son made a great tactical error. He said: "Gentlemen of the jury, if you believe that principal witness, then of course you've got to decide for Pa. But, I don't think you do believe him, and I'll tell you this. I can just hear Pa coaching him now. He gets him there in the back room of his office where I used to work, and he tells him what to say. And I'm telling you, Pa told this defendant what to say! He coached him. That's what he did."

The old man rose, stung by his son's accusation. "Gentlemen," he said, "I missed my calling. I should have been a stock raiser. Didn't I produce one fine jackass?"

When Dad was willing to trust me finally with the trial of a case—a misdemeanor—I was excited, unimportant though it was. It was scheduled before a magistrate, Leb Sewell, a veteran justice of the peace, in Russellville. I never dreamed that nearly twenty years later that short criminal trial would figure in an embarrassing conversation in a campaign for Congress. I must jump to 1942 to describe the impact. I was campaigning in my old home town, and my opponent was Bob Bailey, who was serving his third term as lieutenant governor of Arkansas. Bob had continued to live and practice law in Russellville, and was making considerable headway in that populous area with an argument that went something like this: "Brooks doesn't love you like I do—I stayed here with you, while Brooks moved away."

Campaigning with the people informally, I sought every opportunity to identify myself with them, reminding them of early associations and experiences. One day I saw a group surrounding Judge Sewell. Here was an ideal chance to mention that case, presided over by him, that I naturally regarded as historic. With an audience of perhaps a dozen voters, I said, "Judge, do you remember the first case I ever tried in your court?"

He did! But they were the last words I uttered for many minutes—till he finally paused for breath.

He said, "I'll say I do! How could I ever forget it?"

With rare histrionic effect, he turned to the little assembly, and regaled them to my great discomfort in this fashion.

"Yes sir, fellows, I'll never forget it! They had old man Whittlesby in here, charged with breach of the peace. The boys had been feuding—it was a family row like I never saw one. And Brooks was defending. His Daddy decided to let the kid try one by himself. And would you believe it—right in the middle of that case, while I was listening to the testimony, they broke out in a fist fight right there in my courtroom! They were fighting all over the place. Sounded like a bunch of mules on a plank floor. And in that melee, I looked up to see Brooks standing on a chair shouting at me, 'Your Honor, I demand protection!'"

Here I sought to interrupt, for this was ruinous to a campaigner—being cast in a dubious role, when I was so earnestly seeking to establish the image of a courageous public servant. Actually, if I mentioned protection, I was thinking of my client's daughter, who was almost hysterical. For years I have tried but not figured out a way to vindicate myself. The judge's story was devastating. The crowd enjoyed it hugely, and my only hope of retrieving something finally was to join in the laughter, thinking that exhibiting sportsmanship might help.

The episode closed with my feeble plea, "Now, Judge, don't you remember I said, 'I demand protection *for my client*'?"

"Sonny boy," was his final summation, "you wasn't thinkin' of that client!

"But," he added, "it was a big day for me. I fined 'em all the minimum amount for fighting, but collected costs in every case, and it added up to quite a figure!"

My recollections of tilts with judges bring to mind that hoary old chestnut which was popular fifty years ago. A big league baseball player said to a lawyer, "How do you select your judges?"

"Like you handle baseball umpires," was the answer.

"Why, how's that?"

"When lawyers can't hit any longer, we bench 'em."

I have known judges, however, whose names evoke memories of a totally different character. The one whose friendship meant most to me as a young man was Judge Marcellus Davis, a friend of my father's.

I have already identified him as the former Consul to Yucatan, a post obtained for him by Colonel William L. Terry, who feared the able young lawyer was going to run against him for Congress.

When I knew him he was much older, lame from a fall, and almost ready for retirement after an active life.

His home was in our sister town, Dardanelle, an old river port on the Arkansas River, where he was much loved by his neighbors, though they were not spared his gibes. He came to be considered one of the most colorful characters Arkansas ever produced.

Dardanelle is a picturesque town, lying at the foot of a Gibraltarlike peak, called Dardanelle Rock, which rises from the bank of the river. "Yes," Judge Davis used to say, "there is the Rock and there is the town. Both have been landmarks for a hundred years, and the town has grown as fast as the Rock!"

He was a great lover of dogs and the outdoors, an inveterate fox hunter, a satirist par excellence, and was noted for his quaint way of revealing a love for his fellow man and the rural environment.

One of my first cases was on behalf of the owner of a dog that had been killed. The case was tried before another judge, but Marcellus dropped in to the courtroom to hear me make my argument. Whether this characteristic action was due to his friendship for my father or me or the dog, I never knew, but it affected me like a shot in the arm.

I had planned to quote as my climax and *pièce de résistance*, Senator Vest's famous "Eulogy on the Dog," with which he had once swayed a courtroom. But to my intense disappointment, the judge dismissed the case on a technicality, without hearing either side.

There was nothing that could justifiably be said—but Judge Davis said it anyhow! From his seat on the front row, he commented to his colleague on the bench, "In my opinion, sir, you have committed grave error."

He presided at a court hearing in 1922 in which I participated, and the following day he wrote me this note:

Dear Brooks,

What you did yesterday was refreshingly boyish; but be a boy as long as you can, for the blood of youth is the wine of life, and while a greater prohibition than the 18th Amendment has left me but an empty cup, I love its lingering fragrance still.

And so when my own boys come to visit with me, I cannot find it in my heart to let them understand I am only a broken, crippled old man, and I let them drag me out to ride and hunt and shoot and fish as in the olden, golden days gone by.

Is it any wonder, then, that the poet son (Charles T. Davis) began one of his most moving verses with this couplet:

> This is the ancient law of youth:
> To ride, shoot straight, and speak the truth.

The old gentleman's lameness was due to a fall in my father's law office. Some time later I remarked to him (motivated by a desire to impress him with my knowledge of the law of torts), "Judge, it's kind of you not to sue Dad for harboring a hidden danger in his office."

That brought this mock-serious comment, "Son, the dangers in your Papa's office are not hidden—they are open and notorious! Everybody that goes in there gets hurt, one way or another."

The Judge's fellow townsmen enjoyed his almost daily recitals of his own dog's superior intelligence.

"Dogs think. Yes they do," he said. "Yes sir—they can almost talk. They do talk to each other."

Then he related his walk from home accompanied by his big mastiff, faithful companion of many years. "We were within twenty feet of the office when old Tige stopped short, looked up at me, and I could almost hear the words rolling off his tongue as he turned toward home. 'Well, I'll be danged! I almost forgot that bone.' And would you believe it?" the Judge added, "Not long ago he chased a rabbit under this low slung office, and when he couldn't scrounge under he ran off, and it wasn't three minutes till he came running back with a little terrier, who went right under the house at just the place the rabbit went in! Yes, sir, I tell you they think and talk to each other."

After a few years with Dad, I was appointed assistant attorney general, and I took my family to Little Rock to live. There, my opportunities increased, and my experience widened.

We had a United States district judge in Little Rock named Judge Jacob Trieber. He had a delightful German accent, and was very popular with the lawyers; for though he had a caustic tongue, which he did not hesitate to employ, his barbed comments were often humorous, and his nature was essentially a warm one. Because I was assistant attorney general of the state

I was often in his courtroom, and though there were many times when I felt the sharpness of the judge's tongue, I also knew that Judge Trieber had a basic sympathy and friendliness toward young lawyers.

One day my assignment was to uphold one of the state's laws against the complaint of a corporation that the law violated the Fourteenth Amendment to the Constitution. The Judge interrupted my argument:

"Vait, Mr. Hays! Do you know what you are asking dis Court to do?"

"I'm asking for a declaration of the law, I believe, Your Honor."

"No! You are asking dis Court to overrule de Supreme Court of de United States. Its decision in de Children's Hospital case iss so clear dat not even you, Mr. Hays, could ask such a t'ing except de Courtroom iss full of pretty young ladies, and you vant to make a speech."

There was a burst of laughter from the pretty young ladies, and this young lawyer, his face red, took his seat.

Another characteristic incident may be worth retelling, although it had wide circulation at the time it occurred. Silver dollars were in use then, and perhaps the story, like the dollars, may have passed out of circulation.

Mr. M. E. Dunaway, an able trial lawyer of that period, was so absorbed in his case that he didn't notice how loudly he was jingling the money in his pocket. Judge Trieber noticed it, however, and interrupted the argument to say, "Mr. Dunavay. Please don't rattle your money. It makes de Court nervous."

Mr. Dunaway was contrite, promised to be careful. But again he forgot himself and set up quite a jingle with his right hand and the large silver dollars in his pocket. Again Judge Trieber warned him.

When it happened the third time, the judge said testily, "Mr. Dunavay, how much money haf you in your pocket?"

The lawyer ruefully drew out his hand, and looked at the silver dollars in it.

"Three dollars, Your Honor."

"Vell! I fine you two of dem. Now rattle dat udder von!"

I suppose it was Judge Trieber's impatience with trivia that one day caused him to connive at the escape of a prisoner. The United States Marshall had arrested a young man charged with killing a yellowhammer.

The case was brought to the United States District Court because of a federal statute against killing migratory birds, which statute grew out of a treaty with Canada.

Judge Trieber was probably not in sympathy with the extension into that area of the strong arm of the federal law, and so was doubtless caught off guard by the prisoner's plea of guilt.

The colloquy that ensued, composed of a series of leading questions by the presiding judge and honest but unhelpful answers from the defendant, was very funny to those in the courtroom.

Judge Trieber: Young man, you didn't really kill de yellowhammer, did you?

Young Man: Yes, Your Honor. I'm afraid I did.

Judge Trieber: Vell. So you killed de yellowhammer. Mmmmm. But you didn't know it vas a yellowhammer. Did you?

Young Man: Yes, Your Honor. I knew it was a yellowhammer.

Judge Trieber: So it vas a yellowhammer. . . . But you did not know de yellowhammer vas a migratory bird, did you?

Young Man: Yes, Your Honor, I knew it was a migratory bird.

Judge Trieber: (in desperation): But you didn't know dat killing the little migratory bird was against de federal law, did you?

Young Man: Yes, Your Honor, I knew I was violating the law.

Judge Trieber: Vell, I gif you de minimum sentence of ten days in jail.

Then in a stage whisper to the marshall, he said, "Mr. Marshall, do de Court a favor, and when you get to the door, please let dis prisoner escape."

I happened to be in the courtroom one day when Judge Trieber sentenced a father and two sons who were frequently brought in for making moonshine and other misdemeanors. As the sheriff came forward to lead them out, Judge Trieber said sternly: "Mr. Sanders, the jury having again found you guilty of manufacturing and selling intoxicating liquors, it becomes the duty of dis court to sentence you to the federal penitentiary. But before de court does dat, I just vant to say to you dat you and your boys have given dis court more trouble dan all de people in Arkansas put together. Haf you anyting to say?"

Mr. Sanders, far from abashed, was equally indignant. "Yes, I have! I just want to say that we haven't give you no more trouble than you've give us."

Another judge, whom I knew first as a friend of my father's, and who, like many country judges, was beloved in his section, was Judge Volney Walker of Fayetteville, Arkansas—Vol, to his friends.

One of Vol's lifelong friends was Mrs. Sarah Spillers, who had attended grade school with him. Congressman Jim Trimble, who knows the Ozarks as few others do, told me that he heard the following encounter when Sarah was on the witness stand and Vol was presiding over the trial. The witness kept drifting all over the universe in her testimony, in spite of the repeated admonition by the judge to stick to the relevant matters, and not to talk about just anything that came to mind. Finally she turned in the witness' chair and lifted her arm with an index finger pointed menacingly toward the judge.

"Now, look here, Volney! And you listen to me, too. You can just rap all you want to with that little mallet—you're not going to stop me! I'm going to have my say."

The jury, the lawyers, and the audience were aghast. But the judge relieved the tension. He quietly and slowly laid the gavel down.

"Well, now, Sarah," he said, "you just go ahead and have your say. We want it to be real homelike around here."

During prohibition days, one of Judge Walker's mountaineer friends, living fifty miles from the railroad out in a remote section of a big county, came to see him. He had a quart of what was called "White Mule." It was a colorless concoction and got its name from the fact that it had the kick of a mule. The mountaineer wanted to give Vol a quart of this home-produced potent liquor, and Vol accepted it in the name of friendship.

"Lem, tell me about your boy," the judge said. "You named your lad for me, didn't you?"

"Yes," the man said, "I did, Vol, I named my boy for you."

"How's he getting on?"

"Well now, I'll tell you, Vol, about that boy. You know, soon after he was born, and I give him your name, which I was proud to do, I got sent up to Leavenworth for selling liquor. I was gone three or four years. I hadn't been at home very long when Ted Simms acted up and I had to kill him. They sent me down to the Arkansas penitentiary then, and that boy growed up while I wuz away from home. Out from under my influence, Vol, he didn't turn out so good!"

Incidents in the religious, legal, and political life of the various southern states bear interesting parallels. For example, Senator John Sherman Cooper, a former Kentucky judge, tells this story, which sounds remarkably like an Arkansas yarn. When a rather notorious character called Uncle Billy Bob was arraigned for drunkenness for the nth time, Judge Cooper addressed him: "Uncle Billy Bob, tell the court why it is that you're here all the time for being drunk. First of all, where do you get the money to buy all the liquor you consume?"

"Well, Judge, you know that's just exactly the question the Methodist preacher, Brother Hunter, asked me yesterday, and I told him just what I'll tell you. I said, 'Well now, Brother Hunter, it's just like you getting money from the Methodists. I ask people for money just like you do. They feel sorry for me like they do for you, and they give it to me.' "

The violence of the nineteenth century in backwoods Kentucky had its outcropping west of the Mississippi in that period. It even carried over into the early twentieth century. At a Kentucky political meeting a certain participant in the debate was shot by several of the others at the meeting. The event occurred on the open floor and created a considerable stir in the community.

A northerner, who was in town, asked an acquaintance, who had been present, why the shooting had occurred.

"He made a motion that was out of order," explained the local man.

The visitor was horrified at this excess of parliamentarianism. "You mean to tell me they shot a man in cold blood on the floor of the meeting, just for making a motion that was out of order?"

"Well," drawled his informant, "the motion was toward his hip pocket."

My wife likes the story of the woman being examined in

court for jury service. She looked up at the judge and said, "I am sorry, Your Honor, I can't serve on the jury. I don't believe in capital punishment."

"Maybe you don't understand," the judge said. "This is a civil suit brought by a wife to recover five thousand dollars of *her* money spent by her husband on gambling and other women."

"Oh," she said, "I'll serve on the jury—I could be wrong about capital punishment."

When Senator Sam Ervin of North Carolina, a renowned storyteller, was a circuit judge in his state, he had to decide a case which had been argued by two lawyers. After he had rendered his decision and retired to chambers, the sheriff came in.

"Your Honor," he said, "Jim Spofford's out there on the street cussin' you by sections. He's got a crowd around him, givin' you the dickens. Do you want to cite him for contempt? Shall I bring him in?"

"He's the one I decided against?" asked the judge.

"Yes, sir."

"Well, just ignore it. It's the privilege of a lawyer to cuss the court for a reasonable length of time after he loses a case."

Senator Ervin told this story to the Democratic National Committee in extenuation of the criticism of the United States Supreme Court's school decision. He said the criticism by southern lawyers had not extended beyond a "reasonable length of time."

Another of his stories has to do with a lawyer who resorted to extreme and unusual measures to win a case. His client was charged with stealing something from a hotel, and the lawyer knew he was guilty. Success was a forlorn hope, unless he could pull off a trick he had in mind.

Knowing the judge was in the habit of stopping in the bar of the hotel for a drink around five o'clock, he had no difficulty encountering him there, and "setting 'em up" until his honor was too mellow to take notice. He then slipped into the judge's pocket several pieces of the hotel's flat silver, and bade him a pleasant good-night.

The next day, when the prosecutor stated his air-tight case to the judge, some hotel property had actually been found in the pockets of the accused. He could hardly believe his ears when the judge said, "Mr. Sheriff, let this man go. I doubt if he really meant to steal anything. You know," looking at the two lawyers and shaking his head in a bewildered way, "some of the weirdest things go on at that hotel!"

Don Herzberg has collected a group of true stories concerning eminent American jurists. The following are told in his words:

A recent public opinion survey listed judges as way up on the "esteem scale." People tend to look upon judges as extremely important people. There is also a tendency, because traditionally judges are looked upon as austere and unbending, to assume that they are humorless. This is not the case. Judges, like the rest of us, have their moments of relaxation and humor.

One of the most austere judges in our history was Chief Justice Marshall, one of the most important justices who ever sat on the Supreme Court. He liked to do everything for himself and resisted strongly having anyone do anything to help him. One day the chief justice wanted to do some legal reference work in a law library. The book he needed was on a top shelf. The books were lightly packed in and he was having great difficulty getting the tome he wanted. He gave a great yank and pulled out the volume only to have the entire shelf of books come down on top of him, knocking him to the floor. The law librarian dashed over to him and helped pull the books off him. "Mr. Marshall, sir, are you all right?" he asked.

"Let me alone," Marshall told him, "I am just a bit stunned. I'll be all right." As he pulled himself together, he mused out loud, "I have laid down the law often, but this is the first time the law has ever laid me down."

The story is reminiscent of one told about the great Constitutional law professor, Thomas Reed Powell, of Harvard. He had earned his reputation in part on books written about the Constitution. During his teaching career, Massachusetts passed a law requiring every college professor to take an oath to support the Constitution of the United States and of Massachusetts. When asked whether he would take such an oath, an anathema to professors, Powell said, "Why shouldn't I take an oath to support the Constitution. After all, the Constitution has been supporting me for years!"

Strategy in how cases are presented to the court can oftentimes have a telling effect on the outcome of a case. Justice Oliver Wendell Holmes was reminiscing about the famous lawyer and general, Benjamin F. Butler. Butler was on his way to Boston to try a case before a Judge Shaw. Holmes met him on the train and they discussed the case. Holmes asked to look at Butler's notes. Butler gave them to Holmes who was surprised to see written on the top of the page, "Insult the judge."

"Why do that?" asked Holmes.

"Well, you see," Butler replied, "I first get Judge Shaw's ill will by insulting him. Later in the case he will have decisions to make for or against me. Since he is an exceedingly fair person and since I have insulted him, he will lean to my side for fear of letting his personal feelings against me sway his decisions the other way."

Another story deals with a lawyer from Wyoming, who had the picturesqueness of a cowboy and an even more picturesque method of speech. He was arguing a case before the Supreme Court while Justice Holmes was still on the bench. Despite a most impassioned appeal to the court, full of the language of the frontier, he lost. As he concluded, Holmes who sat on the right of Hughes, leaned over and in one of his loud, hoarse whispers said:

"Can't we hear that old bird again?"

The clerk of the court heard the remark and afterward advised the cowboy that, if he applied for a rehearing, it might be granted. This was done. In the rehearing the lawyer opened his appeal to the court with these words:

"I come to you as John the Baptist saying: 'Repent ye, repent ye.'"

Whereupon Justice McReynolds, who was enjoying the performance almost as much as Justice Holmes, leaned forward and said: "But are you not aware of what happened to John the Baptist?"

"Yes, I am quite aware," was the immediate response. "He lost his head through the influence of a harlot. But I know the Supreme Court would not be so influenced."

When President Franklin D. Roosevelt was a young lawyer just getting started in New York, he was retained to handle a difficult civil case. The opposing lawyer was a very effective jury pleader and completely outshone his youthful rival in the argument to the jury. However, he made one fatal mistake: he orated for several hours. As he thundered on, Roosevelt noticed that the jury wasn't paying much attention. So, playing a hunch, when his turn came, he rose and said: "Gentlemen you have heard the evidence. You also have listened to my distinguished colleague, a brilliant orator. If you believe him, and disbelieve the evidence, you will have to decide in his favor. That's all I have to say."

The jury was out only five minutes and brought in a verdict for Roosevelt's client.

When Thaddeus Stevens was a young lawyer, he once had a case before a bad-tempered judge of an obscure Pennsylvania court. Under what he considered a very erroneous ruling, it was decided against him; thereupon he threw down his books and picked up his hat in a state of indignation, scattering imprecations all around him. The judge assumed an air of offended majesty, and asked Thaddeus Stevens if he meant to express his "contempt for this court?"

Stevens turned to him very politely, made a respectful bow and feigned amazement. "Express my contempt for this court? No sir; I am trying to conceal it, Your Honor," adding as he turned to leave, "but I find it damned hard to do it."

Chief Justice Fuller, when a young lawyer, was practicing before Judge MacArthur of the Supreme Court of Illinois in Chicago. In his speech before the judge he pleaded his client's ignorance of an offense he had committed.

The judge said, "Every man is supposed to know the law, Mr. Fuller."

"I am aware of that," responded Mr. Fuller. "Every shoemaker, tailor, mechanic, and illiterate laborer is presumed to know the law. Yes, every man is presumed to know it, except the judges of the Supreme Court, and we have a court of appeals to correct their mistakes."

We were still feeling the effects of the Great Depression in Arkansas, and the law business was suffering from malnutrition, when I received one of the most welcome and gratifying telephone calls of my entire life.

When the operator said, "Mr. Hays, Secretary Frances Perkins in Washington wants to talk to you," the desk phone seemed to be transmitted into a musical instrument, and Miss Perkins's voice offering me a job was an exquisite melody.

She asked me to serve as legal adviser in the Arkansas office of NRA, and at last I found myself in the type of work for which I was temperamentally fitted—work for and with *people*. The practice of law had not engaged my wholehearted interest as I had expected it to—perhaps under the circumstances it had not had a fair chance—but now with the opportunity to work with both management and labor to elevate the status of the Arkansas wage worker, I had found my element.

My work, adjusting claims, was hard, sometimes thankless, often frustrating; but it had a morale-building value for both workers and employers, and it was not without its humorous incidents. One such was my rise and fall in the estimation of a female factory worker who had looked to me for a miracle.

I sent my assistant, Charles Measel, to see her and get the details; but he reported that she was so anxious to talk to me, it would be a good thing if I could go with him out to the community where she lived. So one morning we got in my old Ford car and drove out there. Charlie went to the door and called, "Lola! Mr. Hays is out here."

In a moment I saw Lola appear, taking off her kitchen apron as she came, her face alight.

"You say my Little Rock lawyer done come, Mistuh Charlie? Oh, I'm so thankful! I want to see Mistuh Hays! You hear, Hattie?" she called to someone in the house, "my Little Rock lawyer done come, Mistuh Brook Hays. I'm countin' heavy on my Little Rock lawyer!"

By this time she had reached the car, where I was sitting behind the wheel. I presume I was not an impressive sight. I was young, and I didn't even get credit for my full age in those days, and slim, and certainly beardless. Lola's face fell visibly.

She responded to my greeting dejectedly, "Good mawnin', Mr. Hays." Then turning to Charlie, she said, "You know, Mr. Charlie, my trust is *really* in the Lord."

I think this became one of Charlie Measel's favorite stories.

6

Laughter in the Sanctuary: The Church

LAUGHTER IN CHURCH, accompanied by the guilty feeling of ir-
reverence and the necessity of subduing it, is one of the universal
experiences of childhood. Nothing more speedily transports me
backward in time—to the days when our whole town, unless
kept at home by illness or some other act of God, was in its several pews on Sunday morning—than the recollection of some of
the unscheduled events that reduced us youngsters to irrepres-
sible giggles.

Like the time that Brother Morton and Brother Wooten (two
revered but aging deacons), each thought he was called on to
pronounce the benediction. Even the grown people were
chuckling as the competition proceeded, each unaware of the
other, until one finished. I had already anticipated and was relish-
ing that moment. Brother Morton concluded his prayer first,
picked up his hat, and started to go. He was deaf, but he wasn't
stupid, and when the congregation stayed where it was with
heads bowed, he knew something was happening. He looked
around for the cause, and saw Brother Wooten's lips moving.
Quickly he ducked his head, and gave an imitation of a man who
has been listening all the time, while I quivered inwardly.

Another small incident that either amused or shocked our congregation, according to whether they were more easily shocked
than amused, was the time the lights went out. It was Sunday
evening and quite dark outside. I was sitting in church with my

parents, when suddenly and inexplicably we were plunged into total darkness.

The minister was reading his sermon that evening, and he came to a full stop. "I don't think this will last long. Let us just sit in prayerful meditation for a few minutes. Then, if the lights have not come on, we'll be dismissed."

Any change from ecclesiastical routine was a boon to me at that age. If there was any praying in my meditations, I'm afraid it would have been that the lights would not come on, but I didn't dream of the rib-tickling denouement that actually took place.

While the congregation waited silently, either prayerfully or, like me, hopefully, "Uncle Bob" Beavers, who was among the most faithful attenders but who invariably fell asleep, was disturbed by the unwonted quiet, and suddenly woke. Finding himself, as he thought, deserted in an empty church, he jumped to his feet and started up the aisle, exclaiming in an outraged tone which carried to every ear of the convulsed congregation, "Well, I'll be damned! They've all gone off and left me!"

In those days there were no street lights in Russellville, and of course no paving, so neighbors usually went in a group to the Sunday night service and Wednesday prayer meeting carrying a lighted lantern. My father did not often attend prayer meeting, so I usually accompanied my mother.

One Wednesday evening when we went into the vestibule, the sanctuary just beyond the closed doors was absolutely quiet. There was no sound of piano or of voices, and no one in view except our small group, so we thought we were the first to arrive. Someone, to put the lantern out, blew at the flame, but instead of going out, it flared up. And it continued to burn stubbornly, in spite of our combined attacks against it—for we all had got into the act, getting noisier and more hilarious as we blew at the flaming wick.

Suddenly the quiet beyond the doors was broken. The notes of "Will There Be Any Stars in My Crown?" came clearly to our horrified ears, followed by the shuffling of feet as the congregation stood and began to sing. It was obvious to all of us at once— we had come in during the prayer! I can see my mother's shocked face at this moment, dismayed that she should have been disturbing religious worship.

With one accord we rushed to the exit, taking the lantern, which now, having had its fun, diabolically went out, leaving us in the dark.

Someone whispered, "Let's go around the block and come in again," and this we did. I sat down by Bill Wooten, a friend and contemporary.

He murmured under cover of another hymn, "The queerest thing happened awhile ago—a bunch of rowdies came into the church, and made the awfullest disturbance in the vestibule, laughing like crazy, and stamping around. Then they went off. They must have been drunk."

I was suitably shocked. "Gee whiz!" I exclaimed. "Sorry I missed it."

Sixty years ago the question of instrumental music in the church house was highly controversial in parts of the South, particularly in western Arkansas. At Dover, Arkansas, an early home of the Hayses, the little congregation voted to install an organ. One good brother was so incensed over what he regarded as terrible heresy that he left the church and vowed he would never return. He called the new instrument "the devil's box."

Some weeks later, lightning struck the church building and the old man was gleeful. He told everyone who would listen, "The Lord was visiting the church with his wrath because of that devil's box."

One auditor spoke up in protest. "But Uncle Johnny," he said, "the lightning struck the *north* end of the building and the organ was in the south end—it wasn't touched."

Uncle Johnny was ready for that one. "The Lord hadn't been there in so long, he's forgotten where it was a-settin'!"

I have known preachers who were deadly serious, some who were unintentionally funny, and some who used humor as skillfully as a good musician uses an instrument—to entertain, to stimulate, and to inspire.

I once spent a delightful evening at Lake Junaluska, North Carolina, after I had spoken there, with a small group, which included Bishop Roy Short. He entertained us with some fascinating tales of his problems and experiences.

One concerned two churches in two southern towns that shared a pastor. One day during his service as district superintendent, long before he became a bishop he was in a remote area in the Southern mountains. A committee from one of these churches called on him and asked that he remove the pastor.

"What seems to be the trouble?" he asked.

"Well, Brother Short, he's just ignorant as he can be," said the spokesman. "For one thing, he thinks the Bible was written in English. And he doesn't even know that language! And he's got a sermon on 'Simon the Leaper' in which he goes on and on about Simon leaping here and leaping there, leaping over this difficulty and over that tribulation!"

Another member of the committee took up the tale. "And when we pointed out to him as gently as we could that it was Simon the leper, he was indignant. He said 'Simon the Leaper' was one of his best sermons, and he had no intention of giving it up."

The district superintendent agreed to see what he could do. But before he had taken any action, he was visited by a committee from the other community. They had heard about the request from their sister church, and were up in arms.

"We don't want him moved," they said emphatically. "He suits us down to the ground! He preaches Hot Hell and Sweet Heaven, and that's the way we like it!"

The late Oscar Johnson, popular pastor of the Third Baptist Church in St. Louis for more than a quarter of a century, took out of this world, upon his departure, something that left us poorer. He had a rare gift for mixing in pulpit presentations a wholesome humor with profound and inspiring theological truths. In private conversations, as well, he added vibrancy and good fun.

One story he used to tell was easy to believe, since in all of his pastorates he was the object of admiration. He reported with a twinkle that a lady parishioner in a Tennessee church he served before going to St. Louis told him that his successor was doing all right and that he delivered good sermons, but, she added, "Oh, but Dr. Johnson, he can't hold me like you did!"

An illustration of his ability to state a point in unforgettable ways was his plea to the congregation one Sunday morning not to come late and leave early. Most ministers would simply have appealed to them in conventional terms to cooperate to this end. But not Oscar Johnson. He won their sympathy and a positive response to his quaint beginning, "Please, won't you cease being postinvocationists and prebenedictionists?"

"Brother Oscar," as he was generally identified, was elected president of the Baptist World Alliance in 1947 at the meeting in Copenhagen. His speech at the closing session was a model of captivating homiletics, mixed with humor of a rare sort seldom heard in European religious meetings. But the laughter of the Danes and others, when the interpreter rendered the Johnson joke in their language, was relished by Oscar. "This is wonderful," he said. "I get two laughs—one when I say it in English and then another, when the other half gets it from the interpreter."

Oscar's excellent sense of humor was matched by a feeling for the dramatic that made his sanctuary a popular gathering place. Once there was a backfire—an incident that will be remembered in St. Louis for a long, long time. Oscar planned a sermon on the Judgment, and had arranged at the climax of the sermon, following the expression "at the sound of the trumpet," to have a trumpeter give a great blast on his instrument. "I must have had that congregation well worked up, and the toot must have been too loud a toot, because the women were fainting all over the place. They were carrying them out faster than we could give first aid. I'll never do that again," said the minister ruefully.

My own pastor in Washington, D.C., Dr. Clarence Cranford, is keenly aware of the advantages of a touch of humor in even the most serious discussion, and is a past master at making an anecdote work for him.

One Sunday when his chosen scripture from the Old Testament included a half-dozen difficult names over which he stumbled a bit, he said, "This passage reminds me of the preacher who hadn't done his homework. It did not seem to perturb him, however, for when he came to the lines in the Old Testament that record the death of a warrior, 'And he hit Abinadad the Hittite that he died,' his version was an unintended departure from the text. He read it like this: 'And he hit Adam a dab; highty-tighty, that he did.' "

It is not unusual, then, for the members of Calvary Church to laugh during the sermon, but those relaxing moments are at the preacher's instigation. Something funny happened one Sunday morning that was not on the program, and was as big a surprise to him as it was to the congregation.

He had referred to Joseph, telling how he had correctly interpreted the chief butler's dream, and forecast his return to favor.

"Did he then—when he was out of prison and back in Pharaoh's palace—did he remember Joseph as he had promised?"

The minister's question was purely rhetorical, but he waited a split second too long. Very softly but clearly from the balcony came an answer in a child's voice, "No-o-o-." It was just above a whisper, but it moved into the silence and floated out over that congregation like the muted but distinct tone of a tiny bell, then died away.

A second longer the audience remained frozen, then broke into helpless laughter, in which the minister joined.

"I always wanted to be able to preach so that a child could understand me," he said. "I think today I have succeeded."

The late, beloved Dr. Forney Hutchinson of Arkansas loved to tell of an incident that occurred in his early ministry, and which he construed as a joke on himself.

He had been sent by his bishop to a Methodist church in DuVall's Bluff. Among his parishioners was a dear and saintly old lady, who was prevented by the ailments of age from attending church often, but who was much beloved by the members.

"Be sure and go to see her soon," some of them advised Brother Hutchinson. "It will do you more good than it will her!"

Rightly considering that this untactful speech was not meant to be offensive, the young minister went the next day to call on the lady. Feeling that the burden of rapport was on him, and desirous of setting the stage for her saintly spirit to emerge and express itself, he asked, "Tell me, Sister Thompson, what it is in your long and saintly life which has given you the most satisfaction, the most real pleasure?"

Almost, but not quite, hiding a sudden twinkle in her eyes, the old lady deflated the pompous young preacher with a word. She did not call him "Sonny," but the effect on him was the same.

"Well, Brother Hutchinson, looking at it up one side and down the other, day in and day out, I 'spect it's been—my vittles."

I had related this story to my longtime friend and colleague, Colgate Darden, when we were both delegates to the United Nations in 1955, and one evening he called for it under unusual circumstances.

We were attending a state dinner, representing our government at the Russian Embassay in New York. Ambassador Henry Cabot Lodge was unable to be present, but the British delegate Harold Macmillan, Pinay of France, and others were present.

The dinner and the service were excellent, and everyone was making a desperate effort to feel congenial and enter into the conversational gambits, particularly the humor, of the dinner companions from other countries.

Colgate, recalling Sister Thompson's appreciation of good "vittles," got everyone's attention at our end of the table by saying, "Brooks, tell 'em about Sister Sarah Thompson."

I was sitting next to one of our hosts, Ambassador Zarubin, who looked at me and waited. It has never been necessary to twist my arm to get me to tell a yarn, so I promptly began. Unfortunately, though, I threw in a gratuitous and wholly fictitious detail right at the beginning, which proved to be a rock on which my tale foundered and sank.

"Sister Sarah Thompson," I said, "was ninety-seven years old. . . ."

That was as far as I ever got.

"Wait a minute!" exclaimed Zarubin. "I know a guy in Russia who is 147." He looked expectantly around the table.

"I should have made her a bit older," I murmured regretfully.

"And what's more, this guy is healthy!"

"Well . . ." I began, *I'm not sure, but I think I was going to get Sister Sarah out of bed.*

Seeing that I was not yet down for the count, but still struggling, Ambassador Zarubin delivered the knock-out blow. "And he had forty-eight sons and daughters!"

He sat back, smug and triumphant, and dared me to top that. I didn't try. I looked at Colgate. He appeared to have found this exchange funnier than the story, particularly when I said to him later, "When a Russian breaks up an Arkansas story like that, the Geneva spirit is dead as far as I am concerned."

The evangelists of my boyhood, who used to hold "protracted meetings" in the summertime, usually in brush arbors, were often excellent entertainers. One of these was the Reverend John E. Brown, a distinguished Arkansas evangelist, who founded the John Brown University at Siloam Springs in our state. I met him at a dinner in Washington shortly before he died, and there he told a story about the embarrassing spot into which a fellow evangelist had once got himself. I imagine only a preacher could fully appreciate the humor of the situation.

When he was a young preacher, just beginning to hold evangelistic meetings, he went to Nashville to attend a revival being conducted by the great George Stewart. One night, in the midst of an impassioned plea for the Christian life, Dr. Stewart dramatically paused, then said, "Brethren, I see my friend George Johnson of Knoxville. Come up here, Brother George."

When the friend, an older man, had come to the platform, the evangelist put his arm around the other's shoulder. "This dear friend was converted in my meeting just a year ago," he said. "He is now sixty-four years old, and he had lived in sin sixty-three years! Now he's lived one year in grace. Brother George, tell the audience—isn't it true you have been a happier man, better satisfied; in fact, you have had *more fun* in the one year you've lived in grace than all the years you lived in sin?"

The old man looked startled, and with a rising inflection said, "Now, wa-a-it a minute, Brother Stewart! You've asked an honest question, and I've got to give you an honest answer! No, I can't say I've had more fun since I've lived in grace. You see, when I lived in sin I had a *lot* of fun!"

George Stewart signaled to his singer to take over, and while the audience roared, he buried his face in his hands. "I can't survive that!" he said, as he too laughed helplessly.

I love stories about church life and its people, especially those that concern well-known personalities.

Even the eminent Harry Emerson Fosdick is not immune to life's little ironies.

Dr. Henry Van Dusen tells of the little lady in Madison, New Jersey, where Dr. Fosdick had his first pastorate. Long afterward, going along the corridor of the church where all the pictures of former pastors had been hung, she saw that of a curly-haired youth just out of seminary.

"Oh, there's dear little Dr. Fosdick!" she exclaimed. She looked at it for a moment, and then said wistfully, "I wonder whatever became of him."

I address many religious groups, and so my opportunities to collect such stories have been extensive, and my use of them has been substantial. Those that provoke a laugh at the expense of some other group are always popular; but I tell more on my own people, the Baptists, than on any other denomination, and I have found them very ready to laugh at themselves. In fact since they are well aware of some of their own characteristics, there are some jokes, both true and apocryphal, I believe they savor a bit more keenly than others.

One I am thinking of is about the couple who moved from the north to a southern city. Several church groups called on them with a view to securing them as members, and eventually they chose one and joined it.

When some Southern Baptists expressed their disappointment to the newcomers, the wife said somewhat wistfully, "We've always wanted to be Southern Baptists, but my husband and I talked it over, and we decided we just aren't physically equal to it."

Once after I had told this in Oklahoma, a friend said, "I'll give you another one to go with that. I know of a church that sent a delegation to the preacher. They said, 'Pastor, you know we're loyal, and we think a lot of you. We want to carry out your program—but we do feel we are entitled to Saturday night off.' "

Some yarns seem to be enjoyed a little more keenly by non-Baptist audiences. Perhaps it is understandable.

One such story, which I began telling thirty years ago and have heard told with variations by other speakers in later years, relates how a Baptist preacher was going home one night after a meeting. In a lonely spot, he was accosted by a highwayman, who pointed a pistol at him, and demanded, "Your money or your life."

Preferring not to argue with a gun, the minister handed over his purse, containing eleven dollars.

The robber counted it, then looked up in disgust. "Is this all you've got?" he asked threateningly.

"Well," said the preacher slowly, "that's all I've got that's mine, and that's all you can have. I am carrying in the other pocket in a little leather pouch three hundred dollars I have taken up as collection for the Mossy Creek Baptist College. But that's the Lord's money. I certainly will not give it to you. The only way you can get it is to kill me and take it off me."

"Well, I ain't going to kill you," said the robber, "and I ain't going to take it off of you, and here's your eleven dollars back. I'm a Baptist myself!"

Another story to which I give a bit of verisimilitude goes like this:

A man from a little community in north Arkansas, calling on my father, said, "Mr. Hays, did you hear about our bad luck? Our preacher done run off with two hundred dollars of the church's money."

Dad expressed the proper sympathy, then asked, "Did you catch him?"

"Yep, he was half way to Little Rock, but we caught him and brought him back."

"What about the money? Did you get that?"

"Nope," said the visitor disconsolately. "He'd done run through it."

"What are you going to do with him?" asked Dad curiously.

"We're going to make him preach it out, every last penny of it."

One of my friends from college days is Chester Lauck, who played the part of Lum Edwards on the radio program of "Lum and Abner." In introducing me at our national Sigma Chi Convention one year, he said "Ole Brooks allus asks me about the Baptist preacher at Pine Ridge and jes today I was able to say this to him: 'Well I went down to hear him Sunday night, and I'll say this about him—once he cleared his throat, took a deep breath, and rared back, he come forth with some of the best out-loud talkin' I ever set under.'"

I have several favorites among the stories that have been effective in making a point.

One I always hang on "Brother Tucker," a middle-aged deacon in our little church. When a merger of the Baptist and Christian

Churches was contemplated, Brother Tucker expressed himself in no uncertain terms:

"I'm a *Baptist*," he declared, "and nobody's gonna make a Christian out of *me!*"

To reinforce the point that the quality of church membership is more important than the quantity, a useful little illustration is the misplaced denominational pride of a country lad who became embroiled with the law. A letter to his mother from the state penitentiary read like this:

Dear Mama,

Don't worry about me down here. I'm getting along all right. They treat me good. And, Mama, you'll be glad to know it's the same here like it is ever'wheres, us Baptists is in the lead.

While I was presiding as president of the Southern Baptist Convention, during the 1959 annual meeting, I used a story to good effect during one of the debates.

A matter of policy was under discussion, and it had reached a difficult stage. Tension among the messengers (delegates) was plainly felt, and the people who packed the great auditorium were getting restless. So many had wanted the floor, they had gotten into a parliamentary tangle, which had to be settled.

Taking the microphone, I said, "The Chair asks your patience. This is all pretty complicated, and he is doing the best he can." Then less formally, I reverted to the first person and said confidentially, "I want to be fair to everybody. I promise I won't run this session like a card game the boys were having over in our hill country."

In deference to my audience, I put in a little apology which had never been in the story before. Baptists view playing cards with disfavor—particularly cards used for gambling, so realizing I had stumbled into a proscribed area, I said "It must have been Rook"—referring to a card game having a very innocent reputation. This struck the audience as being very funny, which was an unexpected bonus.

I went on, "In the middle of the game, one of the players looked up and said sharply, 'Now play the cards fair, Reuben! I know what I dealt you!'"

During my term as Baptist president, I met a dear little lady who said, "Oh, Mr. Hays, I am so happy to meet my shepherd! We don't have bishops, of course, but I call you my shepherd, and I am going to tell them down in Georgia that I met the Shepherd of the sheep."

I then told her about the experience of a minister over in Virginia. He moved from one city to another, where the Rotary Membership Committee came to him and said, "We would like to have you become a Rotarian."

The minister said he would be glad to accept.

The committee then advised him that the classification of Christian minister was filled and asked if he would consider some other classification.

Yes, he said, he would.

Presently they came back with the news that the only opening was that of "hog caller."

"Very well," said the minister. "I will accept that. Over in the city I just left, they called me shepherd of the sheep. But of course you know your people here better than I do."

Another story I have enjoyed telling (changing the locale whenever it suited my purpose) I got from the late Dr. Henry G. Bennett, a native of Arkansas, who became president of Oklahoma A. & M College. One day Dr. Bennett ran into a man he had known over in Arkansas.

"Why, hello, Tom!" he said. "Where are you living now?"

"Over here in Okliehomie," said Tom.

"Well, that's fine! What brought you to Oklahoma?"

"I come on account of my belief."

"Your *belief!* Oh, come now. Arkansas people are not bigoted—they're noted for religious tolerance. What do you mean, 'your belief?' "

"I believed the mule was mine."

A good illustration of the idea that religion has its practical as well as idealistic aspects is an incident that occurred in Yell County, Arkansas. A doleful old deacon, respected by all even though they hated to see him coming, received what was felt to be a merited rebuke when he called on an expiring neighbor who was being kept alive by an oxygen pump.

When the deacon walked into the room, the friend, though

lying under the oxygen tent, was perfectly conscious. The visitor went to the bedside, looked mournfully down, and in a semi-quaver said, "I just want to ask you if there is anything I can do for you during your last hours on this earth."

A spark of indignation came into the sick man's eyes. "Yes," he said feebly, but with an unmistakable tartness in his voice, "you can take your foot off of the oxygen hose!"

Some yarns fit no particular category, but are funny enough to need no pigeonholing. I am fond of the one about two deacons who went fishing on Sunday. Suddenly one of them said, "This is just awful! Here we are playing hooky, and enjoying ourselves, and our pastor's in the pulpit preaching his heart out. We ought to be ashamed."

The other said, "Well, I couldn't have gone to church today anyhow—my wife's sick."

The next day the two friends met on the street. One asked, "Was your wife mad when you got home so late yesterday?"

"Mad! Man, she was plumb *historical*."

"You mean hysterical."

"I mean historical. She brought up things that happened forty years ago!"

A few other favorites speak for themselves:

The grandmother in a certain family got sick. Knowing her reluctance to have a doctor, the family called one without telling her. He was a new doctor in town, and he just showed up and said he had come to see her. He made an examination and a bedside visit and left. Soon one of the daughters went in to see how her mother reacted.

The mother said, "Wasn't that nice of the new preacher to come to see me?"

"No, mother, that was the new doctor."

"*Doctor!*" exclaimed the old lady.

"Yes, he was," admitted the daughter.

"Well," said the old lady reflectively, "I thought he was rather familiar for a preacher."

A minister received a call from the Internal Revenue Department, asking about a member of his church, Mr. Henry Thompson.

"He stated on his income tax return," said the official, "that he had given three hundred dollars last year to the church. Is that correct?"

"I don't have the records here, and I would have to check on it. But I'll say this—*if he didn't he will.*"

A companion piece concerns a lady who called her bank for information. "I want to talk to someone about my bonds," she said.

"For conversion or redemption?" she was asked.

She was silent a moment. Then she said, "Is this the First National Bank or the First Baptist Church?"

An illiterate young mountain preacher had begun to preach with no formal equipment whatever, so uninstructed in the ways of the world that he found himself in the coils of the law without having committed a shockingly criminal act. It was enough of a breach of the statutes, however, to draw a one-year sentence to the Arkansas penitentiary. He fled to Texas (I usually say I don't know why the young man preferred freedom in Texas to jail in Arkansas), where he began to preach in a remote community under an assumed name, thinking his shady past would not be revealed.

However, on the following Sunday, as he was about to begin his sermon, he saw sitting on a back pew a former associate in the penitentiary. He flipped over the pages of the Bible, as he said, "Brethren, under the influence of the Spirit, I'm going to haul off here and change my text."

Looking significantly at the back pew, he said, "My text is," and pretended to read: "If thou seest me and thinkest thou knowest me, say nothing and I will see thee later."

Some years ago the women members of an unsophisticated church declared themselves in favor of installing a chandelier. After they had proposed it, a church conference was held to discuss the matter.

A deacon, representing a faction that opposed this proposal, presented the alternate view.

"We are against this here chandelier proposition for three reasons," he said. "In the first place we couldn't even order one —nobody would know how to spell it! And then even if we got it, there ain't anybody in our congregation that could play it. And third, if we've got a sum of money to lay out, we think what this church needs is a new light fixture."

I have never felt any greater reluctance to enjoy jokes on my denomination than to laugh at myself, and so I did not hesitate to spread it about when I saw something that amused me at Copenhagen, Denmark, when it was host city to the Baptist World Congress.

Another convention was meeting there at the same time, and the city's greeting was hospitably emblazoned on two banners and displayed prominently where they would catch the visitor's eyes when we got off the boat. The juxtaposition might have been thought to be a bit infelicitous, but I enjoyed it, for the two banners, one above the other, read:

"Greetings to the International Association For the Study of Microbes."

"Welcome, Baptists."

My favorite Baptist story is one I told for several years to so many audiences that I met it coming back, whereupon I reluctantly stopped telling it. I believe it to be a true incident, and I just happened to be in the town where and when it occurred.

It was in Abilene, Texas, just after Halloween that I read in the morning paper a little human interest item someone had sent in. A small girl had asked her mother if she couldn't have a "different" costume for that evening. She didn't care to be a devil or a witch or even a ghost; she would rather be an angel. Her mother, entering into the spirit of the occasion, managed a little white costume, and even some heavenly appurtenances in the shape of wings and quivering halo, and after supper she went out with a group of neighborhood small fry.

At one house where she knocked, a man opened the door, saw a very attractive little lady he did not recognize, and exclaimed admiringly, "Well! And who are you?"

"I'm a little angel."

His eyes twinkled, and he decided to tease her a bit. "Is that so? What kind of angel are you?"

She didn't hesitate. "I'm a little Baptist angel."

"Then I think you had better have this great big apple."

He dropped it into her open sack.

She peered down into the paper bag for a long moment, and then raised reproachful eyes.

"You broke every damn cookie in my sack!"

Of course I have been on the receiving end many times, my friends taking the position that (putting it in the vernacular) since I dish it out so frequently I must also be able to take it.

When I was appointed to the Tennessee Valley Authority Board of Directors, a Mississippi editor wrote in his paper, "We don't know how much Mr. Hays knows about flood control or navigation or hydro-electric power, but there's one thing for sure—the Baptists now have access to the largest baptismal pool in all the world!"

During the early days of the Farm Security Administration, when I was often asked to discuss some of the social aspects of the rehabilitation program with church groups, there was considerable pride among Department of Agriculture staff members in the opportunity this afforded the agency to present "the human side" of their work.

When Dr. Robert Montgomery of the University of Texas (on temporary leave for FSA service) was asked about my function, he would always say, "Haven't you heard? Why, he's our Missionary to the Baptists."

An old friend, Joe E. Culpepper, moved an audience in Kansas City, when he once introduced me with the following story:

"One time, when I was driving through Arkansas, I stopped at Russellville for gas, and got into a conversation with the elderly proprietor.

"I believe this is Brooks Hays' boyhood home. Is that right?"

"Yep, that's right."

"Did you know him?"

"Oh, sure. Everybody knowed the boy."

"What kind of boy was he?"

"Well, just an ordinary normal boy."

"Can't you tell me anything special? Anything at all?"

"Well, he loved that little Baptist Church. They just didn't open the doors without finding that boy right there, but it didn't keep him from being an ordinary normal boy. I saw him once

going toward the depot carrying a valise and with a Bible under
his arm.

"I said, 'Where are you going, Brooks?'

"He said, 'Down to New Orleans to the Maddigrass.'

" 'Why you got the Bible?'

" 'Well,' Brooks said, 'If the girls are as pretty as I hear they
are, and if everybody has as good a time as I hear they do
down there, I thought I'd stay over Sunday."

When I have occasion to face other denominational groups, I
usually give them the same treatment I give my Baptist folks. I
think the Presbyterians in these modern times recognize that
their tendency to preserve their historic solemnity makes them
an inviting target, but I try always to respect the limits of good
taste. The Episcopalians, too, with their formality of worship
added to undeniable financial and social superiority, are as
tempting to us of humbler communions as an elegant silk hat
used to be to boys throwing snowballs.

I toss a few verbal snowballs at both groups impartially, not
favoring one above the other. I lean a little toward the Episcopalians when I tell about the visiting clergyman from a very
formal big-city church in the north who preached for the first
time in a southern town. At about his third sentence an elderly
member encouraged him with a loud "A-men!"

The visiting preacher stopped, looked over toward the "amen"
corner, and said politely, "I beg your pardon?"

Another quick gibe at pomposity in the pulpit concerns the
preacher who said condescendingly, when he was speaking on a
verse in Matthew 5, "As our Lord said in the Sermon on the
Mount—and He was right."

These two denominations have not been above firing off shots
at each other, particularly from the home bases of England and
Scotland. Rumor has it that a Scotch Presbyterian labored hard
and brought forth a provocative couplet:

> Pisky, Pisky, boo and bend,
> Up and doon, and up again.

Upon which, an Episcopalian, thus having the last word, mock-
ingly added,

Presby, Presby, dinna bend,
Sit ye doon on man's chief end.

Francis Pickens Miller, famed Virginia Presbyterian with a wry sense of humor tells this one: a backwoods Presbyterian was talking to a neighbor about church work and mentioned John Knox. His friend said, "Who is John Knox?" In shocked accents the other exclaimed, "Man, read your Bible!"

The relationship between economic and political groupings has produced some pleasant and often relevant quips. For example, it was said by one non-Anglican that the Church of England was the Tory party on its knees. And in the United States in a simpler political society it was said that the Presbyterian General Assembly was the Republican party at prayer. In this period, antedating the current patterns when sectarian lines tend to vanish in political organization, it was assumed that Catholic constituents would prefer the Democrats. I once heard two Bostonians chuckle over this conversation:

"Have you heard that Murphy is quitting us to join the Republicans?"

"Oh, I am sure you are mistaken, I saw him at church yesterday!"

Jokes on the Scotch Presbyterians I enjoy doubly, for I like to exercise my Scotch accent.

This one pleases me: In a little Scots Kirk one frosty Sunday morning, an Elder said to his pastor, "Domine, on a bitter-r cauld day like today, 'twould be all r-right for ye to take a wee dr-rap."

The Domine looked wistful, but shook his head. "Nae, Sandy, I canna' do it, for thr-ree reasons. In the fur-rst place, 'twould not be r-right. In the second place, I am pr-reaching on temper-rance. Thirdly—"

He paused. Then, like one closing the door on temptation, said, "I had a wee dr-rap before I left home."

One of the delights of serving on the old time "preaching missions," so popular thirty years ago, was the opportunity to get acquainted with men like Dan Poling and Peter Marshall. Both became my intimate friends and Peter even sought my advice when the Republicans tapped him for the Senate chaplaincy.

"Should I accept?" he came to ask me.

"Why not?" I said.

He was sensitive to the feelings of his friend and fellow pastor Frederick Brown Harris who had served as chaplain for a number of years.

"But," I argued, "it was not inspired by you. The Republicans are making the decision—Dr. Harris will be assured that you have not campaigned for this."

He did accept and his prayers were not only sincere and inspiring—they represented an individual and distinctive approach to the problem of how to pray for a legislative assembly. Few people failed to enter into the spirit of his prayers and few failed to share their fervency and powers.

"Help us Lord to *stand for* something lest we fall for anything" was one prayer, and with petitions like that the minds of senators seldom strayed during the prayers.

Peter Marshall was partly responsible for preserving an incident involving one of his predecessors at New York Avenue Presbyterian Church, Dr. Wallace Radcliffe. William Jennings Bryan, a staunch Presbyterian, occasionally occupied the Lincoln pew.

One Sunday during Dr. Radcliffe's pastorate, soon after the 1896 campaign, when free silver was the issue, just before Dr. Radcliffe left his study to begin the service, one of the elders rushed in to say, "Mr. Bryan is worshipping with us—he is in the Lincoln pew."

The good Doctor was not perturbed. "That's fine," he said, but his mood quickly changed when he stood to read his text and realized that the punch line of his scripture was "Thy silver perish with thee."

Dr. Frederick Brown Harris, who again became the Senate Chaplain after Peter Marshall's death, also possesses a good sense of humor. He told me once that on a wintry Sunday morning he slipped on the ice just as he was entering Foundry Methodist Church, which he served as pastor. Friends helped him to his study and summoned a doctor. His injury was pronounced to be very slight, but word of the accident quickly spread through the congregation, and when he read his scripture, he suddenly realized that it was an unhappy coincidence. The congregation laughed uproariously when he read "the wicked stand in slippery places."

Peter Marshall was succeeded at the famous New York Avenue Presbyterian Church in Washington, D.C., by another able Scotch preacher, Dr. George Dockerty. The church's fame was firmly established when Abraham Lincoln attended it. He never joined, but the old fashioned uncomfortable pew where he sat is marked with a plate, and special guests are often seated there. After one evening, in which my pastor and I squirmed through a long service, he said he could quite understand now why Lincoln never joined!

A Presbyterian minister is believed to have inquired of an elder of this church why they must always go to Scotland for their preachers. "We've got good preachers on this side of the Atlantic," he complained. "Why don't you give us a chance?"

"Well, it's the accent," the other admitted.

"The *accent?*"

"Yes. It makes a difference. If you were going to talk about Barnabas, let us say, you might begin, 'Brethren, I take as my text, "And Barnabas was a good man."' That's not the way a Scotsman does it! He would begin, 'Beloved—I take as my text this mor-rning those thr-r-rilling wor-rds, "And Bairnybas was a gude mon!"' Oh, yes, it makes a difference."

I once heard Danny Thomas say, in the course of a humorous address, that someone had lodged a complaint with him for neglecting the Lutherans when he distributed his birdshot about the church-going landscape.

His answer was, "I just never saw a funny Lutheran."

Now I think this is unfair, and to prove it I'll just cite the Lutheran preacher who confessed to his congregation one Sunday as follows:

"My friends, something unfortunate has happened. My sermon was all ready and lying on my study table last night. This morning I found it on the floor, chewed to bits by my daughter's puppy. So, being without a prepared message, I shall have to preach as the Lord directs. But I promise to do better next Sunday."

Stories that adherents of the three major faiths have told on each other are legion, and form part of the conversational repertoire of people of all countries. It would be repetitious and unrewarding to retell here the fictitious ones, for they have gone the rounds.

With respect to the Catholics I shall limit myself to two favorite samples, one old and one new.

Forty years ago, in Chicago, I attended a dinner where Cardinal Mundelein was guest of honor, and the following story was told:

The Cardinal was in his chauffeur-driven limousine which was going down Michigan Boulevard at excessive speed. He was stopped by a traffic officer, who took out his book to give the driver a ticket.

He had only wet his pencil, however, when the prelate in his churchly robes opened the rear door and inquired, "What's the trouble?"

The book was snapped shut and back in the officer's pocket in a twinkling.

"Oh, no trouble at all, Your Eminence!" the policeman said, "I was just warnin' the driver there was a Protestant cop on the next corner."

The more recent story concerns a mischievous priest who was fond of teasing. One day he called a nun on the phone and, disguising his voice, said, "Sister Margaret, this is Martin Luther."

Sister Margaret was more than a match for him. "Well, Brother Martin," she asked sweetly, "where in hell are you?"

An experience of my own—which I have enjoyed telling, particularly to Catholic audiences who have never failed to appreciate the humor of it—took place in Colombia, South America. I was president of the Southern Baptist Convention, and accompanied by my wife, I visited Baptist missions in several South American countries in 1958. One Sunday evening we were in a small Baptist Church, where the service was in Spanish. The pastor acknowledged my presence, making a little speech about me to the congregation, not a word of which I could understand, until with a flourish of his hand, palm up, he said, "El Papa!"

I whispered to the missionary who was with us, "It's a bit embarrassing to have El Mama sitting here by me!"

One of my dear Catholic friends in Congress was Representative Eugene McCarthy, now senator from Minnesota. He made some devastating comments about my ecclesiastical office, to which I was elected while still one of his colleagues.

"I observe," he said, "that following Brooks' elevation to the 'papacy,' he leans more and more toward the idea of infallibility!" This gibe went over so well among our colleagues, that he included it in an interview for a national magazine, adding that other communions should not view this dogma with alarm. "If the Pope really is infallible, then there is nothing to worry about. If not—well, we are no worse off than the Baptists under Brooks."

On the subject of Jewish and Christian relations I find it somewhat difficult to avoid solemnity. If this seems out of keeping with my theme, let me defend it by suggesting that I cannot help getting a bit serious at the mention of our Biblical heritage, in which the Jewish people had such a substantial part. The impulses of humor in this area are therefore a bit restrained. Let me defend it by a reminder that laughter and tears are never very far apart.

My strong feelings regarding anti-Semitism, going back to college days, account partly for my practice of avoiding Jewish stories. Many of these stories are genuinely funny and carry no hurt, but it is better to leave the telling of them to those of Jewish faith unless one can be sure a story lies entirely outside the stereotype.

I have been extremely fortunate in finding enriching associations with Jews. I served for many years on the Board of the National Conference of Christians and Jews with Roger Strauss, son of Oscar Strauss, one of the famous trio whose father established the family base in New York City in the nineteenth century. The others, Nathan and Isidore, were, like Oscar, highly successful in business, philanthropy, civic leadership, and other lines of endeavor. My friend Roger Strauss was named for Roger Williams, one of our Baptist heroes, and herein lies a story. It began in Talbotton, Georgia, a small town in the central part of the state.

Some years ago my friend Weyman Huckabee, then a vice president of Wesleyan College in Macon, was conveying me from the Columbus airport to his campus when I suddenly realized we were passing through Talbotton.

He says that I shouted, "Stop the car."

He was curious about my excitement and quite interested in the story of the Strauss family, as I later gave him the details, including the legendary aspects that Baptists enjoy repeating.

As I opened the car door, I said, "I want to see if the history of Oscar Strauss' stay in this town has been properly noted."

I had to look only a few moments to find a marker. It carried an appropriate sketch of the little family's residence in that rural area. Not recorded, however, was the fact that in 1858, when the father brought the family to Talbotton, there was no synagogue in the community, for they were probably the only ones of Jewish faith in the area. Wanting religious instruction for his lads, he sent them (aged thirteen, eleven, and eight) to the little Baptist Sunday School. They remained true to their Hebrew faith, however, and re-established their formal ties to the synagogue a few years later, when they moved to New York City.

It is not claiming too much for the Baptists, I trust, to suggest that Oscar Strauss' interest in Roger Williams began in Talbotton, for living among Baptists he gained lasting impressions of the struggle for religious liberty led by one Baptist hero.

As a result, when Oscar found the time to record his appreciation of Roger Williams, he produced a book on the subject, and then he named his son Roger Williams Strauss.

My friendship with that son, who was not of my religious faith nor of my political faith, is one of many symbols of our nation's pluralism, and represents a link between Baptists and Jews, which should be invoked whenever a bigot belittles or assails the faith of Israel.

The sadness I felt in my boyhood when I read of the tragic, though beautifully inspiring, death of Roger Strauss' father and mother in 1912 persists till this day.

They were on the Titantic, and the mother would not leave her husband when offered a place in a lifeboat as the great vessel was sinking. She was in his arms as it went out of sight.

Georgia and the Baptists should be proud of that chapter in the Strauss family history, and a knowledge of it should shame every utterance or action tinged with intolerance.

It has been said by one historian that two of the great theologians of the nineteenth century were "politicians named Lincoln and Jefferson."

I have an addendum: "And one of the great politicians of the twentieth century was a theologian named John." (I use the term "politician," of course, in its broadest and finest sense.) Pope John released powerful forces in our world that will have significance for all time to come.

One of the high points of my career was a private audience with him in 1961. The effect upon my wife was hypnotic. My former congressional colleagues were still occasionally calling me "the Baptist Pope" (a flippant but not irreverent allusion to my two-year presidency of the largest Baptist Convention in the world), and having noted the expression on her face during our audience, I said to her later, "You were adoring the wrong Pope." She had an adorable look herself, wearing a black lace mantilla supplied by Monsignor Ligutti. She hung on every word the friendly little pontiff was saying.

His greeting revealed his marvelous gift for establishing rapport, "Mr. Hays, I know that you are a Baptist and that Baptists and Catholics have not always been as cordial toward each other as Christians should be, but I am Baptist too—I am John. . . ."

(To the rabbis who once visited him he said, "I am your brother Joseph.")

I recall little that was said otherwise in our historic meeting. (I was the first of the Baptist denominational officers to be privileged to meet him in private audience. Later, when I met Pope Paul, the Religious News Service reported that I was the only Protestant layman to have had private audience with both Popes John and Paul, though I must now share the honor with President Johnson.)

The climax of the talk with Pope John was his statement to me, "We are brothers in Christ." For the head of a church which at one time had made much of the doctrine, "Outside the Church there is no salvation," this was an utterance to strengthen the spiritual bonds between us. I have enjoyed relating this to Baptists in the interest of a sound ecumenicity not universally favored by my fellow churchmen. (Some of them say that I am their most vocal "ecumaniac.")

Pope John's humanness was further revealed in his inquiry about our children. I told him that we had a lawyer son, and a daughter who was celebrating her birthday that very day.

It did not escape him, for when we were telling him goodbye he said, "It is my practice in my afternoon prayers to mention persons by name, and I shall pray for you and your family, particularly for the daughter whose birthday it is."

Later, on his birthday, I walked into St. Peter's Cathedral in our block and prayed for him, especially that if he were taken (he was in his last illness), the sweet beneficent spirit we identified with him might continue to bless the human family and be a lasting force for unity.

Monsignor Ligutti, the Pope's adviser on rural life, placed me under heavy debt in arranging the two audiences. I had known him in the United States—our friendship having begun in the thirties when he was a parish priest in Granger, Iowa, and I was working on problems of low-income farmers. A believer in the sanctity of humor and a practitioner of humor in his priestly duties, it seemed highly appropriate that Pope John would have at the Vatican this beloved and amiable helper.

The stories about Pope John build up and circulate rapidly. Many are legendary. One of my favorites is based, I believe, on an actual conversation. Pope John is reported to have asked an American soldier his rank and when told that he was a corporal, the Pope said, "Now that's about the same rank I had in the First World War, and I got so tired of taking orders from lieutenants, I decided I'd get where I could give orders, and I made it."

A companion story is probably not true, but it would have produced a broad smile on his countenance. Attributed to him is this statement: "I was a pompous corporal, and I became a corpulent pontiff."

My visit with Pope Paul had gratifying aspects too, but it lacked the liveliness of the talk with John XXIII. Pope John's successor is a good conversationalist. He responded appropriately to my greetings from President Johnson, and as in the case of my first Vatican visit, I learned that the host has excellent briefings. Pope Paul knew that I was in route to a meeting of

Protestant chaplains in Germany, and he asked me to say to them that he would pray for the success of our meeting. He requested Father Stransky of Milwaukee—one of Cardinal Bea's aides in the ecumenical program, whose assignment was to interpret for us (something that we did not need)—to arrange for me to attend the Council meeting next day.

Outside, Father Stransky said, "The Holy Father doesn't know how much he has put on me to get you in—it will take about five signatures."

I silenced him quickly, "Now look here, Father," I said (he is barely half my age), "Don't you weaken on me—with a personal invitation from Pope Paul, I'm going to that meeting!" And he seemed really pleased that I was that excited about it.

At a press conference at the United States Embassy on the next day, I told newsmen about it. I even described the Mass in nonecclesiastical terms (my knowledge of Catholic nomenclature is quite limited). It was an awesome ceremony, viewed from my front row seat in the visitors section only a few feet from the dais. While the Latin could not penetrate my cerebral incrustations, there were moments, as in the recital of the Lord's prayer, when I felt like a participant.

I explained this to the newsmen. Having paid tribute to Cardinal Cushing and others who reflected a devotion to religious liberty, I could say without offending that I seemed "transported to Baptist meetings where that engaging subject is often discussed."

"But," I said, "in the devotional session I felt as if I were in a Quaker service—the mood of quiet reverence was so penetrating." I added something else, resorting to a pun. "I am not catering to the Quakers, of course. When I was in Congress, I did not have a single Quaker in my district and in 1958 not enough friends!"

The interpreter said, after some understanding smiles from the Americans, "Mr. Hays, I won't even attempt a translation of that one."

We disciples of this philosophy of humor in religion have strong support from eminent theologians who believe that it is theologically wise to encourage humor in the exercises of faith. They distinguish between solemnity and stuffiness.

One of the most respected authorities in this field is Dr. Elton Trueblood, professor at Earlham College, who believes that humor has divine approbation and offers documentation of the teachings of Jesus to prove it in his book, *Christ and Humor*.

Thus I conclude that laughter in the sanctuary is quite consistent with the spirit of the liturgy and that humor is indeed the saving grace.

7

Vacancy in Paradise: Academia

MY EXPERIENCES as Arthur T. Vanderbilt Professor at Rutgers University, and later as visiting professor of Practical Politics at the University of Massachusetts, gave me time to reflect upon the vicissitudes and triumphs (yes, there were a few) of my forty years in public service. Still, the time to rest had not arrived—only to take stock and pause to look out upon our distraught world, mustering my faith in its moral solvency, and plucking from the store of memories, laughter and perhaps some slight enrichments.

It was in this period that I was impressed by the fact that knowledge is never in compartments, and the various areas of mental activity bear a close relationship. As a politician, I had often silently deplored the inability of the profession to provide a sense of specialization; we are generalists, having to know a little about a lot of things. Without aspiring to expertness I have nevertheless made a mild claim to being a multi-specialist as a result of the browsing I have done in many fields during these four decades. At least one New Jersey newspaper man accorded me this status. In a press conference he introduced his question like this, "Mr. Hays, you are a lawyer, a former congressman, an author, a former president of a great Baptist Convention, and a professor. If I asked, 'Will the *real* Brooks Hays please stand up?' which one would respond?"

I was about to say "politician," but I had hesitated a moment and during the pause my wife spoke. "An Arkansas social worker," she said, and that added a little more confusion. Still, I liked her answer, and I gave to the newsmen her reasons for interjecting that idea.

As a bride she had gone with me to live in Russellville and observed both my struggle as a young lawyer trying to make a living by my profession and my constant temptation to divert too much energy to the problems of the poor, particularly the rural poor.

This consuming interest followed me to the state house, where I served for two years as assistant attorney general. In Little Rock, I not only had an outlet in my official assignment as attorney for the supervisor of juvenile courts, but as president of the Tuberculosis Association, and finally as president of the State Conference of Social Work.

These varied interests, law, politics, church, social work and classroom, some of which I have pursued simultaneously, justify the reference to my life having been spent in five worlds. This was made possible by the interrelationship of five areas of living.

It is trite to speak of the folly of letting knowledge be put in compartments, but we Americans, with our zeal for specialization, find ourselves tolerating the reluctance of specialists to share knowledge with the non-elite. Then the problem of semantics arises. The experts prefer their own jargon, and we ordinary people have to have their technical words translated into the vulgate.

In politics, the commerce in ideas has a substantial difficulty when we come to the matter of relating moral and religious resources to the governmental and social issues that plague us. We abhor pietistic politicians. Moreover, the doctrine of separation of Church and State has validity, and must be respected. It is very hard to keep away from this structural area in speculating upon the confluence of religion and politics.

The academician, though generally a bit unorthodox, usually agrees with one of the great scholars of all time, Blaise Pascal, who said, "God has put religion into the mind by reason and into the heart by grace." Incidentally, the professor is saying some timely things to the clergy these days, and the academic person has had enough experience struggling with faculty and campus politics to establish rapport with the professional politician.

Hence, the educator can be a valuable part of the catalyzing forces in society. He can enter other areas without being suspect, unless, being an honorable man, he must disavow detachment, once he has decided to participate overtly in political pursuits.

American politics is full of examples of professors who made good in that field. And more recently there is a flow in the other direction.

President Johnson took an interest in my excursion into academia, indicating that he would enjoy returning to San Marcos, Texas, college campus which he loved as an undergraduate. If he does, he would very likely have the same problem that I have, wanting to give every student an A. That's the politician in us. I related to the President the incident of the finest apple-polishing job I ever heard of by a student. At the bottom of the examination paper was this personal message, "Professor Hays, I am not proud of my performance on this examination. It does not meet my standards, but you see I was up all night. At 6 o'clock this morning, my wife gave birth to a little girl. I was so disappointed! I wanted a boy. I intended to name him for you." A-plus was the best I could do for him!

I can sympathize with those who are responsible for establishing the measurements for excellence. Still, gradations of progress can be fairly uniform. It has been discovered in a survey of law school graduates, for example, for a period which included my senior year, that the A students are still there; they are teaching. The B students are practicing law and are a credit to the profession. The C students are making money in business, and the D students are in Congress.

Currently, this matter of grades engages some good professional minds. I like what one critic of present indexes advances —the idea of *sine laude* honors. If "with honors" is a proper reward, and it certainly is, we ought to work out something for the lads at the bottom who barely make it, not because they don't try, but because being far *below* number two they have to try harder just to stay in the game! Life in this transitory vale of tears will never find us mortals distributing rewards and honors with perfect justice. We should, however, seek an approximation of it.

Occasionally, one encounters an instructor who exhibits a

talent for discovering the latent qualities of excellence in a student. When coupled with the ability to encourage the ones who lack the ability to learn quickly or even to absorb the basic lessons, this marks a teacher for distinction.

I recall, for example, an Arkansas teacher whose classroom I visited, accompanied by her principal. In the course of this brief visit she said to one of her pupils, "Otto, will you please raise the window?" This he promptly did and, in his hearing, she said to us, "I don't know what I would do without Otto. He is the only one who can raise that window."

There was immediately imparted to him an appreciation of his superiority in this simple skill. In the usual tests there was evidence that he lagged. As the principal walked down the corridor, he commented on the teacher's perceptiveness and added—"You see, the window didn't need raising—Otto needed to raise the window. He needed recognition."

In 1943 I was invited as a new member of Congress to appear on a radio program, which was then a continuing series known as "Coffee with Congress," conducted by Bill Herson.

A group of radio men came with all their paraphernalia, which was set up in our dining room. There was coffee, for the background clink of cups and saucers gave it a desired realism, but no one really had time to drink any. It was supposed to be a relaxed, informal chat over the coffee cups, and my wife was told to be herself and comment just as she would if Mr. Herson were a neighbor.

He said, "Congressman, have you ever participated in athletics? Did you, for example, play football in college?"

This struck my wife as funny, and just being herself, as she'd been told, she giggled. As Mr. Herson looked questioningly at her, she said, "I was just thinking how he looked in those days. You see, when I knew him first—that was when he was a freshman at the University of Arkansas—he only weighed one hundred and ten pounds. He was tall, but as slender as a toothpick. He couldn't have played football."

To this I replied reproachfully, "Now, honey, wait a minute! You're doin' me wrong. I *did* play football in high school! I was substitute center on Russellville's third team, and I played fifty-five seconds in the Thanksgiving game with Dardanelle!"

I found after the program was aired that I had at least one sympathetic listener. My office adjoined that of Congressman George Bates of Massachusetts, and his secretary, Wilfred Pellitier, referred to it frequently with tears in his voice. If I were to meet him today after twenty-three years, I believe he would shake his head sadly and say, "Only fifty-five seconds! They didn't let him play even a full minute."

I barely managed to escape graduating from high school in short pants (no one ever said "trousers" around Russellville in 1915). I was one of nine boys in the senior class, all of whom with the single sad exception of myself had a physical stature befitting their age and status. In those days, long pants were never worn by boys, and in physical appearance I was more boy than man. But I felt that the ignominy of being the only boy to graduate in short pants would be too bitter to be borne, and I managed to bring my parents around to my point of view in time for the graduation ceremonies. I judge that my appearance in that beautiful new suit must still have left something to be desired, for on a visit to Little Rock a strange boy who passed me on the street managed a greeting and an insult in two words, "Hi, Breeches."

I received no fraternity bids in my first weeks at college, though a friend confidentially passed on the information to me that the Sigma Chis were interested and would want me "when I grew up." That they changed their time-table and pledged me that fall was probably due less to any radical change in my appearance than to the interest of a few other fraternities.

The fact that I was not only gauche, but shy, in those first months of my fraternity life makes one of my experiences, which I recall with mingled emotions, especially ridiculous. Our chapter had the practice of conducting criticism sessions, the purpose being to point out to individual members that their conduct could be improved.

Soon after my initiation, the evening arrived for the first of these counseling meetings. The first one to take his place in the center of the circle for the customary criticism was a popular junior, Tracy Harrell. The older members had very perfunctory comments to offer; there wasn't much they could say to improve the habits of this admirable student. Unfortunately, no one had told me that the freshmen were not supposed to participate as critics and that any request for a comment regarding the habits or character of the brother being panned was a mere act of courtesy.

So, before the chapter's presiding officer, James Winn, asked Brother Harrell to return to his place in the circle, he turned politely to me as if it were an afterthought, and said, "Brother Hays, do you have any criticism to offer of our brother, Tracy Harrell?"

I know, now, that my answer created consternation and embarrassment. Instead of politely disavowing any such notion, I startled the assembled brothers by saying, "Yes, Brother Winn, I do." Then, turning to the junior in the center of the circle, I went brashly on. "You know, Brother Harrell, I think you use too many cuss words. You ought not to be going around our chapter house all the time using these swear words." Then, raising a finger as the prophet Jeremiah might have done, I said, "Now, you take this little word 'damn' . . ."

That was as far as I ever got. The thirty or more Sigma Chi brothers who had been sitting in a bemused silence akin to paralysis, suddenly, as if at a signal, erupted into a guffaw that might have been heard a mile away. The whole house seemed to shake. Some of the less dignified brothers actually fell out of their chairs.

Only two of us were not laughing. I was aware, too late, of my presumptuousness, and I realized even in that moment that I would never be allowed to forget it. My embarrassment was overwhelming. I wanted to rush to an exit, but I was frozen in my chair. The laughter seemed interminable. It was painful beyond description. All I could do was wait.

The other who did not laugh was Tracy. He just sat there, deadpan, staring back at his convulsed brothers, for all the world like a dignified Great Dane watching a group of frolicsome puppies make fools of themselves.

I was glad I didn't know what he was thinking.

Then came the most refreshing and welcome statement, I am confident, an upper-classman ever uttered to rescue a floundering

freshman. When he could make himself heard, still without changing expression, in a clear voice vibrant with feeling, Tracy said to me, "Let 'em laugh, damn their souls! I love you, and I appreciate you!"

In my second year at the university, I roomed in Buchanan Hall, the oldest of the dormitories, and my roommate was Orland Leach, one of the most remarkable men I have ever known. I thought of him as a man, as indeed he was, for, due to circumstances, he had a difficult time completing the preparation courses for entering the university, and he was among the oldest students in his class. He was at least half a dozen years older than I.

His home had been deep in the Ozark country, some twenty-five miles from the county seat, in a hill-country village that supplied only the most meager institutional services. His early schooling had been rather barren, but he made up for it by vigorous application to his studies and collateral reading, which his imagination and ambition dictated. His rugged life showed in a countenance that reminded me of Lincoln, and his language, like Lincoln's, was colorful and interesting. He was one of the most intellectually honest men I ever knew, and there was an essential goodness in him that was always shining through. Perhaps his character was like that of the one who inspired Jesus to say, "The earth of itself bringeth forth fruit."

Orland was a science student, while I was interested in history and political science and literature. I was interested, too, in the YMCA and the church. Orland was too busy with his physics and mathematics and laboratory experiments to take time out for church activities. Besides, he was not sure that his beliefs about religion were definite enough to justify his making any public avowals of faith. He knew the rules of logic. He was familiar with the methods of confirming or negating a hypothesis. He liked to underscore the *QED* at the end of his experiments. With religious principles it was different. So we argued.

He was patient with me, but the aggressiveness, which most young Baptists of my temperament displayed, must have been a bit irritating, as I pressed my case for a formal commitment upon this uncommitted friend. But he stood his ground, insisting that I was advancing mere theories as facts, and that my "proof" was not impressive.

"Are you *sure?*" he would say. Or, "What tests have you applied to this point?" and "What is the compelling evidence that you are right?"

His avoidance of any semblance of dogmatism was one of his most pronounced characteristics. I challenged him on this one day with a point which I thought might strengthen my side. I pointed to an iron bed in the corner of our room.

It was not an ordinary bed. In those days the university charged us sixteen dollars a month for board, room, and laundry, and for that extortionate figure they did not even supply furniture for the male students. We bought it as freshmen, shopping around for bargains from departing seniors, and when our time came to leave the honored halls we sold it for as much as we could get for it. The bed was our best bargain. It had cost us three dollars. We were so proud of it that we never referred to it simply as the bed, but always reverently as "the three-dollar bed."

On this particular day, when I was trying to goad Orland into some admission or other, I taunted him by saying, "You're so undogmatic, you wouldn't let me say the three-dollar bed can't walk!"

"Well," he answered, "science would not put it like that." Then, without pausing for breath or having to struggle for a phrase to express his idea, he said, "There are no rules known to science whereby in the absence of applied external force the three-dollar bed can change its location; but if without notice the bed should walk out of this room, instead of denying it had occurred, science would begin an exploration of the exciting new forces which had produced such a remarkable phenomenon." And he was only a sophomore!

After World War I broke out, and we went into the armed services, I did not see him for years. In the meantime, he had been a captain of artillery, and after the war had become a professor of science in a great southern college.

When we did finally meet, he said, "I have news for you. I found out in my own way and by my own methods, that you were right—the really vital things of life cannot be measured in laboratories or stated in physical terms. They belong to the realm of the spirit."

Then, summing up his meaningful experience with a capsule use of his mathematical jargon, he said, "You see, Brooks, I am no longer a fraction. I have become an integer."

He died young, at only forty-seven, and while his memory is tinged with grief, I have always been grateful for this association, and for the ideas symbolized by the three-dollar bed.

Law school days in Washington were too hectic for the relaxed enjoyment of campus humor. In fact, George Washington Law School had no campus and little extracurricular activity to supply relief from routine government employment and from prosaic classroom lectures.

The government work week was longer than today, and not even Saturday provided a respite. Classes were conducted six evenings a week. But when the law class ended at seven on Saturday evening, we students were generally found working our way, after a hasty dinner, to the top gallery of a musical show or a movie.

I recall with amusement our first Saturday night, in the summer of 1919. I was the first of half a dozen Arkansas boys to get jobs in Washington, preparatory to entering law school in the fall. Congressman Jacoway of Arkansas had secured a job for me in the Treasury Department.

Someone asked me, "What do you do there?"

I said, "I just count twenty dollar bills eight hours a day, six days a week, and on Saturday night I get one of 'em." I went through the usual motions of counting bills, licking my thumb, and finally shuffling one off to the side. While this account of my labors was a bit fanciful, it was not far from being factual.

Bolon Turner was the first of my Arkansas friends to join me in this adventure—law school combined with a government job. We had rooms near Dupont Circle in a typical three-story row house with a gracious landlady, who took an interest in her "Arkansas boys." Then others came—Joe Barrett, M. L. Miles, Robert Hood, Bobbie Robertson, a congenial Norwegian from Minnesota, and always a floating member or two of our Arkansas colony.

On the first Saturday evening after our group had increased to six, we had had the bargain seventy-five-cent three-course dinner at Fred Sargent's on Fourteenth Street, and standing in a huddle at the Pennsylvania Avenue intersection, we discussed plans for the evening "What'll we do?" was the question to be answered.

I would be more than willing to forget this episode, especially my contribution to the discussion, but Bolon never would let me. For years he told it, in the most libelous fashion, to regale our friends.

"Brooks was the first to come up with a suggestion," Bo would usually begin.

" 'Well, fellows, I think we should take advantage of some of the educational and cultural opportunities that we have here. It's a very wonderful privilege to live in our capital city, and I suggest we make the most of it.' "

As Bolon warmed to his theme with each retelling, I sounded more and more like a prig, but nothing could ever stop him!

" 'Now, for example, there is the Library of Congress, which has a most attractive reading room. And if we become tired of books and magazines and newspapers, we can look at the marvelous murals. It will be a treat, I'm sure.' "

Assuming the role of chairman, Bolon had asked if there was a second to the motion. There was no second. "Any other suggestions?"

There had been—the Gayety Burlesque Theatre on Ninth Street.

"Now, we wanted to be fair and democratic about it," Bolon would say, "so we put it to a vote. The Gayety got five votes, and the Library of Congress one. And so we 'took advantage' of one of our 'opportunities.' If it was not very cultural, at least it might be called educational. And the funniest thing of all was to watch Brooks—he laughed louder than any of us!"

Since 1958, when my Congressional duties ended, I have had more time to indulge my interest in student life, particularly since accepting the Arthur T. Vanderbilt Professorship at Rutgers in 1964, and changing the White House relationship from full-time staff member to consultant. I have had the privilege, during the last few years, of speaking to student groups on more than two hundred campuses, all the way from Assumption College in Massachusetts to the University of the Pacific, in California. In 1963 the Methodist Board of Higher Education asked me to give a series of talks on the application of Christian ethics to contemporary political and social problems at each of sixteen Methodist colleges all the way across the South. To do this, I asked leave from the White House. President Kennedy quickly agreed. As we walked to the door, he said, "Brooks, you've already got the Baptists—are you trying to take over the Methodists, too?"

"Mr. President," I answered, "nobody ever had the Baptists! And I'm afraid I will find the Methodists just as stubborn."

Student contacts are exhilarating. These college assignments have not only given me a lot of pleasure but have provided outlets for my desire to help students who are interested in political careers. My work as a faculty member at the two state universities has been particularly satisfying. I had not realized until I had the tours of duty at Rutgers and the University of Massachusetts that such contentment would be possible this side of Paradise—which reminds me that the title of this chapter needs explaining.

There is a motor court near Fort Smith, Arkansas, named Paradise Inn. As I passed it one evening in my car with my friend, Warren Cikins, I noticed its attractiveness and mentioned it to Warren.

He was more interested in the "no vacancy" sign. "What—no vacancy in Paradise?" he exclaimed. "How sad!"

My answer, prompted by the fullness of my contentment, was, "But as long as visiting professorships are available at colleges like my two, life is so good here, Paradise can wait!"

I have tried to avoid the attitudes that sometimes make student-teacher relations formal and forbidding. I like students to assume that informal comments are welcome. Sometimes there is surprising brashness in a student's remark, as for example when I was at Ouachita College in Arkansas to give the commencement address. It was a terribly hot afternoon (the thermometer stood above 110°) and students, faculty, and staff were suffering in their black robes. My own discomfort was diminished by concern over my speech. I was concentrating on it as we approached the chapel. Stately organ music set the tempo for the academic procession, and the mood of reverence and solemnity captured me. I was just entering the chapel when one of the seniors leaned over and audibly counseled with me, provoking a laugh in the line behind us. "Do us a favor," this unknown senior besought me, "cut it short."

On almost every campus I visit, something occurs to confirm my admiration for modern student character, and my appreciation of student imagination.

There is, of course, an understandable uniformity in the language, customs, and even the traditions on American campuses, and each reflects many aspects of contemporary mores and attitudes. The lines of communication must be pretty efficient. Still, there are "localisms" that make for individuality.

The spate of football stories that found circulation on and off campus some years ago seemed to mushroom. Usually the details were similar, and only the punch lines varied. One of these hung on the idea of a friendly professor rescuing a dull student, who was a brilliant fullback, from flunking a course and thereby being disqualified for the team. One little variation of this story I have remembered for twenty years.

The cooperative professor was giving the dull player a special oral examination, the coach sitting by the student to inspire and encourage him.

Professor: What's the capital of California?
Answer: Davis.
Professor: Too bad. I intended to pass you if you could answer that one correctly, but that's wrong.
Coach: Wait a minute, Professor! Sacramento's the capital. Davis is twenty-five miles from it. Twenty-five from one hundred is seventy-five. Seventy is passing!
Professor: You're right. He passes.

I find, too, that on every campus, stories at the dean's expense are popular. I even find the deans repeating them! A sample is one given me by Dean Stephen Bailey of Syracuse University.

Question by a visitor to the campus: And what is your assignment at the university?
Answer: I'm a Deano.
Visitor: A Deano? What's a deano?
Answer: I don't know, but whenever I say a dean, people say "O."

Another dean told me this one, which makes the poor assistant deans wince:

Question: What is an assistant dean?
Answer: A mouse trying to be a rat.

The tables turned a bit with this little aphorism: The function of the president is to do the talking, the faculty is to do the thinking, and the dean is to keep the president from thinking and the faculty from talking.

One of the delights of my post-Congressional activity is to visit these American campuses, and I have had my share of opportunities. On every campus a visitor will be told about the school's graduates or former students who have achieved fame. At Allegheny College, in Meadville, Pennsylvania, he will be told about President McKinley and the cow that was somehow got into "the tower," a prank for which he was said to be responsible. I felt quite complimented when an alumnus said to me, after learning of my Grandfather Hays' association with William McKinley at the college, "I'll bet your grandfather helped get that cow up there."

At Randolph Mason College in Ashland, Virginia, the students were pleased to hear me quote Walter Hines Page, and they lost no time in letting me know that he was one of their "boys." The line I quoted was that brief indictment of the South: "Next to fried food, the South has suffered most from oratory."

The colleges outside the Ivy League, and without the long history and big endowments that some can boast, have their distinguished alumni to point to with pride.

Such historic institutions as Harvard, Yale, and Princeton have the advantage over our younger hinterland colleges, but we can often speak proudly of a faculty member who has a more prominent identification with us than with his own alma mater.

I recall Dr. Charles Hillman Brough, for example, a native of Mississippi and graduate of Baptist institutions in that state. He was professor of economics at the University of Arkansas when elected governor of Arkansas in 1916. He was a popular orator and, after becoming governor, often returned to Fayetteville for brief visits. He was invariably asked to speak and invariably he used this peroration:

"The harp strings of memory strike a tender chord tonight as I come back to the city of Fayetteville, which I love most of all, and see the people, whom I love most of all. Fayetteville, third oldest city in the state and home of some of its most distinguished citizens, home of the University of Arkansas—Arkansas!—greatest commonwealth in the galaxy of sovereign powers, whose star shines out from our flag like the brightest orb of celestial night."

Also, somewhere in his speech, there would appear this expression of hope for his student auditors, "And now my young friends, as you go out into the world to grasp the skirts of happy chance, may your stream of life unruffled run and the roses bloom for you without a thorn."

His warmth was exuded not only on the platform, but in personal contacts as well. Given the slightest opening, he would identify himself to any stranger and revel in every opportunity for conversation. During my tours of duty in Washington in the thirties, he once invited me to eat lunch with him at Ewarts Cafeteria at Thirteenth and F Streets. As we started down the line with our trays, he saluted the young lady waiting on us, "Miss Myrtle, I want you to meet my young friend from Arkansas, The Honorable Brooks Hays, former assistant attorney general of our state, the Democratic National Committeeman from Arkansas and currently assistant to Dr. Rexford G. Tugwell, the Undersecretary of Agriculture."

Miss Myrtle smilingly acknowledged the introduction and we moved on to the vegetables. Again the gretting, "Miss Frances, I want you to meet my young friend from Ark. . . ." and again, a pleasant acknowledgement.

At the salad counter, "Miss Claudia, this is my. . . ."

Finally, at the dessert section we came upon a new employee and the governor's salutation was a bit different. "Young lady,

I am Charles Hillman Brough, wartime governor of Arkansas and presently a member of the Boundary Commission for Virginia and the District of Columbia, and this is my young friend from Arkansas, the Honorable Brooks Hays, former assistant attorney general. . . ."

The young lady was in the act of dipping into a huge ice cream container, and without straightening, she listened in bewilderment to this unconventional introduction. At last, she pulled herself together, and still firmly holding the ice cream dipper suspended in mid air, she smiled cheerfully and said, "Well, how do you do, Governor Brough. I am delighted to meet you. I am Mary Jones, of Richmond, Virginia. I just arrived this morning to work here and it's a pleasure to meet you and your friend Mr. Hays."

I wanted to say, "Bravo"—perhaps I should have—but I was not as composed as the new girl—I just said (but with sincerity) "Glad to meet you, Miss Mary."

So anything can happen in Washington.

At the University of Arkansas in the quiet pre-World War I days, we occasionally saw distinguished people. I remember the thrill of hearing William Howard Taft speak during that period. It would not have detracted from the impressions of that experience had I known then what I learned later—that he was forced by the necessities of his personal situation, there being no provision by the government at that time for former Presidents, to go on the lecture platform, often traveling great distances to meet engagements.

In Washington, students become somewhat inured to glimpses of the great. The first of the notables of whom I remember having a close-up view was Uncle Joe Cannon, who was elected to Congress in the early 1870's and was still a member of the House in 1919, when I entered law school. A year later, when I served on the debating team, Uncle Joe agreed to act as chairman, and did a very good presiding job for one in his eighties. He made one little flub, which may have embarrassed some people present, but not the congressman from Illinois. There was a short musical prelude, which Uncle Joe had to introduce. He said, "Mrs. Russell Smith will now sing a duet."

When she had finished her *solo*, the famous old gentleman

looked at us debaters flanking him, and said, "Well, boys, I said she'd sing a duet. But she didn't need anybody else, did she?"

In New England I have moved among the state schoolmen more than among the Ivy Leaguers, but the legends of Yale and Harvard and others in their category have circulated on our University of Massachusetts campus. I can easily believe the report of the conversation between Mr. Taft and the receptionist for Dr. Elliott, longtime president of Harvard.

Identifying himself, the former United States President said, "I would like to speak with Dr. Elliott."

He got a somewhat repressive answer. "*The President* is in Washington to see *Mr.* Coolidge."

A former Harvard man vouches for the following incident: Dr. Elliott heard some of the students chanting, "Three cheers for Harvard—none for Yale."

Thereupon he interjected this plaintive appeal, "Young men, let's be fair. Let's say, 'Three cheers for Harvard—*one* for Yale.'"

Among the famous professors was Dr. Brander Matthews who taught three generations of Harvard men. Once, noting a completely idle student, he interrupted his lecture to say, "Young man, you are not taking notes."

The young man replied, "I don't have to, sir. My grandfather took this course—and I have *his* notes."

I picked up a quaint little story in Tennessee. A teacher asked her elementary class to prepare a theme on Abraham Lincoln, and when the pupils finished, she said to one, "Now, Jimmie, you may stand and read what you have written."

Jimmie's theme went like this: "Abraham Lincoln was born in a log cabin in Kentucky, and when he was a little boy they moved to Illinois. He was elected our President in 1860 and served as our President till he was shot and killed by Clare Luce Booth."

In telling this, I expressed the opinion that it was probably apocryphal. However, in words attributed to Louis Brownlow, "one should never dilute the oil of anecdote with the vinegar of fact."

8

Cosmic and Cosmetic Salvation: International

WHILE PRACTICING law in Little Rock in my pre-Congressional days, I was asked to serve as local chairman for a preaching mission held in my city. This was a modern adaptation, and I think an improvement, on the old-style revival meetings. A group of top-notch preachers and laymen would gather in one city, and with the cooperation of local ministers, speak in various churches and downtown auditoriums.

The "faculty" for this series, which lasted for about a week, included among a number of outstanding Americans a distinguished Swiss theologian, Dr. Adolph Keller.

I had heard of Dr. Keller but had never met him, and I availed myself of the privilege of driving him to his engagements about the city during his first day. He addressed the Kiwanis Club at their noon luncheon, and I took him to that, sat by him at the head table, and introduced him to the Kiwanians. When the luncheon was over, I took him back to his hotel to rest. Later in the afternoon at the mission headquarters, Dr. Jesse Bader, who was the national director of the missions, stopped Dr. Keller to inquire, "Well, Adolph, how was your speech today?"

In his delightful Swiss accent, Dr. Keller said modestly, "Ah, I don't know, Yesse. I did the best I could. They were very kind, but. . . ."

"Dr. Bader," I interrupted, coming out of my nearby office, "he was just grand!"

Dr. Keller looked around at me, an expression of mild surprise on his face, and exclaimed, "Oh! Vas you dere?"

Any hopes I might have held of impressing our foreign visitor with my personal charm, or my importance as a rising young barrister, were squelched. However, I put the incident to use, when at the conclusion of the mission, we had a small dinner for those who had taken part, at which time reports and other remarks were made. In my report, I made much of my association the first day with Dr. Keller, telling how I had been with him until the middle of the afternoon, and then of his deflating query.

The response was gratifying, and Dr. Keller laughed with the rest, Then, called on by the chairman for a rebuttal, he said ruefully, "But you Americans all look so much alike! Now if some of you just had beards, like me, it vould be easier!"

He waited for our laughter to subside, and then said more seriously, "Some day I vill be in my home in Zurich, and I vill hear a knock on my door. Ven I open it, I vill see a friend standing there, and I vill say, 'It is Brudder Brooks Hays, from Little Rock!'"

Another incident of that week has had a permanent place in my memories.

Dr. Keller needed some typing done one day, and I called in a public stenographer for him. After the young lady had gone, I found him chuckling over his manuscript.

"What is it?" I asked, smiling in sympathy. "Did she make a mistake?"

"Ja. I dictated, 'Salvation is a cosmic process,' and she has written, 'Salvation is a *cosmetic* process.'"

"Well, Doctor," I said, "you must admit that from her point of view, what she wrote made sense."

"Ja, ja," he said again. "I think she improved the line!"

This was the beginning of a warm friendship with Dr. Keller which was maintained by an international correspondence and an occasional joint appearance on lecture platforms. When I spoke in the chapel in Zurich, which Zwingli had made famous, I was happy to see him in my audience. When he came up to speak to me later, he gave me the greeting he had promised, "It is Brudder Brooks Hays of Little Rock."

The first of my many trips to Europe was in 1944. The British made available to congressmen any unutilized space in their great four-motor hydroplanes on their regularly scheduled trips, and Congressman Walter Judd of Minnesota and I took advantage of this opportunity to have a view of operations in the European theatre.

It was a fascinating experience, climaxed by luncheon with General Eisenhower, in his Paris headquarters, on September 22.

Strangely enough, the greatest hazard of this trip was not enemy fire abroad, although we actually came under it, but keeping out of jail in Ireland! You see, I landed there without a passport.

The way it happened was this: Judd and I met in Baltimore, where our hydroplane was in the harbor, and where I was to pick up my passport. British officials had assured me it would be there, visa attached, in time for our 11 P.M. departure. But it wasn't there, and it didn't come. The plane was held, while we waited for a messenger from the embassy. When one had not arrived at midnight, a State Department official got First Secretary Alan Judson out of bed to make inquiries about the whereabouts of the missing passport.

The First Secretary, who after this unconventional introduction became my very good friend, with a very red face confessed that it had slipped his mind, and was at the moment held under lock and key in his embassy five miles away!

After another hectic conference, it was decided to try to get permission for me to *precede* my passport across the Atlantic, and this unprecedented event actually took place. It required waking up another notable, Undersecretary of State Breckinridge Long, who may have been half asleep, but who did give permission for my flight. It was with the understanding that my passport would be flown to London in the diplomatic pouch on the next flight. What no one realized, under the pressure of circumstantial tension, was that since we would land first in the harbor of Foynes, Ireland, Irish officials would have to be considered. They would have to clear me.

And so, when Walter Judd and I finally took off in the palatial flying boat of the British Airways, I hadn't been so excited since Ringling Brothers came to Russellville in 1911. We occupied the tail cabin, which was as large as some hotel rooms I have seen.

The first night we flew to a North Atlantic base, and the second lap required just thirteen and a half hours to get us into the harbor at Foynes.

In routine fashion the other passengers, practically all British civilians, went past the Irish officials. I walked, as directed, into a small room with a single desk at which sat a stern-faced uniformed Irish functionary.

He looked at me, held out his hand, and mechanically requested, "Your passport, please."

I answered with Jovian simplicity, "I have none, sir."

He erupted with such force, I felt as if a volcano had gone off right under my nose. I wondered uncomfortably if everyone in Ireland heard him shout, *"You have no passport!"*

"No," I miserably answered.

Before I could even begin to explain, he said in an awful voice, "Stand aside."

Help arrived almost immediately, but not before I had had some horrible visions of myself interned for the duration in an Irish gaol. I was in a foreign land for the first time in my life, and not even Judd was in sight. Under other circumstances I might have asked for the pastor of the local Baptist church, but I realized that that appeal would not be very helpful here. Before my spirits could sink any lower, one of the high British officials came in to explain the situation, and to urge in the interest of international comity that I be permitted, as a member of the United States Congress (making much of this fact) to proceed to London. His plea in my behalf was successful, and I was allowed to proceed; but I did not breathe easy till the British placed my "special passport" in my hands, and I slept the next few nights with it under my pillow.

To get from Foynes to Shannon airfield, we rode in a chartered bus for forty miles through County Limerick and other historic localities. I must give Hollywood credit for having faithfully reproduced the Irish villages and the countryside, for when we stopped for two hours at Village Adare to wait on another bus, I found on the streets and in the shops people who seemed to have walked right off a movie set. There was the peasant riding on a two-wheeled cart, urging on a plodding donkey, and beside him was his family, coming in for the ride or for marketing on a small scale. It would have agonized an American milk inspector to see the driver of a milk cart take the bucket tendered by the prospective purchaser and lower it into the can and immerse it completely, drawing a dripping full pail for the lady.

Enroute to Village Adare through the magnificent Irish south country, we passed some vine-covered ruins. The bus driver proudly identified them and brought in historical illusions that were not pleasing to the British "civil servants" riding with us. Pointing to one of the old castles, the driver said, "This is a castle that Oliver Cromwell stormed and captured."

A Briton leaned across the aisle and whispered to Judd and me, his voice tinged with feeling, "It was three hundred years ago and they still hold it against us."

The last lap of our trip had been in a landplane, which was completely blacked out (a concession to Eire), and we landed near London, at Croyden Field, in a driving rain. I had expected fog! In a little while it was clear, however, and we drove with a British colonel to our hotel, The Dorchester, adjoining Hyde Park.

It was late in the afternoon when we registered, and we had had no lunch, but we did not wait to eat. We wanted to see the Parliament buildings and Westminster Abbey and as many of the other sights as possible, so we started out without a guide or even a map.

Almost immediately we came upon an imposing building, in front of which an erect and imposing guard stood, looking straight ahead.

"What place is this?" I innocently asked.

The guard seemed to draw himself up even more, though I wouldn't have thought that possible, and in a voice of contempt that reduced me to the level of a hick, said coldly, "It is Buckingham Palace!"

Walter, who had known no more than I what we were looking at, but who had the sense to let me do the asking, got a great kick out of my discomfiture, and walked off laughing.

I found myself thinking sympathetically of the day I saw two little women of uncertain years standing in front of the United States Capitol. They were holding a guide book, like two sharing a hymnal, and looking from the page to the building.

Seeing me approach, one of them said, "Pardon me, sir, can you tell us what this building is?"

Later that week, in London, I was asked to speak at an informal meeting of the Royal Institute of International Affairs, at Chatham House. (I enjoy giving accounts of this to American audiences—it sounds so important.)

I opened my talk by saying, "It's good to be in London. I was born in London."

I instantly regretted it—the lords and ladies beamed, and I had to let them down by adding, "Yes, London, Arkansas, is a city of 264 people." I then recovered their good will by transporting them from the world's greatest metropolis to the Arkansas hinterland. "I must be fair to my natal city. When I speak of the 264 population, I refer only to the central city—the core community. Greater London, including Bald Hill and Mill Creek, has 314 people."

Early in my talk I told about the trip to Dover, referring to the bombs bursting a few yards from us in the streets of Dover. Congressman Judd interrupted, "A few *hundred* yards."

I answered briskly, "I'm telling the story."

His rejoinder was quick, "Yes, and I'd love to hear it when you tell it in London, Arkansas."

Arkansas came into conversations again at a dinner given by Tom Horabin, M.P., at the Brown Hotel. Aneurin Bevin and his wife, Jennie Lee, were also guests. Congressman Richards of South Carolina had joined us by that time, and he was sitting next to Jennie Lee. She inquired of me, "Mr. Hays, what is your state?"

I told her, and got this uncomplimentary reference, "Oh, my! A terrible state! An awful place! I was thrown in jail there once."

Dick Richards took up for me, "Lady, you're getting off to a bad start with him. That ole boy loves Ahkansaw."

(Later I learned that her jail experience was an episode in the share-cropper controversy, and resulted from a visit she and Norman Thomas and others made to the state at the height of the tension. All were released after a few hours.)

I enjoyed an occasional walk around London by myself after Judd's departure. I admit having had a tinge of envy during the walks with Walter. So many Minnesota soldiers were stationed there that quite often someone would call out, "Hey, Congressman Judd,"—always with a Scandinavian accent, and he would greet Peterson or Swanson or Jenson or Youngdahl.

I longed to hear an Arkansas drawl, "Hey, Brooks." Finally, one day I got it—from Colonel Graham Hall of Little Rock. He gave me a good meal at the Officer's Club. No Spam this time. (That commodity was well termed by the Britons, "America's revenge for George III.")

Departing, I found Graham putting three oranges in my overcoat pocket. One, I served to Dr. J. H. Rushbrooke, president of the Baptist World Alliance, at a breakfast meeting with him, and I gave one to a little French girl. "The first one she ever saw," her mother said.

During one of those walks, I was asked by two women at Grosvenor Square for directions to Piccadilly Circus. What I said probably sounded like this to them (never to me): "Indeed, ah don't know, Ma'am. Ah'm a stranger here mahself."

As they quickly turned away, I heard one say, "I should have known," meaning, of course, that I did not look British. Twenty years later, on almost the same spot, a lady asked for directions, and I presume my reply was about the same; but the difference between "I should have known" and this lady's "Oops!" may typify a change in London resulting from some cultural alterations.

What I say about the Arkansas drawl is probably overdone for bragging purposes. Who doesn't like to have linguistic identification with the homeland? And one final incident on that point. Shortly after World War II one of our native Arkansas lads of Korean descent was stationed in Tokyo. An elder Nipponese citizen asked something that he thought his fellow Oriental would know, only to get an answer remarkably like my answer to the London ladies, " 'Deed, ah don't know, suh. Ah'm a stranger heah, mahself."

The old gentleman was heard to mutter as he turned away, "By the sacred god Buddha, these ancient ears have now heard everything!"

Prior to the arrival in London of other members of the House (Richards, Poage, Horan, Mundt, Ellsworth, Phillips, Stockman, Fisher, and Holifield), Judd and I were invited to spend a weekend at Cliveden, the country home of Lord and Lady Astor. I was glad that Judd had gone on to India, as I feel sure that he and the hostess would have had a verbal brawl over differences in foreign policy. His reputation had gone ahead of him. Lady Astor had scarcely acknowledged my greeting before saying, "And where's that horrible Mr. Judd?"

She and I got along splendidly. As we sat down to dinner, she said, "Now, Congressman Hays, you sit here by me, as far away from those Yankees as we can get." (Congressman Edith Rogers of Massachusetts and Admiral Radford were two of the "Yankees" I can remember.)

Lady Astor's sharp tongue was doubtless a pose, which she assumed people would understand. The barbs were rarely intended to sting. The things that impressed me most were her buoyant spirit, her complete conformity to the wartime requirements of compassion, and her devotion to her husband, "Waldorf." Theirs was no different, of course, from millions of other marriages between two public figures, but her deference to him was noticeable. (He was at that time Lord Mayor of Plymouth.) She asked me to accompany her to the Canadian hospital which adjoined their estate, and we walked across the magnificent grounds and through the luxuriant woodland, each carrying a basket loaded with special food items for some of the patients. She seemed to sense the fact that having been on war rations for a week or more, I was almost drooling as I walked behind her, and her psychic comment made me jump.

"Keep your hands off those grapes, Congressman. They're for the sick Canadians."

On Monday morning I returned to London in a car driven by one of Lady Astor's close friends, Mrs. Mavis Tate, also an M.P. Her last injunction was to Mrs. Tate, "Watch him, Mavis, I believe he's a wolf."

I must not leave London without this addendum on my observations from the gallery of the House of Commons. I was there on the day that Mr. Gallagher, the radical member from Glasgow, drew a reprimand from the speaker for infringing a rule similar to our own against speaking insultingly of a fellow member. The gentleman from Glasgow had been riled by one of his fellows, and showed it. I did not get the words with exactness, as the speaker obviously did, but it sounded like, "The right honorable gentleman is an infamous blackguard!"

After this outburst, he stood in silence as the speaker adjured him in the presence of the Commons members not to repeat the offense, and banned him from the chamber for twenty-four hours, but he still looked so angry as he stalked out that I wondered if he intended to obey the speaker. He needed to study the neat strategy employed in our own House, at times, to escape retribution. I remember one occasion where a congressman, feeling very strongly about something and wishing he could call another a liar, instead said smoothly, "The very distinguished gentleman is guilty of prevarication of the facts." And he got by with it!

A member of the Israeli Parliament tried a different tactic. During a hot debate he was called to order for declaring that half the cabinet were asses. "Mr. Speaker, I withdraw the remark," he said, "half the members are not asses."

The great thrill of our trip came when General John C. H. Lee, who was head of the Communications Division, sent word to us that General Eisenhower had approved our request for permission to visit Normandy and Paris. At the same time, General Eisenhower invited us to have lunch with him at Headquarters. We used air transportation for the trip, and spent the busiest three days of the entire trip on the soil of France.

After returning to London following the meeting with General Eisenhower our party of congressmen went in different directions.

I spent two days in Belfast, Northern Ireland, as the guest of an old friend, Sam Reid, taxing master for the Royal Courts of Ulster. I was given red-carpet treatment by the Belfast authorities, including a luncheon by the Lord Mayor Sir Crawford MacVeigh. This experience gave me some new insights into the protocol practices of that area.

Entering the lord mayor's office at the appointed hour, I found I was the first guest to arrive. Standing a few feet away with great dignity and majestic bearing was a gentleman whose impressive emblems I took to be the symbol of high office. I never doubted it was the lord mayor waiting to receive his guests, so I rushed up, my hand outstretched, with a warm greeting, "Mr. Mayor, how fine of you to ask me. . . ."

The impressive one spoke firmly, "I am *not* the lord mayor," he said, disdaining my proffered right hand.

"Oh," I said, stepping back.

In a moment a door opened, and there emerged one that I felt sure *was* the lord mayor. I became mobile again, and stepping with alacrity toward him, I said, "Mr. Lord Mayor, what a delight. . . ."

I was right about it being the lord mayor, but I had not calculated on the dignified gentleman who had just silenced me.

"Wait," he said—it was almost a shout—"I have not *announced* him."

Again subdued, I stepped back and heard in stentorian tones from this towering third member of the trio (there was no audience—only the three of us were breathing the air of that huge room), "The Honorable Lord Mayor of Belfast, Sir Crawford MacVeigh."

For the third time I spoke, less confidently, but audibly, "Mr. Lord Mayor, I . . . I . . . ."

"Wait!" my nemesis shouted, "I have not announced *you.*"

The lord mayor was frozen in his tracks ten feet from me, and I must have been a pitiful figure by that time, listening and looking at last for an authentic signal to shake hands with my host.

"The Honorable Congressman from the State of Arkansas— The United States of America—Mister Brook Hays."

In retaliation for what he had done to me, I should have shouted, "The name is Brook*s,* not Brook!" But I was in a state of shock, and I recall saying nothing at that stage except, "Howdy do, Mr. Mayor."*

From Belfast I went to Glasgow, and there I met Congressmen Poage and Fisher, both from Texas, and Stockman of Oregon.

Bob Poage, a former Baylor man, suggested that my Baptist ties would be useful in locating an appropriate place to worship on Sunday, which was the next day. This was not easy to do.

* A detailed account of this experience is given in *This World: A Christians' Workshop,* Broadman Press.

The Presbyterians are ahead of us there, but I was able to steer Bob to the Adelaide Street Baptist Church for the eleven o'clock service. When the minister walked into the pulpit in a beautiful flowing robe, followed by a resplendent vested choir, Bob, unused to such formality in Texas, said, "Are you sure this is a Baptist Church?"

"I think so," I replied, but doubts arose when the minister, early in the service said, "Will John and Myrtle Watkins please bring their little daughter Jane, forward for the christening service?"

"I don't think we are in a Baptist Church," Bob said.

I wasn't too sure, but suggested there was some explanation, and was reassured when the service was apparently one of dedication not baptism—water was not used.

"I believe it's Baptist," I said, standing my ground. Next, the minister said, "Brethren, we are to have a church conference here tomorrow night to settle a sharp controversy that has arisen among the deacons."

"Now we can relax," I said with obvious elation, "We know it's a Baptist Church."

Bob was momentarily convinced, but doubts returned immediately when the minister added that the disagreement was over "admitting members without requiring immersion."

The pleasure given Americans as a result of our pluralistic culture should be appealing to our European friends. Exploiting the cleavages of ethnic groups clear across our country is a favorite occupation for lovers of humor. But all genuine, wholesome humor springs out of human nature and human experience, and knows no national boundaries. It has, in fact, a universal quality.

An excellent illustration of this truth was related by Marion Hedges, whose name, a generation ago, was one to conjure with in Washington among administration and labor leaders. He had served as treasurer of one of the electrical workers' organizations, and had attended a few international conferences. He said a plumber responded to a request from a housewife to repair a bathroom leak. Passing through the kitchen he encountered an attractive maid, and at once stopped and tried to start a conversation.

The maid, however, rebuffed him. "Go on about your business," she said. "I've got too much work to do to talk to you."

The plumber fixed the pipes and returned to his shop. Late that afternoon his phone rang. It was the maid.

"You can come over now," she invited. "I'm through with my work."

He answered indignantly, "What! On my time?"

Sitting next to Mr. Hedges at the conference where he told the story was a Swedish delegate who commented, "He must have been one of our boys."

But a Britisher took exception. "No," he said, "it might have happened in any country and in any craft." All agreed.

This cosmic quality in humor is produced by our cosmic human frailties—or perhaps our strengths.

Ever since we have been a nation, we have exchanged jokes and barbs with the British.

President Andrew Jackson once responded gallantly to a compliment from a Miss Vaughn, the niece of the then British Minister to Washington. She remarked that he and George Washington enjoyed a rare quality—they were the only ones to have ever defeated her countrymen.

"That, my dear lady," he answered, smiling, "is because we were descended from your countrymen."

This common origin is also a bond in the matter of humor, although as in most families we enjoy jokes at each other's expense. The Revolution is a natural focus for international repartee. A case in point concerning a visiting Englishman, Lord Coleridge, who was being shown around the country by our Secretary of State, who was William Maxwell Evarts. When they got to Natural Bridge, Coleridge asked if the story was true about George Washington throwing a silver dollar over the bridge while standing on the ground below it.

Evarts is supposed to have looked at the distance and then to have observed that Washington might have been able to do it, because a dollar went farther in those days. However, he denied that he had said this. What he actually said was, "Washington might have performed this deed because, after all, he did once throw a sovereign across the sea."

Another incident, which may or may not have happened, has been a favorite in Washington. A young British visitor was being shown around our capital city. Among the sights pointed out to him were the scars on the Capitol building, with the information, "Those were made when your people burned Washington."

The young Englishman looked surprised. "Well, I knew we burned Joan of Arc, but I thought Washington died in bed."

My British Embassy friend, Alan Judson, was a very popular man among American congressmen, and quite effective in the handling of congressional matters requiring United Kingdom action. His manner was different from our popular notion of Britain's civil servants. Wholly informal and approachable, he deliberately gave his American friends many a laugh, and Washington has missed him since he retired to private life in England in 1964.

One summer day Senator Mike Monroney, needing to talk to Alan, located him at his office in the embassy. The senator said, "Alan, this is the Fourth of July. Are you *working* today?"

"Yes, I am, Senator."

"Well, I'm afraid my government would take a dim view of your pursuing regular activities on our natal day!"

Judson, not at all abashed, said roundly, "Well, my government wouldn't! It expects me to be on the job today. By not being alert one Fourth of July, we lost some valuable real estate!"

Judson once unwittingly involved me in an embarrassing situation in Oxford, Ohio, at an International Affairs Institute sponsored by Miami University. I had agreed at the last minute to substitute for Senator John Sparkman. There was barely time to catch the plane to Oxford. The weather was not favorable. After bucking headwinds all the way to Pittsburgh, and transferring to another flight for a buffeting hour, I reached the Cincinnati airport after dark, in a state of nervous semiexhaustion.

I was met there by the pilot of a private single-motor plane to be flown to a small airport near the university. The pilot had trouble getting the motor started, but finally did, and then just as we reached cruising altitude, the door on my side flew open. This was corrected instantly by the pilot, but he could do little for my state of mind. I reached the auditorium at 10 P.M., two hours late, utterly surprised to find the audience still there!

The chairman, President Hahn of the university was speaking, but stopped immediately and introduced me. I was sure that in their hearts they hated me for being so late, so I took a few moments to tell some of my favorite Arkansas stories, hoping to dilute that feeling before launching into a discussion of foreign policy. I was beginning to feel that I was making some headway at winning my audience, when I lost ground again—thanks to Judson!

He had supplied a quotation from Lord Keynes, which I regarded as an appropriate text. I grew deadly serious as I began, "In the language of a noted British economist, the day is not far distant when economics will take a back seat where it belongs and will be replaced by the really important things of life that have to do with philosophy, religion, and good human relations."

Instead of the silence I anticipated, denoting a reverent response to this solemn sentiment, the audience gave a roar that sent me reeling.

I was plainly bewildered; so the chairman walked to the podium while they were still laughing, and said to me, "I have been holding our audience here an hour and a half with a talk on the importance of economics!"

Then we all laughed some more.

I did the best I could to recover by immediately paraphrasing the text, as follows: "Of course, economics should never be taken from the front seat, but philosophy, religion, and good human relations must be moved up to that front seat to share the priorities with economics." That was the best I could do. If I am remembered at Miami University, I fear it will be for that ten o'clock beginning—nothing else.

With the British, as with us, an ideal time for the enjoyment of humor is at dinner—in the family dining room or at a banquet. This is the way that the famous wits of the past got started. Even the great Winston Churchill, master of wit on nearly every kind of occasion, enjoyed the role. I have observed that something will usually happen at a dinner meeting to stimulate laughter, and a clever toastmaster can exploit it. Churchill had discovered this. But he needed no special stimulus. He carried his own stimuli.

There was the occasion, for example, when he served as toastmaster, and two clever speakers were to follow him. Since they were highly talented, he was able to start like this: "The function of a toastmaster is to make himself so deliberately dull that the ones to follow look good by comparison." Then gazing first at the speaker on his right, then at the one on his left, he said, "I fear I cannot rise to the occasion."

One of my favorite stories is about two aristocratic Britishers who spotted a prominent United States senator on the deck of a transatlantic liner. They were brothers and this conversation took place:

"Do you know I believe that is the distinguished senator who has been visiting in our country."

The brother who was not articulate merely nodded.

"Suppose we ask him," and so the talkative one approached the senator saying, "Would you pardon me, sir, would you forgive this intrusion? My brother and I have just been speculating. Are you not a member of the United States Senate?"

The senator quickly indicated that he was, and he was friendly enough to inspire the Britisher to ask more questions.

"Then perhaps you are acquainted with our distinguished Prime Minister, Mr. Churchill."

"Of course, I admire him very much. He and I have been in international conferences together."

The one turned to his brother with this brief statement, "Knows Winnie. And would you pardon a further question, sir? Are you acquainted with our distinguished foreign minister, Mr. Macmillan?"

"Yes, I am," said the senator, "Know him very well. I have been in conference with him. I admire him, too."

The talkative one turned to his brother again, "Knows Harold." Again to the senator, "And would you pardon this further question, sir? I wonder if by chance you are acquainted with Lady ——?"

To this the surprising answer came, "Sure, I know her. She's a windy old sister, isn't she?"

The articulate one turned to his brother. "Knows mother."

Dr. David Butler, the distinguished young British political

scientist, once served an internship in my office. He told me of going to a Rotary Club in Birmingham, England, to speak about American politics. The president of the club wanted to let Butler know that he, too, knew something about American politics. "You've been studying American politics, have you?" he said. "Let's see, they have two big parties, just as we do. The Democratic party, and—let's see—the name of the other party is the 'Revolutionary party.'"

Speaking of political parties reminds me of the Englishwoman in John Buchan's *Pilgrim's Way* who made a shrewd appraisal of the difference between Tories and Liberals. "A Tory," she said, "thinks he's better born, but a Liberal just knows he's born better."

The funniest comment on politicians, I think, is that of the London woman who was asked how she voted in a recent election.

"Vote?" she snapped. "I never vote. It only encourages 'em."

My service in government—Congress, Tennesssee Valley Authority, State Department, White House—has produced a variety of assignments calling for foreign travel, and I have profited from the resulting contacts in the gathering of anecdotes, many of which appealed to me because of their political flavor.

In 1951 I was a member of a House Committee, headed by Congressman Zablocki, which went to West Germany to study occupation problems, and had a conference with Chancellor Adenauer.

After the usual amenities Chairman Zablocki surprised me by saying, "Mr. Chancellor, I will ask Mr. Hays of Arkansas to begin the discussion, since he is our senior member."

Acting on impulse, I used a rather unconventional opening. "Mr. Chancellor, perhaps there is some logic in my speaking first. You see, I am the only one of this group who lives in a state that was once occupied by an invading army, and so I know that occupation armies just can't be very popular. But if your people think they can never love us, they should view this scene— Here I am, traveling with these five Yankees, and I have come to love every one of them!"

The ordinarily grim-visaged Chancellor broke into a broad

sympathetic smile, and there was obviously sincerity in his hearty reply, "Ja! Ja wohl."

Some years later, during my service in the White House, one of my visitors was a German newsman of whom I became very fond. I had started to tell him this story, but he stopped me after the first sentence. "I know about that!" he exclaimed. "Mr. Adenauer told me the story himself, and he added, 'The Congressman relaxed us all.'"

General De Gaulle has served as the lightning rod for many stories, perhaps starting with F.D.R.'s poignant remark to Churchill that the Cross of Lorraine was clearly their cross to bear. Recently these stories have come to light. One of De Gaulle's aides, it is said, screwed up his courage and raised the important question of where, when the inevitable happened, the general should be laid to rest.

"What recommendations do you have?" De Gaulle demanded.

"We have thought of the Arc de Triomphe," the aide responded.

"What," De Gaulle sputtered, "next to an unknown?"

"How about Napoleon's tomb?" the aide countered.

"Next to a corporal?" De Gaulle said dubiously.

"By the side of the ashes of Joan of Arc?" the aide suggested in desperation.

De Gaulle meditated a while and then finally agreed. "Well, she would be worthy of it."

Another De Gaulle story hangs on the tightness of De Gaulle's last election as President of France. One of his aides rushed in when the results were finally in. "Mon Dieu, the election was close."

De Gaulle replied, *"Mon Général, s'il vous plaît."*

The late Senator Pat McCarran had a good story about a miners union meeting in his state of Nevada some years ago. The members were holding the annual election. The chairman called for nominations for president. O'Flaherty was nominated. Then a Swedish member proposed the name of Swanson. Results of the vote were O'Flaherty 93, Swanson 17. Next came the vice president. Fogerty was nominated; and one of the Swedish members proposed Johnson. Results of the vote were Fogerty 93,

Johnson 17. Finally nominations for secretary-treasurer. O'Conner was nominated and again a Swedish nominee, Carlson. Results of the vote were O'Conner 93, Carlson 17. Going home, one of the Irish members said to his friend, reflecting upon the election, "Those Swedes are a stubborn lot, aren't they?"

Speaking of the Scandinavians who have been highly influential in American politics, the rivalry between Swedes and Norwegians, which was once rather bitter, has softened and the elements of humor indulged in by both groups is a happy release from the tensions of the past. I was having lunch rather recently with my Norwegian friend, Joe Nordenhaug, of the Baptist World Alliance, and another Baptist official, Emanuel Carlson, of Swedish descent. They were having some good-natured ribbing, and at one point I asked Mr. Carlson if Joe ever reminded him of the battle of Copenhagen. "Far too often, far too often," was the sad rejoinder. The result was put in a rhyme by one who is obviously biased. It went like this:

> Ten thousand Svedes ran through de veeds
> At the Battle of Copenhagen,
> Ten thousand more lay on the shore
> Killed by von Norvegian.

Congressman William Tuck, a former governor of Virginia once told a group of his colleagues gathered in the cloakroom how he had used one of my stories to handle some of his constituents, who were upset about his vote on a particular issue. He told it like this:

"Brooks, they were pretty hard on me. They were down on me before I had a chance to say a word, and when they paused, and I could politely get the floor, I said: 'Gentlemen, you have heard only half the story. Let me give you my side. But before doing it let me say that since my side hasn't been presented, I am reminded of one of Brooks Hays' yarns brought back from England in 1944. The conduct of an American sergeant was an issue in a lawsuit in Northern Ireland, and it had to do with the sergeant's operation of a jeep. A farmer's cow had been killed on a country road, and the farmer himself painfully injured. As the farmer was giving the Irish judge his side of the story, the judge interrupted to say, "But, Mr. Ferguson, the sergeant tells me that at the time of this incident you said you were all right. Did you tell him that—that you were not hurt?" "Indeed I did, Your Honor." "Well then," the judge said, "I don't think we need to proceed with the case, if you admitted yourself that you were not hurt." "But, Your Honor, you have not heard my side of the story, please let me tell it." "Well," said the judge, "proceed."

" 'This was his side: "You see, Your Honor, I was going down the road driving me cow and the sergeant come up from behind me, he did, with this jeep. He gave me no warning, he simply banged into us, knocking me on one side of the road and me cow on the other. He stopped, got out of the jeep, came over to me, and said, 'Mr. Ferguson, are you all right?' Now, Your Honor, I was terribly hurt, but I said, 'Please see about me cow first.' He raced over to look at her and called back to me, 'Oh my, this creature is in bad condition, all four of her legs are broken.' And taking out his pistol he quickly dispatched her right there. He walked back to me, bent over, and while the gun was still smoking in his hand, he said, 'Again, I'm asking you, Mr. Ferguson, are you all right?' And I said, 'You're dombed right I'm all right!' " "

At the organization conference of the United Nations in San Francisco in 1945, our United States Senator Tom Connolly, who was chief of the United States Delegation, and the former Australian Prime Minister Mr. Evatt were having a sharp difference at one point, and an interesting verbal exchange took place.

Senator Connolly: "And why are we gathered here from the four corners of the earth in San Francisco, the marvelous city lying like a jewel on the bosom of the West? We have gathered here from the four corners of the earth to write out a charter for a United Nations." [Here he sent a quick glance to Evatt.] "And there are some among us who would tear that document into shreds, so that at the end of our exertions the assembly would look like Madison Square Garden after a prize fight."

Very quietly the Prime Minister said, "Mr. Chairman, if the senator from Texas should ever be defeated, which God forbid, he need not worry about employment. Ringling Brothers would be very happy to have his remarkable talents!"

On another occasion, former Congressman Frank Coffin of Maine and I went on a fact-finding trip for the Foreign Affairs Committee to Canada. We ultimately produced a report known as the Hays-Coffin study. In the course of the trip I had to listen to a speech by him and, of course, he had to listen to one or two by me. But I did pretty well by him because when someone asked me what I had been doing, I said that I had been to a wake. This naturally evoked some comment, "What! A good old Southern Baptist attending an Irish wake?"

"Well," I said, "the dictionary defines a wake as 'sitting silently and reverently in front of a coffin' and I did just that for thirty minutes."

Once when I was visiting with Roswell Garst out at Coon Rapids, Iowa, he repeated some of the things that Khrushchev said during Garst's 1955 visit to Russia. By invitation, Garst was repaying Russian Deputy Minister of Agriculture Matskevich's visit to his Iowa farm with a visit to Russia's permanent agricultural exposition and lecturing on American farming methods for groups in the Ministry of Agriculture. During his visit with Khrushchev, when the Russian leader suggested a drink, Roswell found a chance to say:

"Chairman Khrushchev, I do not understand you Russians."

"In what way?" he asked.

"Well, I have been telling you about American agriculture now for about three hours. I have not told you a single secret. You could have had your Washington Embassy subscribe to about half a dozen farm magazines and you would have known everything I have told you. Furthermore you could have gone to the U. S. Department of Agriculture and obtained bulletins that covered the details—the fine details of every subject we have discussed. You did none of these things.

"And yet, when we had the atomic bomb—and you did not—we threatened to hang anyone who helped you acquire the knowledge—we protected the secrets the best we knew how—you generally had stolen our secrets in about three weeks.

"I just don't understand you people at all!"

The Russian leader laughed—a good belly laugh—held up two

fingers like Winston Churchill did with his V for Victory sign and said: "Two weeks, Mr. Garst. It never took us more than two weeks."

President Kennedy had great respect for the Prime Minister of Nigeria, Balewa. After my return from three weeks in Western Africa, a mission for the President in the spring of 1963, he asked me right off, "Did you see Balewa?"

I did see Balewa in his office in Lagos, and I had a fine conversation with him regarding progress in the field of race relations. He was well informed as to the situation in the South and was particularly interested to learn of the progress being made in admitting the descendants of African slaves to full participation in American society. I gave him an optimistic account of developments. But when he asked me in a rather somber vein about the Negroes, intending to draw me out on the question of their morale and hopes, I told him the story of a community in the deep South at a time when school revenues were very slim and it was not possible to improve physical facilities very rapidly. The school board had accumulated enough money to build a new building, but under conditions of segregation; they were embarrassed they could not build two new structures. So they invited in the leading spokesman for the Negro community and laid the problem before him.

"You see," they said, "we have only enough money for one building, and we wonder how the Negroes would feel if we spent it on the building for whites. Will the Negroes be aggrieved?"

"No, indeed," came the surprising answer. "I can think of nothing that would help our Negro people more than having better educated white people."

My contacts with the chaplains stationed abroad were invariably pleasant and even inspiring. Not many chaplains lack a lively sense of humor and they find it a valuable aid. One whose company I enjoyed was the chief at one of our installations south of London, Chaplain Jack Gober. (My wife called him "goobers" and he smiled even at that.)

One of his staff was a Catholic chaplain with a ruddy countenance, but gray hair, and this gave him the look of middle age.

His appearance added mirth to something that happened when he was driving from London to his post.

Relating it to us he said: "I was moving with the traffic at a pretty good clip, speed being encouraged on this particular boulevard. I was a bit annoyed at one stage when I noticed in the mirror a motorcycle keeping too close to me in the rear. I was watching for the stops, but I feared that the motorcyclist wasn't. Sure enough, he wasn't, for when I stopped as required, at a cross street, he had to swerve. He struck the curb with a terrific impact, and his motorcycle wheels went spinning on the ground. His helmet was askew, and he was almost breathless as he stepped to the side of my car to say this: "You'll have to be more careful, laddie! You nearly got me that time."

These little dissertations on humor and philosophy in international matters were inspired by the typographical slip in Dr. Keller's article on "cosmic salvation." When the stenographer wrote "cosmetic," she unconsciously interjected another element into the discussion.

I seldom hear the word cosmetic without recalling the incident in an old fashioned revival conducted by the famous Sam Jones the "Billy Graham of the nineteenth century." In a meeting in western Arkansas he was inveighing against the practice of women "painting and powdering like Comanche Indians." He came to grief one evening when he asserted, "I'll bet there isn't a woman in this congregation who didn't put on a lot of paint and powder on her face before she came to church tonight."

At this point, a lean hatchet-faced lady arose and brusquely said, "Oh, yes, Brother Jones, *I* didn't."

Sam Jones took one look, turned to his song leader and said, "A little would have helped her, wouldn't it?"

If it kept him from repeating the sophistry that women should not use paint, it was a break for the "true faith."

The dialogue now taking place between the old evangelism and the new is reflected to some extent in the quaint typographical error in Dr. Keller's manuscript, one dealing with the mass man, the other, focusing on the individual. In my own theology, they are easily reconciled.

This observation also applies to political situations in which the avid "organization" politicians exhibit concern for individual support and goodwill. My philosophy is that in both politics and religion, we must seek a balancing of these two interests, the individual and his society. Both government and the church must be concerned with the individual; though I agree that if a distinction is to be made, the church would be regarded as primarily concerned with the individual, and government with the social order. (There are all sorts of exceptions and corollaries.)

The apparent conflict between the two attitudes caught me in a dilemma, once, when I made this observation to my wife, "My old neighbor was right, though his grammar was bad, when he said, 'A man don't know nuthin' he didn't learn.'"

She promptly challenged my statement. "But what are you going to do about that other fellow I've heard you quote, who said, 'No man can live long enough to learn all he has to know just to survive—some things he must inherit from the race.'"

This swept me suddenly into the realm of educational theory, away from both theology and religion, and posed a question for me. I reconciled the two by letting the first theory give ground, for I concede there are some things a man *does know* by inheritance. I could, however, defend both by taking the position that inherited knowledge is faith.

I disengaged myself by suggesting that the stenographer, merely by accident, pointed up the dichotomy of truth. Salvation is indeed cosmic—its universal character has been proclaimed throughout recorded history; and if we think of "cosmetics" as a design for a lady's hope and security, then it could symbolize a concern for the individual.

My political instincts are again overtaking me, and I cannot resist sharing with the reader one of my rejoinders when a friend spoke of my majority of 3,500 votes, in my first election to Congress in 1942, as "a nice block of votes."

"Not a block at all," I said. "Marble maybe; not a block, but a sack of 3,500 little marbles. I had to search out most of the people and convince them they should go along with me."

The individual wins. And I am proud of our country, perhaps most of all, because it makes the individual a focus of deep and profound concern, for certainly, the final values of human existence are centered in the heart and soul of a person.

9

And I Have the Last Laugh

A PASSER-BY, seeing smoke coming from a cottage roof, hammered on the front door.

When, finally, it was opened, the Good Samaritan exclaimed to the woman in the doorway, "Madam, your house is on fire!"

Putting her hand behind her ear, she said, "What?"

Raising his voice, the man repeated, "Your house is on fire!"

Undisturbed, the woman responded, "Is that all?"

To this he replied, "Well, it's all I can think of right now."

What I have written about the uses and abuses of humor in public service is not quite all I can think of right now, but I must spare both the reader and myself.

I recall watching my mother finish the use of her cookie cutter, as she lifted the dough in proper forms into the oven. Gathering up the tidbits of dough left on her kneading board, she put them into more cookies.

"Nothing must be wasted," she always said as she took up the fragments.

I too, have some fragments left that I do not want to waste.

The biggest ones involve my friend, Adlai Stevenson. I could not include Adlai in the chapter on the Presidents, for he just didn't make it. Still, few men in public office in our entire history could equal him in the appropriate use of humor.

I had come away from the Chicago convention in 1952 a Stevenson enthusiast, and a few days after the convention I was asked to serve as his "advance man" in the South. I went ahead of him, making final arrangements for his speaking appearances, keeping in touch with the Springfield headquarters, largely through my friends Oscar Chapman and Senator Fulbright. The latter was spending most of his time in the mansion helping with speech preparation. At that time I had never met our candidate, and I did not see him during the campaign. In fact, three years went by before I met him. He knew, however, of the contacts I had with headquarters, and had adopted some of the suggestions I made regarding the content of his speeches.

I recall, for example, that when I reached New Orleans I was told by advisers there that, since the Republican nominee had said something about the deterioration of French culture, it would be a good idea for our candidate to say something in praise of the French contribution to American life. I immediately relayed this suggestion to Senator Fulbright in a phone conversation, and he readily agreed. He felt sure the governor would want to do this. Adlai not only embraced the idea, but carried it out in style; when he came to that passage in his speech, he gave it in choice French. This was money in the bank for the Democrats!

I finally met "the governor" in the fall of 1955, when I was serving as a member of the delegation to the General Assembly of the United Nations. Late one afternoon I found a message at the Vanderbilt Hotel, which was our home during the session, with the interesting invitation: "Mr. Adlai Stevenson wants to know, can you meet him at the Savoy Plaza Hotel at 5 P.M. today?"

My wife and I were there a little before five, and Bill Blair, his law partner, met us in the reception room, saying that the governor would be out in a moment. When he breezed into the reception room, he greeted me as he would an old friend, "Hello, Brooks."

Since it was apparent that he had not realized that this was our first meeting, I suppressed the impulse to say, "Well, at last there is a confrontation!"

He shook hands with my wife and invited us to sit down. Instead of complying, she said, "Governor Stevenson, I know that you and Brooks have some things to talk about, and now that I have had the pleasure of meeting you, I will go down and wait in the lobby."

He quickly retorted, "Don't be silly! Let Brooks go down and wait in the lobby."

(My wife said later, "If he wasn't already my candidate, he would be now!")

This was my introduction to the famous Stevenson wit. It was only the beginning. Our correspondence picked up after that. One of my prized possessions is a postcard he mailed to me in Africa during the summer of 1957, just after my election to the presidency of the Southern Baptist Convention. It read, "The African drums just brought word that you are the New President of the Baptists. I marvel at your versatility."

The ecclesiastical theme often found its way into our letters and conversations. I remember saying to him in his office in Chicago one day, "I was glad to see that you went to the Presbyterian Church in Lake Forest yesterday. I thought you were a Unitarian."

"Well," he said, "actually I am both."

I became technical. "You can't be," I said. "That's like saying you are sitting on a one-legged, three-legged stool."

I think he enjoyed the occasional theological references. He was fascinated when I told him what Dumas Malone had said about Thomas Jefferson, acknowledging as he did that there was evidence of a Presbyterian influence in the work of the founding fathers, even in Jefferson's contribution. Malone purported to have found the answer, since Jefferson was not a Presbyterian. He attributed it to George Wythe, one of Jefferson's favorite instructors at William and Mary College.

He put it like this: "Whom the Lord did not predestinate by Presbyterian ancestors, he did fore-ordain by Presbyterian instructors."

"Actually, in the book," I added, "it may read as 'Scotch ancestors,' but since Scotch and Presbyterian are practically synonymous, I leave it like this—although Presbyterians are the more synonymous of the two."

Adlai was interested in my story of the Baptist group that flourished a half century ago in the rural South, "The-Two-Seed-in-the-Spirit-Predestinarian-Baptists." This group not only had an awesome name, but an awesome theology, based upon the concept of a predetermined destiny for each individual soul. Another friend who was intrigued by it was Jim Stokely of Newport, Tennessee, and a day or two after I had made reference to the group, which has since virtually expired, I had a letter from Jim with the following reference, "I was fascinated by your story of the Two-Seed-in-the-Spirit-Predestinarian-Baptists. I want you to know that I am a One-Seed-in-the-Spirit-Universalist, Thomas Jefferson, Adlai Stevenson, Estes Kefauver, Brooks Hays Baptist." I transmitted the note to Adlai with a final query, "Do you think he was mentioning us in ascending or descending order of importance?"

The governor seemed to enjoy a comment I made during the 1955 session of the General Assembly of the United Nations, when Outer Mongolia's application for membership was being pressed by the Soviets. I came up with the suggestion that we compromise the issue by admitting Outer Mongolia, and then admit Texas, on the theory that Texas is as autonomous and independent as Outer Mongolia, perhaps more so, and would generally be as loyal to United States policy as Outer Mongolia to the Soviets. Simultaneously, the name of Texas would be changed to "Outer Arkansas."

In the fall of 1955, in the conversation at the Savoy Plaza Hotel in New York, he had raised the question of whether he should be a candidate for President in 1956. In substance, I said this to him: "Governor, why raise the question at all? I doubt that you will feel, when the time comes, it is within your power really to make the decision, since you have a sensitive conscience and your conscience will dictate the answer. No one knows at this moment what the prospects for victory will be; and while I would like to see you spared the torture of this campaign, I don't think that, if the party feels you should lead us again, you will consider declining it. That's the exact situation as I analyze it now." Subsequent events tended to confirm all I had to say to him that day.

In my long association with Adlai Stevenson, I recall only one difference in our political reactions. In a speech in Flint, Michigan, in his first campaign for the Presidency, he said, "When I was a boy, I never had much sympathy for a holiday speaker—he was just a kind of interruption between the hot dogs, a fly in the lemonade." I couldn't understand that—speeches at country picnics were the breath of life for me. And I believe that if Adlai had not had a completely different political environment in his Illinois boyhood, he would have felt exactly as I did. For example, the famous Jeff Davis to whose colorful ways I have already alluded, was a popular attraction at all of the big summer picnics in our state, and could be counted on to meet effectively the competing noises from whining merry-go-rounds, fightings dogs, and bursting balloons. While I was never responsive to the Jeff Davis proposals based on emotionalism for the relief of rural poverty, I did feel a fascination for his style of political oratory and campaigning. He possessed talents for entertaining a rural audience. His appearance alone seemed to stir them. He was a large man, handsome, of florid countenance, dressed always in a long cutaway coat of Confederate gray, and regardless of any other forms of entertainment, the crowd followed him to the speaker's platform. And as he walked through the crowd, he would be greeting old friends, often able to call them by name; if not, he dissembled a bit.

One farmer, hoping he might be remembered, said, "Jeff, you don't know me, do you?"

The governor had an answer because he had learned how to be sensitive to any sign of identity. On this occasion he took a quick look from head to foot, and he noticed, on the inside of the blue denim overalls that the old man was wearing, a few short gray hairs. "Of course, I remember you," the governor said. "I even remember the gray horse you used to ride." That did it.

Jeff Davis' favorite target was the *Arkansas Gazette*. He constantly derided "That Squirrel-Headed Editor and the high-collared fellers around him."

Sixty years ago the following type of story could be counted on to draw gales of laughter from an Arkansas audience.

"Now just yesterday I was driving over to Waldron, and I came on a big crowd in front of a farmhouse where one of my good old friends lived.

"He came out to meet me, and I said, 'Lem, what's the crowd about?'

"'Oh, Governor,' he said, 'I have more trouble than I can

handle. There's a skunk under my house, and he is scenting up the place something awful. I am going to have to move if I can't get rid of him, but I don't know how I am going to do it. I have sent the best skunk dog in Scott County to run him out, but the skunk has *stunk him* out.'

" 'Now,' I said, 'I know how to get rid of him.' I had the morning *Arkansas Gazette* in my pocket, and I folded it up real tight and flung it under the house, and you know that skunk came out of there in a hurry! It outstunk the skunk."

I believe Jeff Davis was careful to tell this story only where skunks were known, and where the *Gazette* was *not* known, because actually the editor of the *Gazette* was one of the state's most respected men. It was an interesting turn in political fortune that the editor, J. N. Heiskell, was appointed to the Senate vacancy upon Jeff Davis' death in 1912, and served about a month of the intervening period before the successor was formally elected and inducted.

The southern counterpart of Chauncey Depew was Tom Heflin of Alabama, whose gifts as a ranconteur I have previously described. It was in the period when the Ku Klux Klan flourished that Tom lost his image as a lovable legislator and entertainer. His daily diatribes against the Catholic Church made him the hero of the Klan. One day, his southern colleague, Joe T. Robinson, provoked beyond restraint, stood in the Senate to attack the Klan, making an eloquent plea for tolerance. Senator Heflin was on his feet instantly to complain about Robinson's attack, concluding with the statement, "The senator from Arkansas won't go to Arkansas to make that speech next summer."

To this Joe Robinson replied, "I will not only go to Arkansas and make this speech, but I will go to *Alabama* to make it."

Then Tom forgot himself, making a fatal slip, "If he does, they will tar and feather him."

With a powerful and resonant voice, Robinson seized the advantage, "Mr. President, the amazing utterance of the senator from Alabama, to which we have just listened, reveals the spirit of proscription which resides within his breast."

He did not need to say anymore than this, although he proceeded with a denunciation of the Klan. Many political observers believe that Joe Robinson's sincere and spontaneous expressions that day, meeting the threat of bigotry, produced his nomination in Houston as Al Smith's running mate.

One other reference to Ambassador Stevenson is in order. Adlai responded sympathetically to my philosophizing on the idealistic approach to the effect of political defeats. He would have agreed with my comments to Rutgers students, "One should never equate success with the ability to get more votes than someone else in a given election." Some of my most gratifying experiences have been in races that I did not win. Of course, I would rather win than lose. Also, I would rather run without an opponent, for then, in the vernacular, "you don't have to laugh when you ain't tickled."

I was not merely theorizing when I talked in this vein to Adlai. I was able to identify myself with him in the pre-1956 campaign. I had a similar dilemma to resolve in 1930 in the race for governor of Arkansas. I knew that the odds were against me, and that it would be a bruising campaign, but I knew that if I did not run I would be failing thousands of people who were convinced of my sincerity in the 1928 race when I opposed the same state administration. If I wanted to keep this image instead of acquiring that of an opportunist, I literally *had* to make the campaign, regardless of the outcome.

I quoted Shakespeare to Adlai—"Tis not always ours to command success, we can do more, Sempronius, we can deserve it."

He was not familiar with that one. He said, "Wait while I get a pencil."

My last visit with Adlai was in Hot Springs, Arkansas. I had asked him to accept the Arkansas State Bar Convention's invitation to give the major address (my son Steele was secretary-treasurer), and he agreed to do it. My wife and I went down for the event—a great occasion for the Arkansas lawyers. I was asked to introduce him.

I began, "I would be glad to bring you the greetings of the President of the United States, but to tell you the truth, he doesn't know where I am."

I warmed to my theme. We had as a guest "one of the great men of our times." I made reference to our long and intimate friendship, my appreciation of his sensitive and noble actions in two national campaigns, his notable achievements as chief executive of his state and as our ambassador at the United Nations. I spoke of his love of the law, of his wistfulness in viewing the opportunities for an exciting practice, an opportunity lost only because as a conscientious man he accepted the challenge of public service, even the hardships of two candidacies he did not relish. I presented him as a distinguished lawyer, a remarkable administrator whose talents had been demonstrated at state, national, and international levels, and the apostle of peace who had won the admiration of people around the world.

He acknowledged it in this way: "Mark Twain said a man can live a month on one compliment. Brooks has assured me of immortality! He will go to Heaven for his charity, unless he goes somewhere else for his exaggerations. I bring you the greetings of the President of the United States. He knows where *I* am. He knows I am at the Security Council."

As I strive to reach that mystic word *Finis* I am reminded of a famous baseball player, Herman Schaefer, who amused, then chilled and thrilled thousands of Chicago fans one summer day in 1906. A member of Detroit's team, the Tigers, he stepped to the batter's box at a crucial stage in a crucial game, turned to the stands, raised his cap, and said, "Ladies and Gentlemen, I am Herman Schaefer—better known as Herman the Great. I shall knock the ball into the left field bleachers." And he did! The ball fell exactly where he predicted it would. But it did not conclude his act. He paused at first base and yelled, "Schaefer leads at the quarter." At second, "Schaefer leads at the half." At home plate, he again raised his cap, bowed, and addressed the stands, "Ladies and Gentlemen, I thank you for your kind attention."

In the same spirit, but not renouncing the satisfaction of reaching home, I too thank you sincerely, Ladies and Gentlemen, for your kind attention.

And now let me come to the conclusion of the whole matter. When we become fully and happily identified with our groups— our families, our churches, indeed with our entire human family —we will recognize that when we laugh at our fellow men we are laughing at ourselves.

Identification is the key to this. I could not have escaped religion's part in this book's thesis even if I had so wanted. "A man's religion or his no-religion," as Carlyle said, "is the most considerable part of him." Life's only lasting values are essentially religious, though not every person defines his cherished values in such terms.

Please let me emphasize the idea of identification. Every truly happy person identifies with the race. I do not mean a "ha-ha happy person" (a phrase borrowed from my friend George Schweitzer of the University of Tennessee), but rather the calm and internally peaceful person who finds his contentment in relating his laughter and his tears to the needs and aspirations of the peoples of this restless world.

There was a whole biography in the sentence alluding to Jane Addams, "She wanted to share with humanity all of her joys and all of its sorrows."

And Safed the Sage (William E. Barton in *The Christian Century*) was digging deep when he defined optimism as "such sorrowful discontent with the good we have done as to give us joy in the pursuit of something better."

Index